Becoming an
Excellent Genealogist
Essays on Professional Research Skills

Edited by

**Kory L. Meyerink, MLS, AG, FUGA; Tristan L. Tolman, AG;
and Linda K. Gulbrandsen, AG**

Contents

Acknowledgments

It is always true that no book is the sole work of just one author, and of course that is clearly evident in the case of a collection of essays, such as this book. The authors of the essays certainly deserve a major acknowledgment because they contributed their insights without direct compensation but rather recognized the importance of professional development; not only for themselves but also for the readers of these essays. Each of them would certainly acknowledge their teachers and mentors throughout their careers. They include the many men and women who have shepherded the accreditation program since its inception in 1964 under the auspices of the Genealogical Society of Utah. Pioneers of accreditation, such as Frank Smith and Henry Christiansen, are represented here by their late colleague, Jimmy B. Parker, who oversaw the program for many years in the 1970s and contributed substantially to the commission through his teaching. We also acknowledge each of the past and present commissioners, as they have provided constant support of this project, with many of them having contributed essays as well.

Lastly, without the dedicated time and effort of my co-editor, Tristan Tolman, this book may never have seen the light of day. Launching a project such as this is one thing, but bringing it in safely for a landing is another, and she has done a wonderful job on the landing.

~Kory L. Meyerink, MLS, AG, FUGA

Contributors

Suzanne Russo Adams, MA, AG, specializes in Italian research. She is a Brigham Young University graduate with bachelor's degrees in Sociology and Family History and Genealogy and a master's degree in European History. Suzanne currently works in content strategy for FamilySearch and was previously employed by Ancestry for more than eleven years. She is a former board member of the Association of Professional Genealogists, the International Commission for the Accreditation of Professional Genealogists, and the Utah Genealogical Association. Suzanne is the author of *Finding Your Italian Ancestors: A Beginner's Guide* (2009) and was a lead researcher for Season 1 of NBC's hit show "Who Do You Think You Are?"

Karen Clifford, AG, FUGA, is a Midwest, Mid-South, and Mountain West AG Professional and an instructor/curriculum developer for online genealogy courses at Monterey Peninsula College in California and the Salt Lake Community College in Utah. She has written several college textbooks on genealogy and computers, as well as genealogy credentialing, and has edited several family histories for GRAonline.com, where she performs research for hire and is the chief executive officer. Karen served in the past as vice president of the Federation of Genealogical Societies, president of the Utah Genealogical Association, vice chair of the International Commission for the Accreditation of Professional Genealogists, and as a commissioner. She currently chairs the Test Development and Quality Control subcommittees of the International Commission for the Accreditation of Professional Genealogists.

Apryl Cox, AG, is a professional researcher, instructor, and lecturer. She is a member of the Association of Professional Genealogists and is a commissioner with the International Commission for the Accreditation of Professional Genealogists where she also serves as co-chair of the Testing Committee. Apryl is an adjunct professor with Brigham Young University where she teaches family history courses. She currently conducts client research and consultation, teaches family history classes, and lectures at national, state, and local conferences.

Jill N. Crandell, MA, AG, is a professional researcher accredited in Midwestern United States research. She has a bachelor's degree in Family History and Genealogy and a master's degree in History. Jill has enjoyed teaching family history at Brigham Young University for the past eight years, and she is currently the director of the Center for Family History and Genealogy. She was a founding commissioner and executive secretary/treasurer of the International Commission for the Accreditation of Professional Genealogists, has served on the board of directors of the Utah Genealogical Association, and was a director of the Salt Lake Institute of Genealogy in 2000 and 2001. Jill and her husband, Bill Crandell, are the parents of five children.

Kathryn M. Daynes, Ph.D., AG, is an associate professor of history and former director of the Center for Family History and Genealogy at Brigham Young University. She received her Ph.D. in American History from Indiana University. An Accredited Genealogist professional of the Mid-South and Gulf-South regions, she teaches classes in general United States and Southern research.

Loretta Evans, AG, has been doing genealogical research for over thirty-five years. She is accredited in Midwestern United States research. A popular lecturer at state and national conferences, Loretta is the author of numerous magazine articles and six published family histories.

Linda K. Gulbrandsen, AG, is a professional researcher and lecturer specializing in Midwest, Eastern States, and urban U.S. research. She is manager of the U.S. and Canada Research Consultation Services Unit for the Family History Library. She formerly managed probate research operations for a law firm in Illinois and has worked with a large private clientele and several research companies. She was an online instructor with Brigham Young University and serves on the Advisory Council for the Salt Lake Institute of Genealogy and as chair of ICAPGen.

Amy Harris, Ph.D., AG, is an assistant professor of history at Brigham Young University. After graduating from BYU in Family History and Genealogy, she received a master's degree in European History from American University and a Ph.D. in British and European History from the University of California, Berkeley. Amy earned her accreditation in English research in 2007. She currently teaches British genealogical methodology and paleography courses at BYU. Her historical research centers on family relations in eighteenth-century England. Her first book, *Siblinghood and Social Relations: Share and Share Alike* (Manchester University Press), will appear in late summer 2012.

John Kitzmiller, II, AG, FSA(Scot), FSG(Eng), is an author, lecturer, and researcher of English, Scottish, Welch, Manx, and Ulster family history. He was elected a fellow of the Society of Genealogists in England. For fifteen years, John worked as the Product and Operations manager for the Family History Department. He is now a senior reference consultant at the Family History Department. He has published eight books dealing with different research aspects of the above countries. He has also done advanced field research in each of the countries about which he has lectured. He is an officer for the International Commission for the Accreditation of Professional Genealogists and a fellow of two other organizations in Britain.

Anne Leptich, AG, has over forty years of genealogical research experience. She was chair of the International Commission for the Accreditation of Professional Genealogists from 2007 to 2009, has served on the board of directors of the Federation of Genealogical Societies, and was first vice president of the Genealogical Forum of Oregon. She has taught at Clark County Community College and is a past director of a family history center.

Ruth Ellen Maness, AG, is a senior reference consultant at the Scandinavian Unit of the Family History Library. She has been an instructor at the Salt Lake Institute of Genealogy and has taught genealogy classes for Brigham Young University, the Federation of Genealogical Societies, the International Commission for the Accreditation of Professional Genealogists, the National Genealogical Society, and the Utah Genealogical Association. She was a professional genealogist for thirty-five years, with field experience in Scandinavia, England, Germany, Poland, South Africa, and the United States. Ruth authored the *Scandinavia-Questions & Answers* column in Everton's *Genealogical Helper* (formerly *Heritage Quest Magazine*); *Passport To Paradise – The Copenhagen "Mormon" Passenger Lists 1872-1894; Legacy of Sacrifice*; and family histories presented to such notables as Odvar Nordli and Kåre Willoch, the prime ministers of Norway.

Marilyn Markham, MLS, AG, CG, has worked for thirteen years in the Family History Library, mostly in the US/Canada Reference area. For an additional twelve years, she worked in other areas of the Family History Department. For five years, she taught New England Research at Brigham Young University and has taught classes at the Family History Library and various genealogical conferences. From 2003 to 2009, she was on the board of directors for the Utah Genealogical Association and was president for two years. She was director of the Salt Lake Institute of Genealogy for two years.

Kory L. Meyerink, MLS, AG, FUGA, is the vice president of ProGenealogists in Salt Lake City. Formerly, he worked with Ancestry and at the Family History Library. Kory is past president of the Utah Genealogical Assocation, founder of the Salt Lake Institute of Genealogy, a nationally known speaker, the editor of *Printed Sources,* and an adjunct faculty member of Brigham Young University and San Jose State University.

Chad R. Milliner, MLIS, AG, was bitten by the genealogy bug when he took an introductory genealogy course at Brigham Young University. After changing his major to Genealogy and then earning a master's degree in Library and Information Sciences, he became a professional genealogist and for twelve years undertook research for clients. For the last six years, Chad has been an employee of Ancestry. Chad is an Accredited Genealogist professional with a research focus on England. Chad is an alumnus of the National Institute of Genealogical Research in Washington, D.C., and has taken several courses at the Institute of Genealogical and Historical Research in Birmingham, Alabama. He resides in West Jordan, Utah, with his wife and twin children, who keep his hands very full.

Nathan W. Murphy, MA, AG, is a research consultant at the Family History Library in Salt Lake City, Utah. He holds a bachelor's degree in Family History and Genealogy from Brigham Young University and a master's degree in English Local History from the University of Leicester. He specializes in English and Southern United States research and has helped many clients break through brick-wall problems using DNA.

Carolyn J. Nell, AG, FUGA, became an Accredited Genealogist professional in 1982, specializing in the Mid-South and Gulf South states. She served as chair of the International Commission for the Accreditation of Professional Genealogists from 2001 to 2007, president of the National Genealogical Society from 1992 to 1996, president of the Fairfax [Virginia] Genealogical Society for three terms, and president of the Utah Genealogical Association twice. In 1998, Carolyn was made a fellow of the Utah Genealogical Association in recognition of her contributions to the field of genealogy. In 2010, she received the Lifetime Achievement Award from ICAPGen for service and dedication to the organization and genealogical community.

Jimmy B. Parker, AG, FUGA, was involved in research for over forty years as an Accredited Genealogist professional for much of the United States, especially American Indian, before his death in 2011. He was a staff member of the Family History Department of The Church of Jesus Christ of Latter-day Saints and manager of the Family History Library prior to his retirement. He wrote and lectured extensively. After his retirement, he was a staff member of the Bountiful Regional Family History Center and a worldwide support missionary for The Church of Jesus Christ of Latter-day Saints. He owned Heritage Plus, a professional research and oral history business.

Tricia H. Petrey, AG, received a bachelor's degree in Family History and Genealogy from Brigham Young University and is an Accredited Genealogist professional specializing in Southern States research. Her experience includes work as a research assistant at the National Archives in Washington D.C., as the research director for a Salt Lake City based genealogy company, and as a genealogy instructor for two community colleges in California. She lives in South Jordan, Utah, with her husband and five young children, where she is consumed with the "other end" of her genealogy!

James W. Petty, AG, CG, is a professional genealogist with over thirty-five years of experience. He is president of Heirlines Family History and Genealogy, Inc., and co-founder of Heritage Genealogy College. He is an Accredited Genealogist and Certified Genealogist professional and has college degrees in Genealogy and History.

Joy Price, AG, has been researching family histories for over thirty years. She became an Accredited Genealogist professional in 1989, specializing in Mid-Atlantic States research. She has taught family history classes and served as a missionary at the Idaho Falls Family History Center for many years, has worked as a consultant for Family History Library tours in Salt Lake City, and was stake director for FamilySearch Indexing. She has served on the Utah Genealogical Association board, the Salt Lake Institute of Genealogy board, and as the executive secretary of ICAPGen. She has published several articles and books. Family here and beyond is her passion.

Richard Woodruff Price, MA, AG, is accredited in English research. He received a master's degree in Family & Community History from Brigham Young University in 1984. His master's thesis studied child-naming patterns in sixteenth- and seventeenth-century England. He was a founder and past president of the Association of Professional Genealogists (APG) and vice-president of APG Salt Lake Chapter in 2000-2001. Rick has lectured at multiple genealogical conferences including NGS, FGS, UGA, Brigham Young University genealogy conferences, and the Wiltshire England Family History Society Annual Conference. He has been a full-time professional genealogist since 1976. In 1981, Rick founded Price & Associates, Inc., Genealogical Services after working for five years at the Institute of Family Research, Inc., in Salt Lake City, Utah. He has taken numerous research trips to England, Scotland, Wales, and Germany, spending more than a year in archives, churches, and record offices there. He is the author of *John Lothropp 1584-1653: A Puritan Biography & Genealogy*. Rick and his wife Nancy are the parents of five children and four grandchildren.

Heidi G. Sugden, AG, is a native of Vienna, Austria. She has worked for the Family History Library for over fifteen years and is an Accredited Genealogist professional specializing in French research. In addition to helping patrons in the library, she also loves teaching classes and doing research on location.

Tristan L. Tolman, AG, is a professional genealogist, author, editor, and publisher. She has a bachelor's degree in Family History and Genealogy from Brigham Young University and received her accreditation in genealogy research in the U.S. Mid-Atlantic States through the International Commission for the Accreditation of Professional Genealogists. Tristan has been actively involved in the genealogical field for over twenty years. She currently serves on the Board of Commissioners of ICAPGen as the first vice chair and is a member of the National Genealogical Society and the Association of Professional Genealogists. She specializes in U.S. research, writing personal and family histories, and preparing genealogical information for publication. She and her husband Blair are the parents of five children.

Judith Eccles Wight, AG, graduated from Brigham Young University and is an Accredited Genealogist professional specializing in Irish and Scottish research. She was a British reference consultant at the Family History Library from 1990 to 2001 and served as director of the Sandy Utah East Stake Family History Center from 1997 to 2000. Judy is a former commissioner of the International Commission for the Accreditation of Professional Genealogists and is a published author, genealogical lecturer, and teacher. She is the sole proprietor of Wight House Research.

Preface

The drive—it's part of us; trying to be the best we can be. It's what brought our ancestors to the New World. It's what propels modern sports teams to become champions. And it's what makes genealogists strive to learn more about history, records, and the human condition. It's an effort to become the best family historians we can be so we can find more solutions to those perplexing genealogical problems.

Such are the genealogists who spend money and time on how-to books, genealogical magazines, conferences, seminars, and institutes in order to learn what they don't already know, or to reinforce what they learned earlier. These are the genealogists who volunteer at libraries, historical societies, archives, and family history centers, knowing that by helping, they too will be helped. These are the genealogists who join genealogical societies, attend their activities, and serve on committees and boards. These are the genealogists for whom this book was written.

Basic genealogical instruction is becoming more and more plentiful as the popularity of family history research continues to grow. Mentors, librarians, volunteers, and others provide carefully planned materials to teach about records and beginning the research process. However, genealogical research can be complex. There is a myriad of possible records to consider, find, and use in our research. There are an even greater number of circumstances in which our ancestors lived. Just as every family is different, every lineage is different. Every genealogical problem to be solved varies, to some degree, from every other problem.

Successfully navigating those difficulties is challenging. It takes certain aptitudes, as well as certain knowledge that may not be readily available. Unfortunately, among the vast number of books and other sources of genealogical instruction, there is very little that takes the researcher very far beyond basic, introductory instruction. Two major guidebooks provide in-depth treatment of sources (*The Source* and *Printed Sources,* both from Ancestry). Some journals provide useful examples of solving difficult problems (notably *National Genealogical Society Quarterly*). But even these sources only scratch the surface when it comes to helping the experienced beginner or intermediate researcher become a better genealogist.

Formal courses of study (currently three genealogical institutes and a few college programs) provide some assistance, but that help is limited by its very nature. They are expensive, time-consuming, and geographically distant from most of their potential students.

The avocation of genealogy has grown. It is time to provide a higher level of instruction to more family historians in a convenient and inexpensive format. Yes, it takes time, effort, and (indeed) money to become an excellent (or advanced) genealogist. But there has to be someplace to turn to begin this process.

Becoming an Excellent Genealogist seeks to serve this purpose. Conceived, encouraged, and published by the International Commission for the Accreditation of Professional Genealogists (ICAPGen), this book brings together hundreds of years of the authors' combined experience in brief, easy-to-read essays. The authors of these essays have contributed some of the most important lessons they have learned in their years of experience. Their clear, succinct instruction, illustrated with brief examples, teaches concepts and methodology not usually taught in classes or other books. Each essay is an individual expression by an individual author; thus, each one has a distinct voice and presentation style. This is as it should be. There is not just one right way to say or present a concept. This book aims to reflect the unique experience and voice of each author.

The ICAPGen Commission is very pleased to present this guidebook to the genealogical community. It does not seek to be the "final word" in genealogical methodology. Indeed, it seeks rather to be one of the first steps in taking family history "enthusiasts" (as one organization terms today's practitioners) to the "next level" in their pursuit of this popular avocation. It does not cover every possible topic—nothing could—but the lessons learned by these tested, professional genealogists can help all to become excellent genealogists. We sincerely hope it meets your needs and helps you become the best genealogist you can be. Best wishes for success in all your genealogical activities!

~The International Commission for the Accreditation of Professional Genealogists

1

What Makes an Excellent Genealogist?

Kory L. Meyerink, MLS, AG, FUGA

So, what is an "excellent" or an "advanced" genealogist? This is a question that experienced and professional genealogists have been asking themselves (and each other) for years. With very few college degree programs oriented to genealogy, virtually no government licensing of genealogists, and few salaried positions with job descriptions, how do we know if someone is an advanced genealogist?

Maybe the first question should be, does it matter? From the undercurrent of discussion, it seems to. Certainly the prospective client of a professional genealogist would like to know if the person he or she is contemplating hiring is an advanced or experienced genealogist. But wait, if they are professionals, aren't they advanced? Shouldn't they be experienced?

At first thought, that might seem logical, but further consideration indicates that such assumptions are not always true. With no governmental oversight or required licensing, anybody can claim to be a "professional" genealogist. Many people with only a modicum of genealogical experience and/or training begin to develop a client base and accept money to research a family tree. By most definitions, this makes them professional genealogists. But, does it make them good (let alone, excellent)?

Yes, the genealogical field has established standards, thanks in large part to the National Genealogical Society and the Board for Certification of Genealogists. Yes, there are organizations for professional genealogists. However, the Association of Professional Genealogists (APG) has no membership test—anybody can pay membership dues and belong, though they do require members to adhere to a Code of Ethics. Yes, two major organizations in the United States exist that provide competency tests for genealogists and grant those who pass the test a credential to acknowledge their success. Both the Board for Certification of Genealogists (BCG) and the International Commission for the Accreditation of Professional Genealogists (ICAP-Gen) test for ability and competence in adequate (but different) ways. Those who pass either of these tests may call themselves advanced genealogists.

As of 2012, however, a minority of practicing professional genealogists have acquired even one credential from either of these organizations. Only ten percent of APG's membership claimed one or more of the accepted genealogical credentials. Some professional genealogists have chosen not to test for one of those credentials, yet many of them are clearly "advanced" genealogists. So, as important as testing bodies and credentials are, many genealogists simply do not want to obtain them. Therefore, credentials alone do not define an advanced genealogist.

Practitioners of genealogy have been using terms such as novice, beginner, intermediate, and advanced without any mutually agreed-upon definitions. Such terms appear on conference registrations, evaluation forms, institute application forms, class descriptions, and elsewhere. Unfortunately, words without clear meanings simply add to the confusion. So how can we determine when someone is an advanced genealogist? How does one become an excellent or advanced genealogist?

There are no easy answers to such questions. It takes time, knowledge, experience, and a certain aptitude, among other things. There is no certain path, no proscribed regimen to obtain that status, but this book offers part of the answer. It provides a "bridge" from the traditional topics learned in classes, seminars, conferences, institutes, magazines, journals, and books to the accumulated years of actual experience of "excellent genealogists."

An excellent genealogist (or one who wants to become excellent) will achieve a higher level of proficiency by adopting the research approaches and tactics often associated with an "advanced" level genealogist. To begin this task, the introduction to this book outlines some key foundational principles of advanced genealogy by considering the following concepts:

> An excellent genealogist (or one who wants to become excellent) will achieve a higher level of proficiency by adopting the research approaches and tactics often associated with an "advanced" level genealogist.

- Nature of Advanced Research Methodology
- Elements of Advanced Research
- Continuing Self-Education

Nature of Advanced Research Methodology

It's not just about the records. The same records are out there for all researchers to use, from the novice to the most experienced researcher. Rather, advanced methodology is about principles, procedures, attitudes, and understandings. It is the *approach to* the records, the problem, and the research process that separates an excellent genealogist from the less-successful researcher.

Using Sources and Information Better

An excellent genealogist has a deeper and more complete understanding of genealogical sources and information than the less-experienced family historian. This understanding comes from experience with the records, from studying the records themselves (not just the people in the records), and from learning from the research of others. It combines with the natural curiosity that must exist in the mind of a diligent and excellent researcher.

This curiosity compels a researcher to ask *how* and *why* something happened, not just when and where. It urges the excellent genealogist to seek to understand why a record was created, what it says about individuals, and what it *was not* designed to report. Thus, such a researcher does not automatically decide a man died or moved just because he was no longer listed in a tax list. Rather, depending on the nature of the list (what was being taxed), he could have sold that property, he may have been eligible for tax abatement (due to age or infirmity), or the laws could have changed to the extent that he was no longer in a taxable class.

Another example is in the approach to indexes. Experienced researchers know that bigger is not always better. Large indexes, so desired by beginning genealogists, are sometimes the bane of good genealogy. They often provide too many "hits" to fully evaluate the information. Spelling variations of surnames are difficult to spot when those variations are pages (or screens) away from the "preferred" spelling. For example, the equivalent surnames Thompson and Thomson may be separated by dozens (or hundreds) of Thompkins, Thomsens, and other variants. The situation is even worse if the spelling variations begin with the first or second letter: Thompson versus Tomson, or Cline versus Kline. No known computer algorithm can find all possible spellings of every name, and most miss even the most obvious.

Indexes can also provide a false sense of "completeness." Not knowing what *is* and what *is not* in an index, the less-experienced researcher may think a thorough search was done, when indeed it was not. For example, an Internet search engine may find 13,985 hits for your query, and that seems pretty thorough. If you narrow it down with just the right words to a more manageable 78 hits, and carefully evaluate each of those hits, you might think you have searched "everything online." Well, you haven't. Perhaps you didn't narrow the hits as well as you thought you did, or perhaps there are other parameters you could use to search the Web.

Therefore, the excellent genealogist will also consider smaller indexes; those which focus on only one source. Often they index the information in greater detail. They surely will have fewer hits, so if the search target was recorded in the indexed source, there is a much greater chance of actually identifying him or her. Consider the well-known and deservedly popular *Periodical Source Index* (PERSI). With about two million entries for genealogical periodical articles, it is a researcher's dream index. However, it does not index every name in *any* of the thousands of periodicals it indexes. For that, you need to go to the annual, or cumulated, indexes for a specific periodical.

But it's not just about using indexes better, it's also about using records better. Excellent genealogists study the entire record and pay attention to the myriad of details in the record, even if some of those details do not pertain to the reason for reading the record. Consider the commonly used U.S. census records. Each census is different from the other censuses and includes different information. All researchers quickly learn that all household members are named only on censuses in and after 1850. However, excellent genealogists know, for example, that the 1870

Excellent genealogists study the entire record and pay attention to the myriad of details in the record, even if some of those details do not pertain to the reason for reading the record.

census includes a column identifying whether an individual's parents were of foreign birth and a column indicating if the individual was eligible to vote. Thus, for persons born outside the United States, this census indirectly indicates whether they were naturalized. Answers to these and dozens of other questions can and should impact the direction of research but will only do so if the researcher pays attention to such details.

Another record type with many important details is the death certificate. When using death certificates, genealogists are trained to see who the informant was and determine his relationship to the deceased. But it is just as important to learn where the person was buried, which funeral home attended to the deceased, and whether or not a coroner's report was filed. Noticing and using details in the records are what help separate excellent genealogists from average researchers.

Some details aren't even reported on the records themselves, so excellent genealogists must know the history of the records and the rules with which they were created. The census again provides an example. Each census had a legally established date for which the information was to be recorded. While the actual date of the enumeration is given at the top of the page, the form does not tell you that no person born after 1 June (for the 1850 through 1900 censuses) should be listed on the census. This information is not written on the form, it's only given in the instructions to enumerators. It's this detail that explains why a child, known to be born 23 June 1860, was not enumerated on the census that year, even though the census taker dated that page 5 July 1860.

Elements of Identification

All genealogists know to search for the name of a relative, along with that relative's birth date, birthplace, and parents' names. But that's just the tip of the iceberg. Proper genealogical identification is so much more.

Names. Excellent genealogists don't stop until they understand a person's full name. Just what does that middle initial stand for in a great grandmother's name? Could it be a family name, or a clue to a relationship? Even the complete name is not enough. Did the person use a nickname or variants during her lifetime? Was a woman married more than once and thus listed under other names besides the name of the man (or men) with whom she had children? When tracing immigrants, it's not just the name that is crucial but the name in the foreign tongue of the immigrant. Cultural names are equally important. Many Roman Catholics were given a saint's name at baptism that may not appear in other records. Not knowing this may cause a family historian to overlook the very record of birth for which he is searching. Jewish immigrants (and those of many other cultures) often radically modified their names to sound more "American."

Dates. Depending on when and where a person's ancestors lived, there may be big problems with reading and understanding the associated dates. Quakers chose to use numbers for the months, rather than the commonly accepted names that were derived from pagan gods. How does the inexperienced genealogist interpret an obituary or letter that says someone died on the 4th ult.? Researchers in France and parts of Germany and the Netherlands have to deal with an entirely different calendar developed by Napoleon. Far Eastern cultures, as well as many non-Christian religious groups, had calendars different from those used by most North Americans. And what about "double dating" and the calendar change of 1752? There's much to be learned about the chronological aspects of genealogy, including the not-so-simple process of determining a birth date from a person's age in a record or the appropriate spacing of children in a family, or the ages of mothers at children's births. Excellent genealogists know, for example, not only what a perpetual calendar is but how and when to use one and where to find one when it is needed. Proper identification of ancestors and other relatives demands that an excellent genealogist understand and accurately apply correct dates.

Places. North American genealogists quickly learn that county (and other) boundaries and jurisdictions changed over time. Excellent genealogists understand that such changes have an echo effect even today. Where were deed, probate, court, and other records kept, both before and after boundary and jurisdictional changes? Were the records kept in the old courthouse, transferred to the new, or sent to the state archives? How does the genealogist accurately reflect place changes in a database or article written about the family? Towns and counties (and even some proposed states) have gone out of existence. Names have been changed. Tryon County, New York, is long gone, but does the pre-Revolutionary War researcher know that all of its records are still extant, just hiding under the name Montgomery County?

Relationships. Of all four key elements of genealogical identification, relationships are at once the most important and the most complex. Ultimately, relationships are what genealogy is all about. The exact birth date or place of an ancestor may never be known and perhaps not the complete name. But without understanding relationships, that person has no place on the family tree. Relationships are the heart and soul of genealogy, and so it is relationships that all genealogists are trying to identify and prove. To forget this key aspect and focus instead only on names, dates, and places often leads to incorrect linkages—assumptions of relationships based on "right name, right place, right time frame."

Thinking (and Searching) Broadly

If the concept of understanding the details in a record are so important, how much more important is it to apply that type of mindset to the entire research process? Too often, beginning genealogists limit their searches to a few common and popular records, such as the census or government vital records. Perhaps she does most of her searching online, or he seldom goes beyond the sources of the famous Family History Library. While there is nothing wrong with online searches or the microfilms of the Family History Library, limiting one's search to such records is not the way to success with the really tough problems.

One of the wonderful aspects of North American research is the veritable cornucopia of records, most of which are readily available to any researcher. While our friends searching European records may spend most

Always be sure to use ALL available records.

of their time in civil vital records or church registers, there's so much more for the North American researcher. Always be sure to use *all* available records. Most genealogical issues can be substantiated (and should be) by two or more records, so don't stop just because the cemetery tombstone includes the birth and death date. The more circumstantial the evidence is, the more sources should be used to support a proof statement (or argument). Be sure to check the sexton's burial record, if extant, along with any church baptismal entries, obituaries, and death records. This habit is especially critical when records are not available or don't provide the expected information. "Substitute" records are a way of "thinking broadly": Tax lists for lost census records, land deeds for missing probates, naturalizations for passenger lists, and so many more.

Thinking broadly also applies to the way a record is searched. Be sure to search a wide range of years. Watch for children at least until the mother was fifty years old. Certainly also search a year or two before a marriage. Check neighboring counties or church parishes if the marriage is not where it was expected. With the advent of larger databases, it's possible to search the census across the entire country, not just a state at a time. It was just such a search some time ago that turned up a missing Arizona man in Washington, D.C., where he was working for the federal government. "Broad searches" also means checking a wide range of spellings for the name, both the given name and the surname. Even if the family always spelled their name the same way, that does not mean the clerk spelled it that way.

Too often, genealogists tend to focus on "the record." What record will give the wife's maiden name? What source will name his hometown in the old country? The excellent genealogist approaches the research from the other direction: Focus on the solution and the variety of ways of finding the answer. To find that maiden name: Should you search land records for a deed of gift to a son-in-law? Or, review probate files for a daughter with the right married name? Or, analyze the naming pattern of the woman's children for clues to her father's name? Maybe you need to do it all. Maybe the name of that foreign birthplace is attached to a neighbor who traveled with the family, or a history of the locality will identify where the early settlers came from. There's almost always another way to get to the answer, if you think broadly enough.

Elements of Advanced Research

Despite the lack of a universal definition of an "advanced" genealogist, there are some traits common to all advanced or excellent genealogists. The purpose of this book is to share many of those traits or elements. As an introduction to the concept that various elements of advanced research can be identified and described, consider the four following approaches.[1] Many aspects of these concepts are developed in greater detail in the essays in this book.

Changing Your Thinking

Excellent genealogists are not locked into just one way of thinking, or of approaching a research problem. Rather, they go out of their way to develop alternative theories and to find uncommon sources to search. They are willing to "pay the price of success." Paying the price does not just mean researching longer or attending another conference, although that is part of it. Even more importantly, it means moving away from one's "comfort zone"—literally, changing how they think about finding solutions.

This means that they are also willing to change their attitude about how they research and how willing they are to continue promoting their pet theory about an ancestral connection. When someone challenges their conclusions, excellent genealogists are humble enough to, with an open mind, consider that challenge and, as needed, change their own conclusions. In order to change their thinking, excellent genealogists are willing to step outside themselves. A shy, retiring, bookworm kind of researcher will make a conscious effort to develop personal networks of other researchers, knowing that the knowledge and experience of the network will likely lead her to solutions she would have never found on her own. It impels the "know-it-all" genealogist to seek out further education opportunities and to become more humble, recognizing that he really does not "know it all."

Changing one's thinking means learning how to develop, *and prove,* credible hypotheses about genealogical situations. When research problems become so great that "easy" solutions don't work, one of the first steps for the experienced genealogist is to develop a hypothesis that incorporates all of the known information, considers the culture of the time (such as slavery in the antebellum South), and does not violate natural life cycles (having children at too old or young of an age). A careful and well-developed hypothesis will often lead to solutions faster than just digging through more and more records.

Another way to change one's thinking is to realize that names are not just identifiers. Rather, they have meaning, in multiple ways, for the genealogist. A rare surname is often easier to search, but beware that such names are often misspelled in a wide variety of unpredictable ways. The uncommon given name of a sibling may be the easier way to find a family in large databases, rather than the common name of the direct ancestor. Genealogists quickly learn that Polly is a nickname for Mary and Jack for John. But, how quickly do they search for Ted when an ancestor's name was Edward or Theodore, or Rick for Frederick? Sure, names may change at marriage or after immigration, but they often change at other times in life that are unpredictable. One girl switched to using her middle name in school because three boys in her class shared her first name and she did not want to be considered a boy.

---

[1] Thanks to David E. Rencher, AG, FUGA for partnering with the author in the development of these concepts for the Salt Lake Institute of Genealogy.

And name issues are not just about personal names. Place names suffer some of the same problems; for instance, too many places in England named "St. Mary," or the inability to recognize the German city of Köln as Cologne in English. In Ontario, Canada, the city of Berlin changed its name to Kitchner during World War I (guess why), and it remains so today, causing some confusion for people seeking records for a town that "disappeared."

Thinking also changes when the researcher realizes that records and information about an ancestor's neighbors, friends, and even distant relatives may yield important facts about the ancestor. People did not live in a vacuum, so it is crucial to "cast a broad net" in order to gather as many clues as possible from the records. Those witnesses on a church christening record may have migrated from the same previous county as the family being researched. A woman with a different surname may be a married sister. One of the farm hands who appears in a census record may have later married the owner's daughter. Think carefully about what to record when abstracting a record. Those "other" names may not be as unrelated as at first assumed.

Taking the time to understand items such as migration patterns and alternate jurisdictions is also an important change when thinking about the family. How, when, and from where did the early settlers come to the family's county? Knowing the government jurisdictions (town, county, state, etc.) is all well and good, but what were the boundaries of the school district or their favorite church? Which newspaper(s) served that town? If there were two mortuaries in a southern town in the 1920s, which one served the black population?

Times change, people change, society changes, boundaries change, even geography changes (how many cemeteries have moved or disappeared to make room for a new reservoir, now called a lake?). Therefore, the researcher's thinking needs to change as well. Not *just* because of changes over time but because of differing approaches to problem solving. One final change to keep in mind: The vast majority of genealogical problems *can be solved!* Yes, there are times when records run out (typically in the 16th century) and counties were burned, but even with burned counties there are alternate sources and strategies. The excellent genealogist does not give up on a research problem; rather she changes her approach, often by changing her thinking.

Dealing with Sources

In addition to thinking differently, excellent genealogists also deal with sources in ways the less experienced researcher may not have considered. Researchers quickly learn how to glean ancestral information from a myriad of sources, but it is also possible to "turn the tables" and use those same sources to find descendants of an ancestor. The value of descendant research is often overlooked, but a distant cousin who still lives in the ancestral town may have the family Bible or other papers with key information. Modern DNA testing can be helpful if a

In addition to thinking differently, excellent genealogists also deal with sources in ways the less experienced researcher may not have considered.

line of descent can be traced forward to a living great-great grandchild. Therefore, when reading an obituary, the excellent researcher does not just read to learn where the ancestor was born and when but also notes where his children were then living. A death certificate is not just an avenue to a birthplace or parent's name. Rather, it also identifies the informant, typically a family member. Census searches can be used to bring descendants forward as well as to trace an ancestor to an earlier resident.

Those same sources can be used with greater agility to discern the parents and ancestry of female lines, not just the easier-to-find males. Even records that do not name the wife or mother of an ancestor do provide important clues to previous residences, where the female family members may be found. The 1850 Ohio census record of a widower with children, all of whom were born in New York, makes a very strong suggestion that their deceased mother was also born in that state. A careful analysis of all the families in the 1830 census of a town for girls of age 15 to 29 may suggest some candidates for the father of a young lady known to have married about 1832 (based on children's birth years).

Using sources better is not just about "genealogical" sources. In addition to the original and derivative sources everyone uses, background information is also necessary to success. One can use the *Handybook for Genealogists* or *Ancestry's Redbook* to learn when a county was created and from which parent county. But, how many scour the Library of Congress catalog to identify a local history that's not in the local library? How many have found an article about the World War I draft registration records to know which men were excluded from registration? When the term "lancepesade" shows up in an early New York record, the excellent genealogist does not just assume it's some obscure Dutch term but rather finds an unabridged dictionary that explains its meaning and origin. Background information helps the immigration researcher understand why his Italian ancestor did not naturalize, yet his Irish grandfather did. Researchers, by their nature, love to question. The best ones also use a wide array of background information sources to find the right answers, thus allowing them to make better assessments of the research circumstances.

The issue for an excellent genealogist is to carefully dissect the record to learn as much as it can reveal about the family, including understanding what it does not say. The Pennsylvania tax list that names a man as an "inmate" is also saying that he was married but did not own land. The absence of a man, known to be in his mid-30s, from the local militia list may suggest that he was sick or had physical (or mental) limitations that excused him from service. Date references to the 4th or 7th month may well suggest that Quakers were involved. For such researchers, city directory research means a careful and thorough search through every published directory for the entire span of time the family lived in the city. It's not enough to check a couple of years for the family, or even worse, to believe that "I already know where they lived and who he worked for; it won't tell me anything new." That is *not* an effective way to deal with sources.

Using Repositories

No one library, archive, or Web site has all the needed records for research. Of course, this is not news to any but the most novice of family historians. However, the expert genealogist has a much greater understanding of the wealth of repositories that hold records about families. She knows that the state library has the most complete collection of county histories for the state and that the early tax lists are at the state archive. But, it's more than that. He also knows which out-of-state archive holds important records for research in the family's state. She knows that one of the best collections for early Kentucky research is at the Wisconsin State Historical Society. He has learned who, at the county clerk's office, knows where the delayed birth certificates are filed.

How do they know all this? They have visited those repositories and regularly check their Web sites for new information about new collections. They use library catalogs and archive inventories to understand the breadth and scope of a repository's collection. Most of them have volunteered (or still do) at a local library or society. In their insatiable search for knowledge and information about sources and repositories, they read articles in *Prologue* (the magazine of the National Archives) and converse with colleagues about their onsite research experience. They have visited more mortuaries than all eight of their great-grandparents combined.

Libraries may be a genealogist's best friend; after all, their mission is to share information with the public. But the excellent genealogist also understands the rules of each library as well as the nature of its collections. She understands the mission of the library and the subsequent limitations of its collections. By respecting the professional status of the library staff, that same staff is sometimes able to "go the extra mile" to assist the researcher or notify him when new materials arrive. Extensive and careful use of libraries will expose the genealogist to a wide variety of reference tools that point towards other sources of value. And, when a local library does not have a needed source, the staff member running the inter-library loan system can be an important resource.

Archives, of course, are much different than libraries and need to be understood as such. Their mission is *not* to share information but rather to *preserve* it. Their records are often not public, although the public may be permitted to use them. In most cases, neither the archive nor the archivist owns or controls the record, and this is a critical distinction that experienced family historians understand. The records often still belong to the agency or institution that created them and may be restricted by that creator. When access is limited, knowledge of the archive is even more critical for the genealogist. What kinds of indexes or descriptive catalogs are available? Are they posted online? Have the original records been microfilmed or scanned for Internet access? If the archive is private, is membership needed to access the materials?

Without repositories, genealogists don't have the records they need to conduct their research. Therefore, repositories can't be ignored by excellent genealogists. The very same record may be (and often is) in more than one repository, but one of those may provide better access for a particular researcher. Of course, researchers don't stop with libraries and archives. There are many other kinds of repositories to become familiar with, including historical, genealogical, or fraternal societies, museums, publishers, private record holders, government offices, and, of course, the world's largest repository, the Internet. Understanding them all takes time but pays great dividends in experiencing success in research.

Understanding repositories means that missing and destroyed records don't deter the excellent genealogist for very long. Rather, understanding and properly using a wide variety of repositories is one of the key ways to get past the "burned county" problem. Land records lost? Check with the local title companies. Census missing? Search the tax lists. Since no one entity made all the records about the population, no one repository housed (or lost) them all. Alternate repositories will house alternate sources, so becoming familiar with all kinds of repositories will expose the family historian to yet other records about the family.

> **Understanding and properly using a wide variety of repositories is one of the key ways to get past the "burned county" problem.**

Handling the Information

Of course, good genealogy is not just about dealing with sources (records) or using repositories. Rather it is about the information found in the sources housed in those repositories. Ultimately it is the information that family historians seek, and the excellent ones know how to use the information they find. It starts with avoiding "Information Overload." While some may believe you can never have too much information, that's not true, especially if the researcher is not well enough organized to know how to manage and retrieve the information. When the tombstone, family Bible, obituary, and death certificate all disagree on the date of death, which one gets recorded in the database, and what does one do with the others? When the ancestor Dirk Jansen had four sons and each son named one of their own sons after their father, how does the genealogist keep the four Dirk Jansen cousins separate from each other? Certainly the field of genealogy has developed some standards for numbering people in published accounts, but what about personal filing systems? Plenty of advice exists, but the excellent genealogist has to determine what works best for her own note-keeping system.

Then, once one has gathered information from a variety of records, how does the researcher know where it came from? Genealogists call that concept "documentation," but even in a world of evolving standards, there are many different ways and levels of documentation. While novice researchers may not even think much about that concept, experienced genealogists know that they need to know *how* they have come to know certain information. This, of course, also means that they will be adequately citing their sources, but what does "adequate" mean? Sure there's a rule of thumb: Provide enough information in a citation so that someone else could find that same record. But, how much information does that "someone else" need to have? Many researchers may know what TAG 34:15 means, but others may not. Other "citations" are even more obscure. Abbreviations such as GSU and FGRA were once understood by many genealogists, but today very few know what they mean, let alone the level of credibility they may, or may not, have had. The CFI became the IGI, and even this has evolved to a different program. At that point, citations using such abbreviations will become virtually meaningless. Excellent genealogists won't let that happen to their citations.

The information the genealogist obtains from various records in different repositories becomes evidence when applied to a genealogical situation. Each piece of that evidence needs to be carefully evaluated and any discrepancies resolved. The four different death dates just mentioned above don't only need to be recorded in some fashion, but a decision should be made regarding their accuracy. Which one has the greater weight? The information may be primary in each of them, recorded at or near the time of death. The experienced genealogist knows what other factors to examine and weigh in order to make a decision. Those with some experience may say: Let's get another record and see if that "resolves" it. It's not just "getting more records"; correct evaluation of each record is the answer. That's how the excellent genealogist handles that kind of information.

Eventually the researcher finds enough acceptable evidence that the genealogical situation seems clear. The evidence is "convincing" and maybe it is finally time to stop researching. But, is it really? Would others be so confident, or is the researcher just too tired to look further? Or, is she so enamored with her own theory and interpretation that she's no longer an impartial judge? It's human. Everyone wants to "be right" and to solve the problem he's been working on for some time. So, now we have the Genealogical Proof Standard coming to the rescue. That will measure all our evidence and pronounce a verdict, right? No, not at all. It still takes careful and experienced application to achieve that standard. How does one define "reasonably exhaustive research"? What records are reliable, and who determines whether they were correctly interpreted? Is the rebuttal of contradictory evidence adequate? The skills to answer those questions are the skills that the excellent genealogist has developed. These are some of the elements of advanced research.

Continuing Self-Education

Without a doubt, an excellent genealogist never stops learning. Unlike many fields of endeavor, each genealogical problem is unique. The combined circumstances of time, place, surname, religion, ethnicity, occupation, geography, economics, society, intelligence, culture, health, emotions, personality, and nature make each person and family different. These differences translate to their ancestors or descendants, as well. Sources and research methods that worked for one family often do not pertain to the investigation of the next family.

> **Without a doubt, an excellent genealogist never stops learning.**

Unlike lawyers who have case law to set parameters for their work, or accountants who have laws and regulations governing their activities, genealogists need to develop a different research plan for every research situation. There may be similarities to previous cases or commonly used sources (such as the U.S. census) to consider, but they don't always apply.

The excellent genealogist recognizes the differences of each situation and the limits on her own knowledge. Therefore, the excellent genealogist never stops learning. Such researchers consider all of the following arenas in their ongoing efforts to become as educated as possible in their chosen avocation.

Personal Assessment

Education always begins with some form of personal assessment. Individuals decide they need to learn something. Unfortunately, all too often that assessment is subconscious, or barely conscious. Researchers, in particular, need to take the time to review their own personal needs. Genealogists seldom have enough time to do all the research they want, so how could they possibly have enough time to get the education they need? Well, that's a bit of a fallacy. Excellent genealogists understand that more education will make them better genealogists, as well as faster and more successful researchers. So, what is it that needs to be assessed? Consider the following:

- **Research needs.** What specific needs will help current and projected research? If a genealogist wants to explore Italian ancestry, then learning Italian becomes a research need. If a recent discovery has shown that the family lived in Alabama, then it may be time to learn about the resources and repositories of that state.
- **Time available.** No one has enough time, but for what's important, everyone makes time. How much time the researcher has will dictate some of the choices. Perhaps an evening class can be fit into the schedule for a few weeks. An accumulation of vacation days at work may allow attendance at an institute or conference.
- **Funds available.** Yes, good education costs both time and money, but the researcher controls both of these elements. Some forms of education are low-cost, but it may be time-intensive to visit the local library and read all the books on the subject of interest. Many moderate-cost options are available, but nothing worthwhile is totally free.
- **Areas of interest.** In addition to research "needs," every researcher has areas of interest. They often overlap with "needs" but even then, take time to identify them in this assessment. Specific interests may dictate the available educational avenues. For example, relatively few instructional opportunities surface for Welsh research, so books and periodicals may be the best alternative.
- **Resources available.** Ultimately, education usually comes down to what's available. Time and cost may prevent traveling to a distant location to learn more. Perhaps there is no published material on the topic of interest. However, in most cases several different resources are available. Take the time needed to identify them all, so appropriate choices can be made.

Books

One of the most popular forms of self-education in genealogy has always been books. They are often readily available and cover a wide variety of topics. Identifying and selecting the right ones, however, can be more challenging than originally thought. Some books are out of date and/or include incorrect information. Seek the advice of experts in the field, starting with the local genealogical society and library, but don't stop there. With virtually every library's catalog now available on the Internet, it should be possible to identify books on almost any topic. Make sure the book is up to date and the author has the necessary credentials for the subject. While there is no single source list or bibliography of genealogical instructional books, the catalogs of major genealogical libraries will aid in identifying them. Consider the Family History Library, the Library of Congress, the Allen County Public Library, and others. An advanced search at WorldCat may unearth local, unheralded books on obscure topics.

Periodicals

Along with books, periodicals are a popular way to learn more about genealogy topics. Literally thousands of local, state, and national journals, magazines, newsletters, and other periodicals are published in the field of genealogy. All of them include "how-to" or background information articles among their contents. The major peer-reviewed journals present research findings that make excellent case studies from which to learn research techniques. Although several of the popular, general-interest genealogy magazines have ceased publication in recent years, society periodicals will continue to be an important source of education for successful genealogists. The availability of a subject index that includes "how-to" references in the *Periodical Source Index* (PERSI) can help researchers find both current and earlier articles on a variety of topics.

Reviews

Book reviews are an often overlooked yet important aspect of self-education. Reviews alert the readers to the existence of new books, an important service in itself. In addition, the critiques provided by qualified reviewers help readers assess the strengths and weaknesses of the book under review, often comparing the book to ones with a similar focus. A careful reading of a review will also reveal what aspects the reviewer believes are most important to understand about both the book and the subject. Almost any book may be reviewed, but usually the most significant books are reviewed the most. Many of them are guidebooks and instructional books, making them excellent self-education material. Check the major, peer-reviewed journals, such as the *National Genealogical Society Quarterly* and the *New England Historical and Genealogical Record*.

Electronic Media

The loss of some print magazines has been more than countered by the rise in electronic media as a source of educational material for genealogists. Delivered through the Internet, articles on all varieties of "how-to" topics appear on hundreds of Web sites. The major subscription and free websites all provide instruction, with the largest volume likely being the Wiki at FamilySearch.org, which will surely continue to grow. The articles at such Web sites are joined by a large and fast-growing collection of personal opinions and experiences reflected in hundreds, if not thousands, of blogs by genealogists, both professional and rank amateur. A slightly more planned and formalized version of blogs, with audio accompaniment, are podcasts and webinars dedicated to teaching genealogical sources and strategies. The electronic media as a vehicle for education will continue to grow as more and more instruction is delivered in written, audio, and visual form over the Web, both for free and for a fee.

Instruction

For serious and in-depth education, genealogists often plan on paid, programmed instructional opportunities offered primarily through local genealogical societies and similar institutions. Seminars are typically a one-day gathering sponsored by a local organization with a single theme and speaker, or perhaps a couple of concurrent classes. Genealogical conferences are usually multiday events with several concurrent sessions to choose from in a smorgasbord approach to education. Most often, these are held by state organizations, but two national conferences must be considered. Held in different locations each year in major cities across the country, the National Genealogical Society's conference is held in the spring while the Federation of Genealogical Societies has a conference in late summer. Prominent genealogical speakers, teachers, and lecturers from across the country share their understanding and insight to sources and techniques.

For greater depth, consider one of the three major annual genealogical institutes where students spend a week and about twenty hours of correlated classroom instruction focused on a single topic. Designed to take intermediate to advanced genealogists and provide them with additional tools and information, each week is intensive and in-depth. The oldest such gathering is the National Institute of Genealogical Research held at the National Archives in July. The Institute of Genealogical and Historical Studies is held in Birmingham, Alabama, at Samford University in June, and the Salt Lake Institute of Genealogy takes place in January, just blocks from the Family History Library in that city.

At the college level, genealogical instruction is rare but is slowly growing. The only four-year university degree program is offered by Brigham Young University within its History Department. Many of its courses are also offered to the public through the university's Independent Study program. Brigham Young University-Idaho offers a two-year Applied Associate degree in Family History Research. All courses are online and taught during academic semesters. The University of Toronto supports the National Institute of Genealogical Studies, which is a "distance learning" program with a full range of courses leading to a Certificate of Genealogical Studies. A few other colleges and universities, such as Boston University, across the country offer a few courses or a certificate program in genealogical research.

Membership

Genealogical and historical societies and related organizations exist in every state and most counties and major cities. These non-profit organizations consist of like-minded persons who gather together to teach each other, share experiences, and provide help and assistance to each other. They typically meet on a monthly basis at a local library or other public venue and offer instruction and direction for research. They are very much the "grass roots" of genealogy. The excellent genealogist generally belongs to at least the local society and often the society in an area of ancestral interest, as societies generally publish periodicals and other materials dealing with local or topical research.

Publishers

While libraries are a wonderful place to find a variety of previously published books about genealogical topics, news about current books is best obtained from publishers. Genealogy continues to be a cottage industry in publishing circles with few general-interest publishers offering any titles beyond the somewhat standard introductory books. However, well over a dozen specialty publishers focus on publishing genealogical sources as well as some instructional and background books. For many years, the two most prolific publishers have been Genealogical Publishing Company and Heritage Books.

Repositories

As noted earlier, understanding repositories is critical for genealogical success. Another reason they are important is because of the support network they provide to genealogists. Not only do many genealogical groups hold meetings at the local library, but their members often volunteer at the library, helping family historians seeking to find their ancestors. Libraries often acquire the books their patrons suggest and may hold classes on genealogical and historical topics, providing yet further means of self-education.

Other avenues exist to help the genealogist learn what she needs to know to be a successful researcher. The key is to always be seeking ways to learn more. With each family having different backgrounds and circumstances, there is no end to the need for further education.

Key Steps to Becoming an Excellent Genealogist

So, can this process of becoming an excellent genealogist be digested down to a few simple steps, so that, once completed, one can call oneself an "advanced genealogist"? Probably not. After all, we may learn much about one particular genealogical topic, say Quaker research, and yet know virtually nothing about another topic, such as colonial Gulf Coast families.

However, while knowledge is a key, the excellent genealogist also conducts research in a more thorough and complete manner, including obtaining new knowledge when the situation demands it. To that end, there are many "hallmarks" of an excellent genealogist, even more than can be covered in a book such as this. In digesting the various concepts discussed in this book, develop a personal checklist of areas where improvement is needed. Consider the following as a starter checklist for improving genealogical research skills. These are concepts followed by virtually all successful and excellent genealogists:

- *Watch* for changing jurisdictions. Even outside North America, boundaries changed, and that impacts where records were made and are stored.
- *Re-examine* the records and get more out of them. Take time to learn their limits, strengths, and coverage.
- *Seek* additional sources. There are more sources that the genealogist does not know about. Ask others, read voraciously, and keep learning about new or different records.
- *Avoid* "right name, right place" syndrome. Many people share the same name, even within a locality, and sometimes within an extended family. Genealogists will be more successful when they take the time and make the effort to fully identify persons.
- *Analyze* friends, neighbors, and extended family members in research. Watch for them in the records, add them to your database, and look for patterns of migration, settlement, names, and relationships.
- *Practice,* practice, practice.
- *Research* non-family lines. Even those who never plan to do research for hire will become better when they begin researching the families of those who are not related to them. This exposes them to new situations and encourages deeper thinking about research methods.
- *Write* about the findings (and what was not found). This practice organizes one's thinking and forces a confrontation of gaps in the research. Then, have the writing reviewed by others for clarity, logic, and completeness.
- *Subscribe* to and read the genealogical journals. Include the national journals and ones for regions or areas of interest. Experts learn much from seeing how others have solved different problems.
- *Enjoy* the journey! Genealogists have chosen this activity. No one has forced them to pursue their family history. Both the thrill of the hunt and the joy of discovery will be greatly enhanced by better preparation and careful application of the principles outlined in this book.

For Further Study

Mills, Elizabeth Shown. "Working with Historical Evidence: Genealogical Principles and Standards." *National Genealogical Society Quarterly* 82, no. 3 (September 1999): 165-184.

Rising, Marsha Hoffman. *The Family Tree Problem Solver.* Cincinnati: Family Tree Books, 2005.

Sperry, Kip. "Indexes" in *Printed Sources: A Guide to Published Genealogical Records,* ed. Kory L. Meyerink. Salt Lake City: Ancestry, 1998.

2

Elements of Genealogy

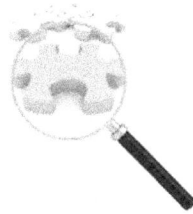

Kory L. Meyerink, MLS, AG, FUGA

Modern genealogy can be seen as consisting of six important and inter-related elements, each of which needs to be understood to maximize success in research as well as in the accuracy of a researcher's conclusions. Most genealogists, amateur and professional, are not consciously aware of these elements but have had at least minimal exposure to their nature and importance. Unfortunately, many family historians think of genealogy primarily in terms of records: What record will prove a relationship? What record gives a wife's maiden name? What record proves I have Native American blood?

This is a short-sided view of genealogy, especially as it is practiced by the best genealogists today. Records, to be sure, are the core of genealogy, in any place and time. However, without a firm understanding of the other five elements of genealogy, the information in the records cannot be used as effectively as possible in reconstructing families and establishing relationships. Each of these topics could be treated in much greater depth, but the following is an introduction to the key concepts. Some aspects of these elements are addressed in other essays in this collection. Other guidebooks may touch upon some aspects. The expert genealogist continues to develop an understanding of all these elements:

- Genealogical Research Process
- Boundaries and Jurisdictions
- Repositories
- Records
- Technology
- Sharing

Genealogical Research Process

Genealogy, like all academic research pursuits, follows the scientific process of research. As an adjunct to history, genealogy uses a "humanities" version of the research process, adapted to the specifics of genealogical research and records. The core concepts of all forms of scientific research include: First, understand what is already known about a subject. Second, determine what one wants to learn. Third, gather information about the subject. Fourth, evaluate the research findings. Fifth, report the results of the research.

As with any process, genealogy can be divided into however many "steps" the author wishes to use, depending in part on the simplicity of the presentation. For this brief introduction, it is sufficient to mirror the five steps above, with a genealogical application.

Identify What You Know

Whether a rank beginner who has just become interested in her own family history or a 40-year professional genealogist, every research situation begins by carefully identifying what information is already known. For the beginner, it means scouring family sources for the names and dates and places of immediate relatives, such as grandparents. For the seasoned researcher, it means reviewing what previous research efforts have produced. The modern genealogist uses one or more computer databases to centralize the gathered information. In addition, an organized system is needed to maintain the inevitable paper and other materials that are collected during research.

This step includes learning and applying the nature of genealogical information and understanding the standard ways in which data is recorded. Genealogists, of course, are seeking information about family members. Most specifically, their names, relationships to others (child, parent, etc.), and the dates and places of key life events (birth, marriage and death). Other information of interest may include military service, occupations, immigration, land ownership, religion, civil service, and any other biographical aspects of a person. Traditionally, dates are recorded in day, month, year order, with the month always spelled out or with a three letter abbreviation but never reduced to a number. Places are generally recorded from the smallest to largest jurisdiction, such as town, county, state (see the Jurisdiction discussion below). While these are foundational concepts that every genealogist should quickly learn, they are also emblematic of the fact that some standard acceptable practices exist that excellent genealogists use.

Decide What You Want to Learn

Successful research must have a goal: something the researcher wants to learn. While this is not a problem for the genealogist, the step of goal setting is often not done carefully. Too many new genealogists only have a nebulous idea of their family history quest. They want a family tree, but what does that mean? Goals must be clear and concrete and, of

> **Successful research must have a goal: something the researcher wants to learn.**

course, achievable. Understanding one's long-range goal is often easy but certainly not sufficient. The genealogist who wants to know where his Irish ancestors came from in Ireland has a quest. The goal must be the initial part of a plan to achieve the quest. For example, first learn which ancestors came from Ireland. Then, learn when they arrived, etc. To be effective, genealogical research goals should pertain to a specific person or family and be clearly defined, such as "When did great grandfather Jones die?" Such goals set up the rest of the research process to lead to success.

Select Records to Search

With a specific goal in mind, it is much easier to select the best records to search, especially when the researcher understands the nature of records (see the discussion below). This step can be very complex and deserves the careful attention of the excellent researcher. Selecting a record based just on one's past experience ("Let's see what the census says") can lead to erroneous conclusions and be a waste of time. This is equally true when the choice is made based on access to a record ("It's at the local library, so I'll check it."). Neither the Internet nor the Family History Library, both with huge collections of records, has all the records a genealogist needs. Indeed, they never will. It takes time, effort, and experience to gain a full understanding of the contents and access to records. Fortunately, there is no shortage of books that discuss records.

Yes, the chief selection criteria includes the content of the record as well as access (where is the record available?). However, the first rule of thumb is to examine compiled records before original records. So much genealogy has already been done in North America, the British Isles, and elsewhere that it is very possible someone else has already found the answers the genealogist is seeking. Only after carefully seeking and searching the research of others does the research usually turn to the vast number of original records preserved in numberless repositories.

Obtain and Search the Records

With the right records for the research goal selected, a researcher then determines where to obtain them and how to search them. Often, in the selection process, the location of the needed records is known, but sometimes it is not. All records reside in one or more repositories, which are discussed further below. Researchers access the needed repositories by visiting, corresponding (phone, e-mail, letter), or having someone else search the records of interest (for free or for payment). In addition to the many considerations relative to obtaining the records, perhaps one of the most important is the realization that many records can be obtained through various means. The earlier advent of microfilming and the recent addition of the Internet have greatly multiplied the options for this important part of research.

Searching the record is often not as simple as it may sound. Many of the essays in this volume address a variety of needed search techniques. For example, while searching for the person(s) of interest, it is important to take note of other persons with the same surname; future research may find them closely related to the family. Broadening the time period of the search, or the geographic area, may locate the right family when the original search appeared to fail.

Of course, learning about available indexes will generally make the search much easier and in many cases, the genealogist needs some facility with a foreign language and/or an archaic form of handwriting.

Use the Information

Having made it this far through the research process, the genealogist now has new information. Even if the subject of the search was not in the records, that is new information and will likely require an adjustment of one's understanding of the family. That new information must be captured, typically in the genealogical database where the new dates, places, and names can be entered. Excellent genealogists will, of course, cite the source of that information as Amy Harris talks about in her essay on documentation in this volume (see Chapter 8). It is also critical to evaluate that information; determine how accurate it is and what it says about other aspects of the family being studied. Does it conflict with previous information? If so, how does the genealogist decide which information is right?

As the researcher uses the new information, it is also critical to share those new findings. Virtually all scientific knowledge is gained, in large part, by building on what others have learned earlier. The same is true of genealogy. It is not possible for every genealogist to "re-invent the wheel" or to research, from scratch, all of her own family. There is simply not enough time. Often the only extant information about a person or family resides in an older compiled record, gathered by someone long ago who had access to now-destroyed or lost records. The importance of sharing elevates that concept to one of these six elements of genealogy and is discussed further below.

Boundaries and Jurisdictions

By their nature, genealogical records have jurisdictional limitations. That is, they apply only to a certain geographic area and/or to certain events and/or families. For example, marriage records in the United States are usually recorded by each different county. A wide variety of jurisdictions exercise authority over which records are created or kept about our ancestors and their families.

After a researcher selects one or more record types that may contain the desired information, it is then necessary to consider which jurisdiction(s) are most likely to have kept those records. Guidebooks, librarians, and fellow genealogists can help determine the most likely jurisdictions for a given record in a certain time period. It is crucial to know which jurisdictions kept the records being sought before one can select specific record(s).

Wherever people settled, civil, religious, and other leaders exercised some level of authority over them, and most created records of genealogical value. Some of the key concepts about jurisdictions include:

Jurisdiction is

- the power, right, or authority to legislate, interpret, and apply civil and religious laws or social habits and traditions.
- the physical boundaries of an organization's authority. For example, a probate court may have jurisdiction over a county or over several counties.

Jurisdictions may have several levels. Large jurisdictions (such as churches or governments) may be divided into smaller ones: a nation is divided into states; a state into counties.

Geography. Earth's physical features, such as rivers, mountains, and lakes, affected jurisdictional boundaries. Indeed, they often became the physical boundaries of a jurisdiction.

Jurisdictions overlap. People usually live in many overlapping jurisdictions at once, such as school, church, or town boundaries.

Imprecise jurisdictions. Some jurisdictions are not defined by clear boundaries. This is notably the case with businesses, societies, and many churches. Rather, they are defined by the choice of a person to affiliate with that organization. However, even most such organizations still operate in a geographical setting, such as a city for a newspaper, or a town for a mortuary.

Jurisdictions change over time. Today's boundaries may have changed many times since an ancestral family lived there.

Records of Jurisdictions

The following jurisdictions created or kept records useful to the genealogist:

- *Governments.* These are the most common records and include records of birth, marriage, death, land ownership, court decrees, military experience, population counts, taxes, and so forth. There are usually several levels, such as national, regional, state, district, local, and municipal. See the chart below, "Typical Government Jurisdictions."

- *Religious Organizations.* Churches usually have a local jurisdiction, such as a parish or congregation. Several local groups usually belong to a conference, association, diocese, or synod. They kept records of events that were sacred or essential to their members' salvation, such as baptisms, christenings, and meeting minutes. Each denomination determines what records were created and at what level they were kept.

- *Families.* This fundamental unit of society is usually informally organized into immediate, extended, or ancestral families. They often possess family Bibles, journals, letters, and other records.

- *Business/Employment.* Commercial companies, unions, and professional associations kept records of commerce, personnel, pensions, customers, etc. As noted above, their "boundaries" are likely to be less precise.

- *Institutions.* Libraries, archives, and other repositories generally collect records for a specific jurisdiction but also create some records, such as catalogs or inventories. Other institutions, such as hospitals, prisons, and schools, kept records of people they served.

- *Societies.* Groups based on similar interests or goals (including ethnic, patriotic, fraternal, and genealogical societies) often kept valuable records and membership lists.

Typical Government Jurisdictions

Nation	Regional	District	Local	Municipal
Canada	Province	County	Township	Town or City
England		County/Shire		Town or City
France	Department		Commune	Municipality
Germany	State (Land)	Bezirk	Kreis	Stadt or Dorf
Ireland	Province	County	Civil Parish	Town or City
United States	State	County	Township	Town or City

Repositories of Family History Sources

Family history research requires the use of a variety of records that provide information about either living or dead relatives. All of those records must reside somewhere, and in order to successfully use genealogical records, researchers must also learn about the places records are kept. The many places that house records are collectively called repositories. No one library or archive has all the records needed to locate ancestral families, so the excellent genealogist learns about the wide variety and different kinds of repositories, each with different rules and methods of access. The following are the most common repositories for North American records, as well as the records of many European countries.

No one library or archive has all the records needed to locate ancestral families, so the excellent genealogist learns about the wide variety and different kinds of repositories.

Original Record Creator

Every record used in family history research was originally created by an individual, institution, organization, company, or similar group. Some record creators are public organizations (such as local governments), while others are private persons or companies (such as a local funeral home). That creator may still be the custodian of the record. This is particularly the case with private organizations, where laws and regulations regarding the storage and preservation of records may not pertain. It is often useful when seeking genealogical records to determine who created the record of interest and then contact that creator regarding access to the records of interest.

County Courthouse

In North America, many records of genealogical value were (and are) created at the local county level. Typically such records are housed in courthouses. They may include land deeds, probate files, court cases, marriage records, birth and death records, and a wide variety of lesser-used records. These are the records created in the day-to-day operations of a county. They are generally considered public records and can usually be obtained by visiting the local courthouse, although more of these records are appearing daily online in indexed or digitized image format. These records may be hosted by the record creating agency or by a larger Web site that features many collections. Some more recent records, typically vital records, might be restricted for use, for privacy reasons, to persons who are the subject of the records or immediate family members.

Archives

The primary purpose of an archive is to *preserve records* that have historical value. In general, when the original record creator (usually a governmental agency but also private organizations) determines that some of the records created in the past are no longer needed for day-to-day operations, they seek a place to store those records for possible future use. Usually these are the original records, such as marriage records or probate files of government agencies. Therefore, governments at all levels (federal, state, county) establish an archival system. Working in conjunction with archivists, the record creating agency determines which records will be kept under what conditions and for how long.

The records are then transferred to the custody of the responsible archive but are still considered the property of the agency/organization that created them. Usually that agency will determine who can access the records and under what conditions. After the records have been kept for the duration of their retention plan (often 20 to 70 years), they may be destroyed, discarded, or given to another organization with interest in the materials. Some records have permanent value and are kept forever. In the United States, these include land transactions, probate files, census records, vital records, immigration documents, etc.

Archives usually store records based on the way in which they were created. Often this is chronologically, so indexes are usually needed to identify records pertinent to a specific person. The records themselves, with appropriate finding aids (indexes, guides, etc.), are described in collection inventories that identify the specific record group, box, shelf, collection number, or other access number(s) assigned by the archive.

Often key records are copied onto microfilm (or a comparable storage medium). This practice aids in storage space issues, helps to preserve the records, and provides reasonable access to all persons entitled to view the records. Once microfilmed or otherwise copied, the retention schedule may call for the original documents to be destroyed.

Libraries

Libraries are the record repository most familiar to the beginning family historian. Typically considered a "home for books," libraries are actually an incredibly designed system for *sharing information*. As such, they have a much different purpose than archives. Libraries primarily collect published materials. In today's world, that includes books, magazines, journals, newspapers, some microfilm, and electronic media (CD-ROMs and DVDs). Libraries also provide Internet access to the public.

The specific collection of a given library is determined by the audience the library serves. Most libraries are operated by a city or county and serve the general public, including genealogists. Some public libraries, especially those serving larger populations, have excellent genealogical collections. Academic libraries at colleges or universities, as well as some special libraries (often privately funded), may also have very good genealogical collections valuable to family historians.

Among the genealogical materials at libraries, researchers will find published histories of families and localities, indexes to records, abstracts and extracts of key records (such as probate, cemetery, or tax records), periodicals, and a wide variety of reference materials. Like all the holdings of a library, these materials are described in the library's catalog, which organizes material by the author, title, and subjects (content) of the publication. Effective use of libraries is a hallmark of excellent genealogists, as well as the topic of Chad Milliner's essay in this collection (see Chapter 17). Most libraries post their catalog online, which may include part or all of their collections. Contact a librarian of that particular repository if you are not certain of the completeness of its collections.

Historical Societies

Historical societies exist for many counties, towns, and other local and state jurisdictions. These may be government- or membership-funded organizations whose objectives are to preserve and explore the history of the locality, or of a specific subject. They often serve as an archive for material pertinent to the institution's designated mission. Historical society collections will often include publications, making such societies a blend of both library and archive in nature.

Publishers

An often overlooked repository for genealogical material is the publisher who provides both print and/or electronic versions of significant genealogical material. While many such works are self-published (by the author), most are issued by a number of small publishers who focus on family history materials. In addition to selling copies of these works to genealogical libraries, they sell to individuals through their own catalogs, Internet sites, and vendors.

Internet

The single largest repository for genealogical material today is the Internet. As discussed in many available guidebooks, the Internet includes a vast number of genealogical Web sites with a wide variety of information. Although the amount of genealogical data on the Internet continues to grow at an accelerated pace, there is still only a small percent of available genealogical records on the Internet. All of the different kinds of records found in archives and libraries may appear on the Internet, including compilations of dubious quality. However, the ease of access through general search engines, along with major and minor genealogical Web sites, makes the Internet one of the first repositories to search for family history information.

Records

Records are the core of genealogical research and, as such, are the focus of most genealogical discussion, instruction, training, and questions. Therefore, there is less need to delve deeply into a discussion of records than the other elements of genealogy. It is useful to briefly point out some of the ways expert genealogists think about records as a whole, which may be a bit different from the less experienced family historian. It is, after all, a thorough understanding of records, both in the specific and in the general, which facilitates a successful outcome of the research process. If a record possesses the information a genealogist needs, but she can't obtain or interpret that information due to a misunderstanding of the record, then the success she could have as a researcher may evaporate.

The records used by genealogists are not disparate sources with little or no connection to each other. Genealogical sources are actually often quite dependent on each other and with careful, integrated use to provide the success all genealogists seek. Since all the information a genealogist seeks and finds comes from a large yet finite pool of record types, it's useful to consider how to understand that pool. Since the researcher seeks records with the purpose of learning specific information about a person, group, or family, records are best understood and used according to their content. Thus, a census record has a similar genealogical use regardless of whether it was created by a town, state, or federal government, or in 1820 or 1920. Specific differences exist among these records, but the genealogical use is similar.

Furthermore, when different types of records have similar content, those records can be used in a similar manner. Since tax lists and censuses both provide a list of residents, usually in rough geographic order, they can be used for similar research purposes: establishing when and where a family lived. In like manner, city directories or voter lists can be helpful where they exist. In this way, types of records with similar content can be grouped together, making it easier for the researcher to quickly review what similar records might be available for a specific place and time. Government vital records may be the preferred way to obtain information about a person's birth, marriage, or death, but they are of comparatively recent vintage; almost all of them were started less than 180 years ago, many only in the last century. Therefore, similar records, such as church registers, cemetery records, or obituaries, can be grouped with vital records.

This kind of organization is most helpful if all possible records can be categorized in some manner, to facilitate understanding and record selection. To that end, all records that a genealogist uses can be broadly divided into four categories, as represented by the following diagram:

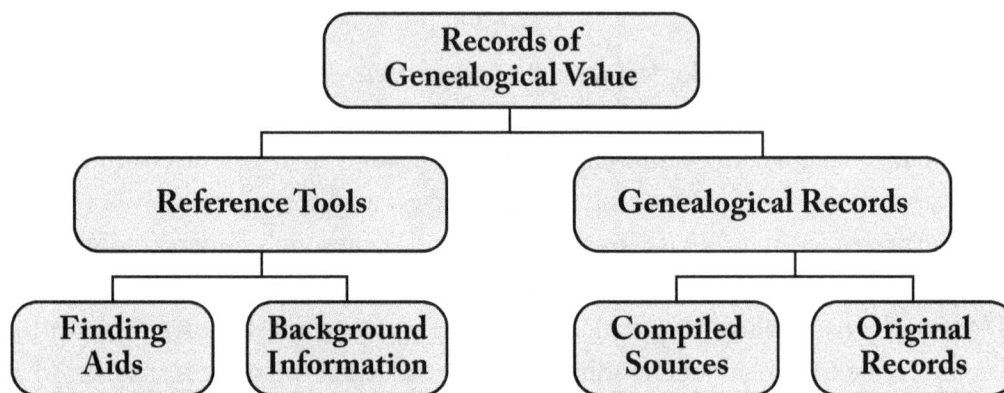

```
                    ┌─────────────────────────┐
                    │      Records of          │
                    │  Genealogical Value      │
                    └─────────────────────────┘
              ┌────────────┴──────────────────┐
     ┌────────────────┐              ┌────────────────────┐
     │ Reference Tools │             │ Genealogical Records│
     └────────────────┘              └────────────────────┘
      ┌──────┴──────┐                  ┌──────┴──────┐
 ┌─────────┐  ┌────────────┐      ┌──────────┐  ┌──────────┐
 │ Finding │  │ Background │      │ Compiled │  │ Original │
 │  Aids   │  │Information │      │ Sources  │  │ Records  │
 └─────────┘  └────────────┘      └──────────┘  └──────────┘
```

Finding Aids

When researchers need help to identify *names* of people within a record or to identify which *records* are out there to be searched, they turn to finding aids. Such records do not provide significant information about a person or a family but are essential aids to finding the information needed. They include the many kinds of indexes all genealogists seek and therefore demand a careful understanding of the many ways to successfully use indexes. They also include several record types that identify records. Specifically bibliographies, or lists of records, along with library catalogs and archive inventories are popular finding aids with excellent genealogists, for they are all lists of records that the researcher may find of value. To ensure success, genealogists also study institutional directories to learn of other repositories and the kinds of records they maintain.

Background Information

Since no one can know everything, the best genealogists frequently turn to background information to enhance understanding or to answer questions. *Geographic* sources include gazetteers, maps, postal guides, and other records that establish the physical setting of a family. *Instructional* sources provide guidance about records and include handbooks and articles. *Historical* sources have important background information about settlement issues and include histories, encyclopedias, yearbooks, and other sources. *Language* tools, such as dictionaries and handwriting tools, assist in the understanding of the meaning of certain words in the records. *Cultural* aids deal with cultural life, ethnology, religion, and other related aspects of the families being researched. Lastly, *factual* sources are occasionally needed to confirm or clarify specific general information and include tools such as almanacs, etymologies, heraldry, etc.

Compiled Sources

As discussed above in the discussion of the research process, compiled sources are the findings of previous researchers, with their conclusions about people and relationships. If others have already studied a family, clan, or group and constructed the family groups, it would be folly not to review and consider such findings. They are generally grouped with a broad, international scope or with a more local focus. *International* sources are generally searched by surname and include book-length family histories, electronic family trees, and similar collections with no particular geographic bounds. *Local* sources focus on the compilations that pertain to a specific geographic area, such as a state, county, city, or other area. Local histories are a prime example, as are genealogical dictionaries or compendia, as well as most biographical sources and periodicals.

Original Records

By far the largest category, original records are those sources created by some organization or entity (such as a church parish, county, local business, family, etc.), in the course of their activities, that recorded information about a person or family at or near the time a significant event occurred, in which the organization was interested. In this way, a county recorder recorded a land deed near the time the property was transferred from one owner to another or an immigration official created or obtained a list of passengers at the time they arrived in (or departed from) the harbor.

Such records can be placed into nine distinct groups, each with several different types of records:

- Personal records include diaries, journals, letters, and autobiographies; those records created by individuals about themselves and their families.
- Vital records document the births, marriages, deaths, or divorces of individuals and may occur as government vital records, church records, cemeteries, Bible records, funeral homes, and similar records.
- Residency records, such as censuses, tax lists, and city directories, provide documentation of where people lived and typically are lists of persons in a locality.
- Ownership sources are primarily probate, along with land and property records; they prove when individuals transferred ownership of property and can be very helpful in establishing relationships.
- Occupational records, such as military and business records, deal with the information gathered as part of a person's occupation.
- Immigration sources document arrival in a new country and consist of passenger lists, naturalization records, alien registrations, and similar sources.
- Civil action records pertain to the records of governments as they manage the affairs of the people through court, public, notary, and guardianship records.
- Institutional sources include records kept by schools, prisons, orphanages, hospitals, and other institutions.

- Specific populations is a group of different record types that exist because special or unique records were created by different groups in the population, including Native Americans, slaves, Jews, and other minority groups.

It is by understanding the creation, purpose, and use of genealogical records, as reflected by their category and then their content groupings, that excellent genealogists can then effectively use, interpret, and evaluate the information in those records. Fortunately, since records are so central to genealogical research, most instructional material spends significant time and verbiage discussing the many different aspects of research.

Perhaps the most comprehensive discussion in print is found in three companion volumes from Ancestry. *The Source* focuses on the major original records used by American genealogists. *Printed Sources* explores the published material, especially the reference tools and compiled sources that are so frequently used by all genealogists. *Hidden Sources* provides summary information about a host of much lesser known and seldom used records. These first two volumes have been integrated into Ancestry.com's Wiki site.

Technology

Technology has radically altered the way people conduct genealogy. It has enabled more people to find more records about more ancestors and their families than ever thought possible just a few decades ago. Today, every effective genealogist will use a computer, even the very few individuals who do not own one personally. Library catalogs and Internet databases

> **Technology has radically altered the way people conduct genealogy.**

can only be accessed by using a computer. Further, it is important to understand technological issues in general terms in order to be an effective modern genealogist.

Hardware

The home office of an excellent genealogist often rivals the most up-to-date commercial office in terms of the variety of new technology hardware, including popular "gadgets." There is, of course, a personal computer and often more than one, including a laptop or smart device for research "on the road." External storage devices, including portable hard drives and the ever-present flash drives, help keep genealogical data on hand. A printer/copy machine makes it easy to make duplicate copies of the various documents found in research. If the copy machine does not also scan documents, then a separate scanner is close at hand for sending records by e-mail and preparing photographs and other material for preservation and sharing on the Internet.

Onsite research trips are carefully planned to include a digital camera or a smart device such as a smart phone or iPad, a GPS device to help locate cemeteries, one or more cell phones, a digital recorder (for taking notes), and sundry other personal favorites. Don't be surprised, especially in the near future, to see genealogists with electronic readers (such as Amazon's Kindle) on which they have loaded copies of the many public domain local and family histories and other genealogical books.

Software

Specially designed computer programs (software) are available to help genealogists more easily compile the following:

- Lineage-linked databases (files that can be searched by name, date, place, or relationship and that show a person's ancestors and descendants).
- Reports and charts.
- Blank forms (for example, Research Calendars).
- Autobiographies and family histories.
- Indexes.
- Transcriptions of records such as censuses.

When selecting a computer program to help with genealogical database management, consider these factors:

- Is it a lineage-linked database and can it print the reports and charts desired?
- Does the program support GEDCOM (**GE**nealogical **D**ata **COM**munications)? This will enable easy data exchange with new-found relatives and other researchers.
- Does the publisher have a good record of answering user questions and helping to solve problems?
- Is the program easy to use?
- Is the program reliable?
- Is the price of the program reasonable? (Some offer "basic" versions via a free Internet download).
- Does the program offer all the features and capabilities wanted? Modern programs have a wealth of features and options that can create a wide variety of reports.

Other software programs support genealogical research in multiple ways, without creating a database of names. They may add reporting capabilities, enhanced output, organization of notes and research findings, or even suggestions of sources to search. Expert genealogists are also adept at using word processing software, spreadsheets, and picture editing software and can quickly make PDF copies of their computer documents. Software apps for smart phones or iPads provide many other features that assist the genealogist's work. And, of course, e-mail, to keep in touch with all those new-found relatives and fellow researchers.

Databases

Technology has brought a wonderful flood of databases for the modern genealogist to use and appreciate. Whether online, on disc, or on their own computer, databases help genealogists find and manage the information they need for their research. Therefore, knowing how to effectively search and use those databases is critical to successful research. Keeping the difference in mind between static and active databases and knowing what data was included and excluded when records are abstracted into a database helps bring success to researchers. A variety of search routines may be used in any given database, but seldom are all of them used. Understand how Boolean searches work, when proximity searching is possible, and how to effectively use truncation, stemming, wildcards, phrase searches, the Soundex, and other phonetic searches to maximize the power of a database to provide hidden information.

Today's databases also include electronic text files, as well as image files, to broaden the options for the researcher. Each of them has their strengths and weaknesses. Was the text file created by an unedited optical character recognition (OCR) program, or was it keyed by human hands? If the latter, how well did the operator/indexer/abstractor know the language or handwriting of the record? For image collections, how complete and legible are the images? How much information was indexed and by whom? Great tools are only as great as the hands that use them.

Internet

Clearly the Internet is one of the most marvelous technological advancements of the last half century. Computers, as great as they are at speedy computations, are just that: machines that do things fast. But, the Internet (yes, driven by computers) allows virtually instantaneous communication and collaboration anywhere in the world. Web sites provide data most researchers had never even heard about, before finding a link. Genealogists are better informed about sources than ever before and have improved access, but that also exposes family historians to all the mistakes that have been made in the history of research on a family.

The wealth of information and the tools for communication on the Internet actually place a burden on the genealogist to be more vigilant in finding and using these sources as thoroughly as possible. No longer can a researcher depend on one data site or link list to provide all the answers. As expansive as FamilySearch.org and Ancestry.com are or as helpful as Cyndi's List and Linkpendium are, the amount of information they don't have or don't point to is overwhelming. Expert genealogists also can't depend on an Internet search engine to find all the data. Google may be deservedly the most popular search engine in the world, but it can't search much of the Web. Most private Web sites, subscription sites, and database collections cannot be searched by Google or other search engines.

Social networking has pushed communication beyond the wildest dreams of the most optimistic genealogist. It's now possible to be in touch with a relative while she is photographing tombstones a thousand miles away or a family's professional genealogist while she is in an archive in Europe. Indeed, they can send instant pictures of the cemetery, the archive, and even the tombstones and church registers. Better communication can lead to less misunderstanding, confusion, and errors in the research—clearly a trait of an excellent genealogist.

Sharing

In every field of study, researchers benefit greatly from the work of their predecessors. This is how scientific and cultural progress is made. In genealogy, there may be several researchers interested in the same ancestors. Because genealogists rely so heavily on the findings of others, sharing information is a way to progress the research, as well as to "pay back" for all of the information gathered from previous researchers. Sharing information allows others to learn what is already known, thus allowing them to apply their research skills and time to finding answers yet unknown. There are many ways to share the results of genealogical research.

Family

Many genealogists share newly discovered information with family members who provided information and with others who may be interested. A family reunion or family newsletter can be an excellent way to share information and help locate others who are interested in your family history.

Database Submissions

One important way to share research findings is to contribute linked family information (pedigrees and family group records) to one of the many online collections of such databases. Most online databases are freely available to the public so that other researchers can easily learn what has already been researched by others. Examples of online databases include:

- Ancestry's Public Member Trees
- World Family Tree
- GenCircles
- One Great Family
- FamilySearch Family Tree

These files consist of information contributed by many researchers. They provide a central storage place where research from multiple contributors can be linked together. Submitted information is not verified by the managers of such collections, so it is important to be reasonably sure that the information is accurate before submitting it. Few, if any, pedigrees will ever be completely finished or completely accurate, so waiting until research is "done" will deprive others from building on what the researcher has learned. It is acceptable to submit information when it appears to be as accurate as possible. Focus on submissions to databases that allow supporting documentation.

Publish a Family History

A well-researched family's history can be a source of enjoyment and education for near and distant family members. Writing a family history can be an effective way to evaluate, analyze, and organize research findings. There are at least three common means of writing a genealogy.

Books. With the growing popularity of "desktop publishing," it is becoming very easy to publish a book about a family's genealogy, or a "family history." Genealogical computer programs can produce various forms, charts, and text to assist in the process. Local publishers will help, especially when the family can give them "camera-ready" copy. Extended family members often want copies and will usually be willing to help pay for some production costs. Even if the interest and money is not there to publish a book, it is possible to print only a copy or two from the computer software for interested individuals.

When compiling a book or manuscript, be sure to donate copies to key libraries that may be interested in the family, such as:

- The local public library and the library where the family's ancestors lived.
- The historical society where the family lived.
- Major research libraries in the region where the family lived.
- The Family History Library in Salt Lake City, Utah. Be sure to grant permission in writing for the library to digitize the book, so it can be made available to researchers everywhere.

Periodical Article. If there is not enough information or funding to write a book, researchers might consider writing a short article for a genealogical periodical. This is especially useful if the article solves a long-standing genealogical problem that may interest other researchers; for example, the birth of an ancestor in the 1700s who may have many descendants. Perhaps the solution and sources are unique, and others could learn from the researcher's experience.

Internet Site. A growing number of researchers are creating their own Web sites where they can post their findings, complete with pictures, charts, and even interactive options (discussion boards, file sharing, etc.). This method is relatively inexpensive and can permit free access by anyone, anywhere in the world without the expense of designing, printing, and publishing a book and then having others have to pay for that cost.

However, Internet sites are not a permanent means of preserving the hard work that went into finding all the family information. Consider having at least some of the key information published in a more permanent form and distributed to several major genealogical libraries for the sake of posterity.

For Further Study

Meyerink, Kory L., ed. *Printed Sources: A Guide to Published Genealogical Records.* Salt Lake City: Ancestry, 1998.

Pfeiffer, Laura Szucs. *Hidden Sources: Family History in Unlikely Places.* Orem, Utah: Ancestry, 2000.

Szucs, Loretto Dennis and Sandra Hargraves Luebking, eds. *The Source: A Guidebook of American Genealogy,* 3rd ed. Provo, Utah: Ancestry, 2006.

3

Genealogical Analysis

Marilyn Markham, MLS, AG, CG

The great detectives of literature, such as Agatha Christie's Hercule Poirot, carefully collected facts about each crime.[1] The facts would often indicate additional avenues of inquiry. After Poirot asked the right questions and gathered the facts, he used his mind, his "little grey cells," to analyze the evidence effectively and create a strong case to capture the right culprit. Analysis made the difference between success and failure.[2]

Genealogists, like great detectives, need to gather pertinent data about ancestors, ask the right questions, and then correctly analyze and correlate the facts in order to put ancestors solidly into correct families. Each part of a history for a family or an individual should be analyzed to determine which data might be correct, which seems unlikely, and which is illogical.

Three key elements should be considered when analyzing genealogical evidence in a research problem: (1) the validity of the sources used,[3] (2) the likelihood that the data found is correct, and (3) a determination of whether the data applies to that ancestor or ancestral family.

Analyzing the Validity of the Sources and Data

The first two elements of genealogical analysis are handled well in other sources, so will be discussed only briefly here. To analyze the validity and trustworthiness of a source, a researcher

---

[1] A fact is "a presumed reality—an event, circumstance, or other detail that is considered to have happened or to be true. In historical research, it is difficult to establish actual truths; therefore, the validity of any stated 'fact' rests upon the quality of the evidence presented to support it." Elizabeth Shown Mills, *Evidence Explained: Citing History Sources from Artifacts to Cyberspace* (Baltimore: Genealogical Publishing Company, 2007), 822.

[2] Analysis is (1) "separation of a whole into its component parts," and (2) "an examination of a complex, its elements, and their relations." *Webster's Ninth New Collegiate Dictionary* (Springfield, Mass.: Merriam-Webster, 1986), 82.

[3] A source may be a living person, a diary, a certificate, a photo, an heirloom, a family Bible, a published family history, a magazine article, or anything else that may give information about a person or family.

must determine how close the creator of the source was to firsthand knowledge of the event described and the accuracy of the creator's memory when he or she finally described the event. A researcher must also determine if the creator was telling the truth without bias or creative additions. Few creators give full, unbiased truth, so the genealogist must analyze which parts of the evidence may be true, partly true, or inaccurate.[4]

Several excellent articles and sections in books have been written explaining ways to determine the validity of sources and the accuracy of data.[5] A few are listed in the bibliography. Most define original and derivative sources; primary and secondary information; and direct, indirect, and negative evidence. Reading and reviewing these articles and chapters is an excellent course of study for any genealogist.

Steps to Proper Analysis

Information about a family should be reviewed and analyzed even if it has been accepted as true for years. As new research is done, this data should be carefully analyzed and compared with known information. The following steps provide guidelines of analysis to determine if and how new information applies to an ancestor or an ancestral family.[6]

Gather Information

Gather whatever information is currently available about the family, which may be found in such sources as family papers; previous research; family histories; birth, death, and marriage certificates; etc. Look at multiple documents, because more information improves the analysis. Records that are not checked may contain the necessary information that would prove or disprove a hypothesis.[7] Be sure to extract all clues from each document.

Evaluate Information

Evaluate the validity of the sources and the reliability of their data. Compare and contrast the information from the various sources, looking for agreement and contradictory data.

Organize Information

Organize the information on a family group record, and create a timeline for the family. The family should be analyzed in its entirety, not as separate individuals. A family group record

---

[4] Evidence is "information that is relevant to the problem." Mills, *Evidence Explained*, 822.

[5] Thomas W. Jones, "A Conceptual Model of Genealogical Evidence: Linkage between Present-Day Sources and Past Facts," *National Genealogical Society Quarterly*, 86 (March 1998), 5-18 and Mills, *Evidence Explained*, 24-25; Val D. Greenwood, *The Researcher's Guide to American Genealogy*, 3rd ed. (Baltimore: Genealogical Publishing Company, 2000), 65-78; "Evaluation of Evidence," *BCG Genealogical Standards Manual* (Washington, D.C.: Board for Certification of Genealogists, 2000), 8-13.

[6] One excellent discussion about analyzing data and applying the data to ancestors is Greenwood, "Analyzing the Pedigree and the Place," *The Researcher's Guide to American Genealogy*, 47-64.

[7] Hypothesis is defined as "a tentative assumption made in order to draw out and test its logical or empirical consequences." *Webster's Dictionary*, 594.

pulls together the information for an entire family. A timeline puts that information in chronological order, allowing the researcher to visualize and analyze the events more efficiently. A timeline should include not only birth, marriage, and death information but also any important events for the family members, such as military service, land transactions, and moves. (See the essay on timelines in this book for further information.)

> **Genealogists, like great detectives, need to gather pertinent data about ancestors, ask the right questions, and then correctly analyze and correlate the facts in order to put ancestors solidly into correct families.**

Study Information

Study each piece of information on the timeline and family group record singly, in conjunction with each family member, and within the context of the larger community. Look for inconsistencies, clues, and gaps, and develop hypotheses to account for the inconsistencies and gaps. Always be open to other possible explanations.

For instance, if a family group record and timeline showed a gap of eight years between the births of two consecutive children, one hypothesis could be that children are missing from the record. Other hypotheses to explain the eight-year gap might be that the parent died and the succeeding children originated from a second marriage, or that the father was involved in a war or a profession that kept him away from his family.

Since a timeline shows events by date, it is a good tool to use in analyzing a family's movement from one place to another and to show approximately how long the family stayed in one place. Analyze any change in location to see if the move makes sense for the family at the time listed. This will help to determine which records to search in which location.

Develop and Test a Hypothesis

Determine what each piece of information might suggest about an individual or family. Create a hypothesis around what seems the most likely scenario, and then search records to determine if data supports that hypothesis. Keep in mind that a hypothesis may be wrong. Search for truth rather than support for a favored idea. A good way to determine the validity of a hypothesis is to try to prove it wrong.

For example, if one child was born in Germany and two years later the next child was born in Michigan, a good hypothesis would be that the mother immigrated during those two years. Additional research may prove or disprove this hypothesis. If disproved, other hypotheses could be that the data about one or both of the children is wrong or that they had different mothers.

Review the facts based on the new research and decide if they prove or strengthen the hypothesis, or if they disprove or weaken it. If the hypothesis is proven or strengthened, continue with research plans. If the hypothesis is weakened or disproved, create a new hypothesis, determine additional research that is needed, and search for more data about the ancestor and/or the family. For instance, if a mother appeared on an immigration list soon after her child was born in Michigan, either the information was wrong about one or both of them or the wrong woman or child was found.

Think Outside the Box

Consider different interpretations for information given about an ancestor. For example, one couple who were born, married, and died in Indiana had a daughter born in California in the 1850s. Possibly the family went to California for the Gold Rush. Another hypothesis was that they stayed in Indiana. A gazetteer showed a California township in Indiana, and further research found a record of the daughter's birth there. Another researcher spent years looking for her ancestors in western New York, not realizing that there was a town in New Jersey named West New York where her ancestors actually lived.

Write Reports and Research Summaries

A critical part of research is writing reports and research summaries. Errors, problems, and weaknesses in logic will become apparent while writing. Reports can be written at any time, not just when research is complete. Intermittent report writing helps with analysis.

Points to Consider During Analysis

When analyzing data about an ancestor, consider the following:

Biases

Learn to recognize your own inherent biases, as well as any bias of the creator of a document or compilation. A bias may be as simple as being adamant on how a name is spelled or as major as changing the date of marriage or birth of a child in order to preserve a reputation. Genealogists must acknowledge problems or contradictions within any hypotheses.

Spelling Variations

Consider spelling variations not only of people's names but also of place names. Names could have been spelled phonetically or changed. A census taker from England may not have spelled a German name the same way as someone from Germany. Names could be spelled many ways, even by someone who knew the language.

Culture

Become familiar with the culture of an ancestor. An ancestor's culture impacted what he or she did. In the seventeenth century, a couple in the New England culture was more likely to marry a year before the first child was born than a couple living in Scandinavia or Germany, who often started a family before the wedding.

Time Frame

Consider if the information was logical for the time when an ancestor lived. A seventeenth-century couple was likely to have met near the homes of their families. After the advent of cars, railroads, and airplanes, couples could more easily meet hundreds of miles from their families.

History

Learn the history of the area where the ancestor lived. Analyze how that history could impact an ancestor. Wars, droughts, epidemics, and financial crises would all cause people to take certain actions. Knowing what went on in the ancestor's world helps with analysis of what was known of their lives and with determining hypotheses of what they might have done. This can lead to finding needed records.

Jurisdictions

Learn when and how jurisdictions[8] began, changed, or ended. Think of ways this would impact an ancestor and the records of his area. Boundary changes altered where an ancestor voted, recorded land transactions, etc. The genealogy of a place determined when records were kept where. Also consider nearby jurisdictions where an ancestor may have conducted business, attended church, bought land, or been married or buried.

Typical Ages

Events generally happened around certain ages of people's lives. Using the family group record or timeline, calculate the ages of people when events happened to see if they were typical of when people generally married, had children, served in the military, etc. Determine the ages of a mother and father when each of their children was born. If a family group record shows a woman as age 79 when a child was born, either she could not be the mother, her birth date is wrong, or the child's birth date is wrong. If a man died fourteen years before his child was born, he could not be the father or his death date is incorrect.

Relatives, Neighbors, and Associates

Information for collateral relatives may have data or clues about the focus ancestor. Information about neighbors and associates may do the same. Often an ancestor's neighbors and associates were relatives by blood or marriage.

Occupational, Educational, Financial, and Social Status

Status can help distinguish an ancestor from other people with the same name in the same area. A city merchant listed on one census as being able to read and write probably will not be listed on the next census as a rural farmer who cannot read or write. Since status can change with time, track people over many years to determine if the progression is logical. Records such as tax, land, probate, and business can help with this analysis.

---

[8] The main jurisdictions considered by genealogists are towns, counties, states or provinces, and countries. Additional jurisdictions to consider are church, census, voting, and school. Also see Loretta Evans's essay on Jurisdictions in Chapter 15 this book.

Military

Find a list of the wars or other military actions that occurred in the ancestor's area. Compare the ages of the ancestor and any sons during the years of the wars to determine which might appear in military records.

Religion

Religion played an important part in our ancestors' lives. Many events were only recorded in records of a church, synagogue, or other religious body. Therefore, it is important to determine an ancestor's religion. Many people belonged to the same religion all their lives, while others changed denominations, sometimes more than once.

Since descendants often kept the faith of their fathers, the descendants' religion would be a good indicator of which religion to try first. However, if this does not seem to have happened in a family and no other family clues exist, use a history of the appropriate area to determine the dominant religion. Search for the ancestor using that religion first. If the ancestor is not located, check the records of the church closest to where he lived.

The table below shows some of the predominant religions in various locations. Use it only as a starting point. Many ancestors were exceptions to this table.

Table
Predominant Religions in Various Locations

People In:	Usually Were:
England	Church of England
Scotland	Church of Scotland; Presbyterian
Ireland, except Northern Ireland	Roman Catholic
Northern Ireland	Church of England, Roman Catholic
Scandinavia	Lutheran
Northern Germany and Northern Switzerland	Lutheran
Southern Germany and Southern Switzerland	Roman Catholic
The Netherlands	Dutch Reformed
Latin America, Spain, France, Portugal, and Italy	Roman Catholic
Russia	Russian Orthodox
United States	
New England	Congregational
South	Baptist, Anglican, and Methodist
Northern Midwest	Lutheran
Other regions	Various religions
Canada	
Quebec	Roman Catholic
Ontario	Church of England
Other Provinces	Various religions

Case Studies

The Daniel Markham Family

The Daniel Markham family group record showed:

- Daniel was born in 1588 in Enfield, Hartford, Connecticut, died in 1690 probably in Cambridge, Middlesex, Massachusetts, and was buried in Norfolk, England
- Daniel's wife was born about 1590, also in Enfield, Hartford, Connecticut
- Daniel's son was born in 1641 in Norwich, Norfolk, England

This information might appear correct until the history of the area is considered. Daniel could not be born in 1588 in Enfield because the first European settlers did not arrive in that area until 1674, eighty-six years after Daniel was born. Since transporting dead bodies in the 1600s was extremely difficult, it is unlikely that Daniel died in Massachusetts in 1690 and was buried in England. In addition, the mother would have been about 51 when the son was born, which was highly unlikely in the 1600s.

The Charles Hartley Family

The Charles Hartley pedigree chart showed:

- Charles was born in September 1817 in Wakefield, York, England
- His father, Richard, was born March 1785, also in Wakefield, was married 2 December 1811 in Wakefield, and died 2 December 1811

Accepting the above information as fact would mean that Richard died on his wedding day almost six years before his son was born. Richard's death date is probably an error.

The Jeremiah Meacham Family

The Jeremiah Meacham family group record showed:

- Jeremiah's first three children were born in New Salem, Franklin, Massachusetts and baptized in Salem, Essex, Massachusetts
- James was born 10 March 1733 and baptized eight days after birth
- Elizabeth was born 12 October 1735 and baptized the same day
- Jeremiah was born 9 July 1738 and baptized the same day

New Salem and Salem are about 73 miles apart. In the early 1700s, there was no way for a new baby and its mother to cross that distance on the same day or even within eight days. Three hypotheses that might resolve this discrepancy are: (1) the children were born in Salem, but their births were recorded in New Salem records with their family; (2) the children were born in New Salem, but their births were recorded in Salem, possibly because their father was from there; or (3) the creator of the family group record made errors.

Histories of New Salem state that New Salem was first settled in 1737, and two histories report that Jeremiah Meacham came with his family to New Salem that same year.[9] A new hypothesis could be that the first two children, James and Elizabeth, were born and baptized in Salem in 1733 and 1735 respectively, while the third child, Jeremiah, was born and baptized in New Salem in 1738, the year after the family settled there. A reference book states that New Salem was established in 1753, which seems to disagree with the 1737 date given in the histories.[10] The reference book may be stating the formal establishment of the town, as opposed to the date of the first settlers that is used in the histories.

Summary

Analysis is a way of looking at information about ancestors logically and creatively. What do the facts say? What could they mean? What do they suggest? Thoughtful analysis based on well-researched data will help genealogists think like a master detective, such as Hercule Poirot, and create strong hypotheses to solve genealogical mysteries.

---

[9] *History of New Salem Massachusetts 1753-1953, Prepared for the Celebration of the 200th Anniversary, August 7, 8, 9, 1953* (Amherst, Mass.: Hamilton I. Newell, [1953]), 5-6. This history also has a photo of a gravestone of Samuel Southwick who died in 1745, p. 33; *New Salem, Massachusetts: Forgotten Franklin County Town*, http://www.yeoldewoburn.net/index1.htm; *Wikipedia*, http://en.wikipedia.org/wiki/New_Salem,Massachusetts.

[10] Marcia D. Melnyk, ed., *Genealogist's Handbook for New England Research*, 4th ed., rev., (Boston: New England Historic Genealogical Society, 1999), 96.

For Further Study

Board for Certification of Genealogists. *BCG Genealogical Standards Manual.* Orem, Utah: Ancestry, 2000.

Cox, Florence Cogswell. *History of New Salem Massachusetts 1753-1953: Prepared for the Celebration of the 200th Anniversary, August 7, 8, 9, 1953.* Amherst, Mass.: Hamilton I. Newell, [1953].

Eichholz, Alice. *Red Book: American State, County, and Town Sources.* 3rd ed. Provo, Utah: Ancestry, 2004.

Greenwood, Val D. *The Researcher's Guide to American Genealogy.* 3rd ed. Baltimore: Genealogical Publishing Company, 2000.

The Handybook for Genealogists. 11th ed. Logan, Utah: Everton Publishers, 2006.

Jones, Thomas W. "A Conceptual Model of Genealogical Evidence: Linkage between Present-Day Sources and Past Facts." *National Genealogical Society Quarterly* 86 (March 1998): 5-18.

Melnyk, Marcia D., ed. *Genealogist's Handbook for New England Research.* 4th ed. Boston: New England Historic Genealogical Society, 1999.

Mills, Elizabeth Shown. *Evidence Explained: Citing History Sources from Artifacts to Cyberspace.* Baltimore: Genealogical Publishing Company, 2007.

4

Avoiding the Assumption Trap

Apryl Cox, AG

From the moment we spot that end-of-line individual on the pedigree chart, we begin making assumptions about every piece of incomplete or missing data that we consider crucial to positively identifying the ancestor. Assumptions as to age, birth year, place of origin, and marriage formulate in our brains.

Assumptions provide focus. They are necessary to create the starting points for future research. They assist us to develop our initial hypothesis and create a research plan. Often, our assumptions are based on past experiences that reached successful conclusions in other similar situations. But our assumptions may also prevent us from finding the correct answer to a problem when our vision is too narrow. Assumptions that substantially limit the range of acceptability can effectively hide many valid possibilities wherein our problem's solution may lie. In essence, we may assemble our own barriers and fall victim to our own assumption trap.

Common Confining Assumptions

When developing assumptions upon which we will base our research plan, we must consider whether our expectations concerning the ancestor's age, marital status, name, occupation, or religion could be too confining. Could this ancestor be on the fringe, or even out of bounds, of what would be considered typical?

We have all heard that men usually marry at about age 24, and women generally marry at about age 21. In our search for an acceptable marriage for an ancestor, we allow for a few years before and at least a decade after these "average" ages. But do we regularly limit our accepted range to the exclusion of the woman who marries for the first time at age 42? Is a candidate quickly eliminated because according to his age at death, he would have fathered a child at the

47

age of 58? If our ancestors were significantly younger or older than the "standard" when they married or bore children, we might exclude them from consideration simply because they don't meet our assumptions. We could end up looking for their births in the wrong decade.

Too often we fail to consider that the parents of the target ancestor could have been previously married and therefore may have been much older than we originally thought. Somehow, we tend to believe (or at least hope) that the parents of our ancestor married only once. In reality, our ancestor could be a product of his father's second marriage and his mother's third. This scenario not only affects our assumption as to the age of the parents but also is vital to the correct identity of the mother or father. And, as many marriage records do not include the marital status of the couple, we may be looking for the birth of the wrong woman if the bride was listed in the marriage record under her previous husband's surname.

How certain are we that the name on the pedigree chart is the actual legal name of the ancestor and the same name under which the individual will be found in census records, a birth certificate, a burial record, or tax records? Names may change throughout life for a variety of reasons, such as convenience, personal preference, the "Americanizing" of a name, or illegitimacy. If we are not aware that our ancestors could have changed names during their lives, we could miss them in an index or not recognize them in original records.

> **How certain are we that the name on the pedigree chart is the actual legal name of the ancestor and the same name under which the individual will be found in census records, a birth certificate, a burial record, or tax records?**

Similar assumptions could be made regarding an ancestor's residence. As much as we would like our ancestors to have remained in one location for generations, that is not often reality. Perhaps our ancestor was employed in an occupation that necessitated frequent moves. Perhaps opportunities for land, wealth, or freedom coaxed family members to migrate elsewhere. Perhaps the thrill of living on the ever-changing frontier beckoned to the adventurous. People moved much more often than we tend to believe. Yet as we formulate our research plans, we may consistently assume that our ancestors were born or married in the same general vicinity where they lived as adults.

Avoiding the Trap

So how can we avoid being trapped by our assumptions? First, we need to develop a healthy skepticism about the validity of information upon which we rely. Of necessity, we make assumptions about the integrity of the data upon which we base our research. Unless a glaring error presents itself on the pedigree chart or a primary source document, we may tend to accept the data as presented. We need to remember that any information could be inaccurate due to mistakes, sloppiness, guesswork, or tradition.

The pedigree chart or primary source document could be flawed because people lied or falsified information, or because of a simple mistake such as a typographical error, transposed data, or a transcription error. Perhaps a previous researcher presented guesswork as fact. "Born 1790" is not the same as "born about 1790." Instead of using key words such as "of," "about," "estimated," or "calculated" to express the researcher's thoughtful evaluation of evidence, he may have presented uncertain data as if it were solid and factual.

Tradition can sometimes sway our minds to accept events or data as being valid when they have not been proven. Basing a research plan on the assumption that a family tradition that has existed for generations must be true can lead us astray. The declaration that "everyone in the family knows that's true" is peer pressure that can seem overwhelming to criticize or doubt. But the fact is, everyone in the family *can* be wrong.

Whatever the cause, inaccurate data can be difficult to spot. It can send us hunting in the wrong areas or tracking the wrong families, or simply send us into oblivion. Inaccurate data may be caught early during the pedigree analysis phase but is often revealed only after significant efforts have been invested and the accumulated evidence just "doesn't make sense." It would be unprofessional to assume that data must be correct because it is published, found on the Internet, or validated by others who have never actually verified what they propose to be true.

> ## Whatever the cause, inaccurate data can be difficult to spot.

Second, we must cultivate a broad mind that recognizes when we may be limiting viable options. If we begin a search using a "normal" range of assumptions, we must always be willing to expand our acceptance range to include all feasible possibilities.

Third, we must foster a questioning intellect that considers what *could* have happened and does not limit itself to our own values and experiences. Our minds are unique. Each person is shaped by his own training, experiences, values, and perspective. As we interpret data, make assumptions, and consider what might have happened in the lives of our ancestors, we do so through our own distinctive filters and thought patterns. Our ancestors were just as unique. What made sense to them may not seem reasonable to us. How many of us would consider falsifying information on our marriage certificate or abandoning our children in order to pursue a future spouse half our age? Yet some of our ancestors did just this and more. Events occurred in their lives about which we may know nothing, because the incidents have been swallowed in history. A debilitating illness or accident, a distant job offer, a family disagreement that led to separation, a "hushed-up" incident of suicide, an illegitimacy, and a criminal offense that led to imprisonment are all events of which we may be clueless. Yet these experiences deeply affected an ancestor's decisions. The results may be occurrences that do not meet our expectations and therefore are not considered in our hypothesis. Seeking another researcher's opinions about a genealogical problem may help us recognize possibilities that we might not have realized on our own.

Making assumptions is a necessity. But when our assumptions are too confining, they may blind us from seeing the truth. When our assumptions result from creative contemplation of a variety of scenarios, they assist us to develop a careful research plan that offers flexibility and allows for multiple options.

5

Demography as a Tool for Genealogists

Kathryn M. Daynes, Ph.D., AG

Eager genealogists have occasionally professed that they wanted to bypass studying history so that they could learn how to trace their own families. This may work as a short-term strategy but quickly founders on the shoals of inadequate knowledge. Knowing patterns of behavior in the past alerts genealogists to what they may expect as they research specific families. Although some ancestors may not conform to the then-current social patterns of births, marriages, and deaths—demography—most ancestors, by definition, will tend toward the average, so knowing the patterns of average people who lived at the same time and in the same place as the ancestors sought eases the search for them. What is more, it provides an understanding of the nature of their lives and culture in which they lived.

Most family historians understand the necessity of studying history to become acquainted with migration patterns. Such patterns are important, of course, but no more so than demographic patterns. Demography is simply the study of population change created by fertility (births), mortality (deaths), and migration. The study of average age at marriage, average number of children, life expectancy, and rate of migration are all patterns with which genealogists should be familiar. Such patterns are researched by demographers, those who study population change. The formula for population change is

Population at Time 2 = Population at Time 1 + (births - deaths) + (in-migration - out-migration)

Births, deaths, and migration are all crucial to genealogists, so knowing the changes in patterns of fertility, mortality, and migration is useful in understanding what a researcher may expect to find in various periods and places.

Take, for instance, this genealogical information: Ralph Josselin, born 26 January 1617 in Chalk-End, Roxwell, Essex, England and buried 30 August 1683 in Earls Colne, Essex, England was married on 28 October 1640 to Jane Constable, who was christened 26 November 1621 and buried in 1693. Nothing seems remarkable in this standard recitation of genealogical facts. What sets his life apart is that he meticulously kept a diary, a record that, when combined with demographic studies of the population in which he lived, reveals patterns in the life of a seventeenth-century English family. The following table, showing Jane Josselin's pregnancies and births, adds to our understanding of these patterns.

Table 1
Children of Ralph and Jane Josselin[1]

Name	Birth	Interval (months)	Marriage	Age at marriage	Death	Age at death
Mary	12 Apr 1642	17.5			27 May 1650	8.1
Thomas	30 Dec 1643	20.5			15 Jun 1673	29.6
Jane	25 Nov 1645	23	30 Aug 1670	24.9	Unknown	
Ralph	11 Feb 1648	25.5			21 Feb 1648	10 days
Ralph	5 May 1649	15			2 Jun 1650	13 mos
John	19 Sep 1651	29.5	Oct 1681	30	Unknown	
Anne	20 Jun 1654	33			31 Jul 1673	19.1
Miscarriage	Jun 1656					
Mary	14 Jan 1658	43	10 Apr 1683	25.3	Unknown	
Misscarriage	May 1659					
Elizabeth	20 Jun 1660	29	5 Jun 1677	16.9	Unknown	
Miscarried 3 times by 24 December 1661						
Rebecka	26 Nov 1663	41	6 May 1683	19.6	Unknown	

By comparing this family's experiences with those of the society in which they lived, we find that this family's patterns tended toward the average.

Marriage Age

The one Josselin male child who married did so at age 30, two years older than the average of 28 for England in the first half of the seventeenth century. One reason the marriage age was fairly high was the expectation that married couples would set up their own households within a few weeks of the wedding, necessitating young men to have established their economic niche

---

[1] Alan Macfarlane, *The Family Life of Ralph Josselin, A Seventeeth-Century Clergyman: An Essay in Historical Anthropology* (Cambridge [Eng.]: Cambridge University Press, 1970), 82, 93-4, 199, 203.

with sufficient resources to support a family before their marriages. The Josselin female children married on average at age 21.7 years, considerably younger than the then-current average of 26, although their circumstances are revealing. Elizabeth, who married just before turning 17, received only some household goods from her father. On the other hand, Rebecka was given £500 when she married at age 19; her father was ill and did not expect to live much longer (he died less than four months after her marriage) and he gave her inheritance to her as her dowry.[1] While the mean marriage age was relatively high, children could marry young if they were willing to forgo financial help from parents—not generally a wise policy—or if their fathers died, leaving them their inheritance.

The mean marriage ages in seventeenth-century England may not seem high because they are only slightly higher than those in the present-day United States. In relation to many areas outside of northwestern Europe, however, the marriage ages were high. In southern and eastern Europe, the Middle East, China, and India, for example, women married young, usually before age 21 and often soon after menarche (beginning of menstruation, which was then frequently at age 15 or 16). Their husbands were older than their brides, often by seven to ten years, and the couple moved into the household of the groom.[2] But northwestern Europe had a long tradition of a different pattern, so divergent that it is called the Northwest Europe Marriage Pattern, which included adolescents leaving their own homes to enter service in others' homes to accumulate resources and then setting up their own separate households when they married in their mid to late twenties. Unlike elsewhere, a substantial proportion, about 20 percent, never married.

To be sure, marriage age in northwestern Europe was influenced by the economy. In sluggish times, people spent more time in service, and the percentage who never married increased.[3] Based on the work of E. A. Wrigley and R. S. Schofield, mean marriage ages over time in England are given below.

Table 2
Average Age of Marriage in England[4]

Group / Location	Years	Male	Female
England	1600-1649	28.0	26.0
England	1650-1699	27.8	26.5
England	1700-1749	27.5	26.2
England	1750-1799	26.4	24.9
England	1800-1849	25.3	23.4

[2] Mary S. Hartman, *The Household and the Making of History: A Subversive View of the Western Past* (Cambridge: Cambridge University Press, 2004), 6.

[3] Roger Schofield, "The Impact of Scarcity and Plenty on Population Change in England 1541-1871," *Journal of Interdisciplinary History* 14 (1983): 278.

[4] E.A. Wrigley and R.S. Schofield, *The Population History of England, 1541-1871* (London: Edward Arnold, 1981), 255.

Migrants to America brought with them the traditions of service, relatively high marriage ages, and neolocal[5] residence for married couples, but circumstances in the New World also influenced when couples married. Availability of land in America provided economic niches for men earlier than they generally found in Europe, making younger marriages possible. On the other hand, men were more likely to immigrate than women, creating a high ratio of men to women and thus providing fewer opportunities to marry. In early seventeenth-century Virginia, for example, the ratio was six men to every one woman of marriageable age, although the ratio became more even as the century came to a close. Men thus married in their late twenties, if they married at all, while native-born women, being so much in demand, often married soon after puberty. Female indentured servants could not marry until they had served their time, but then they married quickly. In Massachusetts, where the sex ratio was not so skewed, mean marriage ages were lower than in England but not so high for men or so low for women as in Virginia. Circumstances in different places at various times impacted the average ages at which people married for the first time. Below are some examples of marriage ages in America.

Table 3
Average Age at Marriage in United States for Selected Groups[6]

Group / Location	Years	Male	Female
Massachusetts	1700-1750	26.00	23.00
Virginia	1700-1750	24.00	18.00
Delaware Valley	1700-1750	27.00	24.00
Backcountry	1700-1750	20.00	19.00
Whites	1880	27.00	23.27
Whites	1920	26.06	22.70
Whites	1960	23.18	20.18
Whites	1990	27.26	24.84

Demographic Transition

Overall patterns of births and deaths before 1800 did not differ between northwestern Europe and elsewhere, although those patterns differ considerably from those of today. Currently, many parts of the world, including the United States and Europe, are characterized by low birth and low death rates. Two centuries ago, however, high birth and high death rates prevailed. The change between these two differing patterns is called the demographic transition. The illustration below charts this change.

---

[5] Definition: living or located away from both the husband's and the wife's relatives. Dicionary.com, http://www.dictionary.com.

[6] David Hackett Fischer, *Albion's Seed: Four British Folkways in America* (New York: Oxford University Press, 1989), 813; Michael R. Haines, "Long-Term Marriage Patterns in the United States from Colonial Times to the Present," *History of the Family* 1, no. 1 (1996): 23. (The figures for 1880-1990 are calculated using the formula for singulate mean age at marriage.)

Chart 1
The Demographic Transition[7]

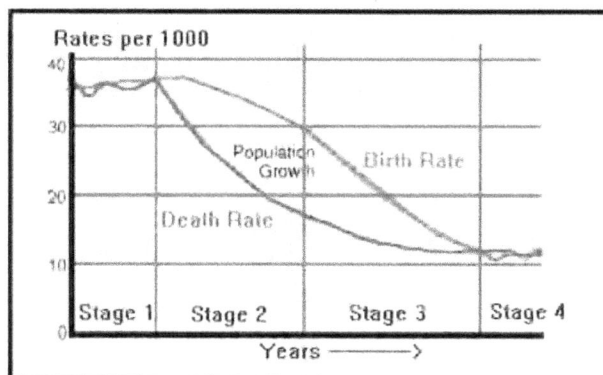

A rough equilibrium between births and deaths characterizes the first and last stages. Change begins when the death rate begins to decline in Stage 2. With the birth rate higher than the death rate, the population grows rapidly, as was the case in much of nineteenth-century Europe. Nevertheless, the birth rate also declines, until in the last stage the population again reaches a rough equilibrium. While this model describes a number of European countries, such as England and Sweden, the United States and France have a different pattern in which births began declining in Stage 2 rather than Stage 3. But the United States also varied by region, so that while birth rates began declining in the Mid-Atlantic states at the beginning of the nineteenth century, they remained high on the frontier. Nevertheless, the model provides a means for family historians to understand what to expect about number of births and life expectancy if they are aware of timing and length of the demographic transition in the region they are researching. For example, the demographic transition in the United States and France extended from about 1785 to 1960, in Germany and Italy from about 1876 to 1965, and in Mexico and India from about 1920 to almost the present.[8]

Fertility

Before the demographic transition, the number of children born to a couple was considerably higher than currently, as the Josselin family illustrates. But Jane Josselin married over five years younger than the average woman in early seventeenth-century England, giving her time to bear three more children than her contemporaries who married at age 26. In fact, the total fertility rate (TFR)[9] for her contemporaries was about 4.5 children.[10] With the onset of the Industrial

---

[7] Internet Geography, http://www.geography.learnontheinternet.co.uk/topics/popn1.html.
[8] Jean-Claude Chesnais, *The Demographic Transition: Stages, Patterns and Economic Implications, A Longitudinal Study of Sixty-Seven Countries Covering the Period 1720-1984*, trans. Elizabeth and Philip Kreager (Oxford: Oxford University Press, 1992), 305, 312.
[9] Total fertility rate indicates total number of children a woman would have by the end of her reproductive period if she experienced the currently prevailing age-specific fertility rates throughout her childbearing life.
[10] Peter Laslett, *The World We Have Lost: Further Explored*, 3rd ed. (New York: Charles Scribner's Sons, 1984), 116; Rodrigo R. Soares, Demographic Transition in England, (University of Maryland), http://www.econ.umd.edu/~soares/616_files/pop&hk&health_figs.pdf.

Revolution, the traditional brake on early marriages was lifted, and the TFR rose to over six children in the early nineteenth-century England, wavered at about five children from the 1830s, and began a steep decline beginning in the late 1870s.[11]

In the United States, the constraints on early marriage were not as great as in Britain, and the number of children per couple was larger. In the late eighteenth century, 12.8 percent of wives had two or fewer children, while 19.3 percent bore at least ten children. Women who married in the 1870s had sufficiently curtailed their births so that less than 1 in 200 had 10 or more children, and over half had only one or two children.[12] The relatively high numbers of children in colonial America compared with the declining numbers in the nineteenth and twentieth centuries can be seen in the following table.

Table 4
Children Born to U.S. Women, by Birth Cohort[13]

Group / Location	Years	Total Fertility Rate
Hingham, Massachusetts	Pre-1660	7.5
Waltham, Massachusetts	1731-1740	9.7
Middlesex, Virginia (white)	1650-1654	7.0
New Jersey and Pennsylvania Quakers	1756-1785	5.0
United States	1867-1870	4.000
United States	1886-1890	3.137
United States	1906-1910	2.286
United States	1916-1920	2.574
United States	1936-1940	2.950
United States	1951-1955	1.920

An analysis of birth patterns shows that birth rates declined either through spacing (longer intervals between births) or through truncation (births at regular intervals until the optimal number of children was achieved and then no other children, even though the woman was young enough for additional births). Truncation not infrequently results in the last child being born a number of years after all the other children.

How couples achieved these patterns has been the subject of considerable scholarly work. Whether the increasing intervals between the Josselin children was a natural result of Jane's ad-

---

[11] Chenais, *Demographic Transition*, 325.

[12] Robert V. Wells, *Revolutions in Americans' Lives: A Demographic Perspective on the History of Americans, Their Families, and Their Society* (Westport, Conn.: Greenwood Press, 1985), 92.

[13] Norman B. Ryder, "Observations on the History of Cohort Fertility in the United States," *Population and Development Review* 12, no. 4 [1986]: 622; Fischer, *Albion's Seed*, 71, 277, 483.

vancing age or the use of abortifacients cannot be determined from Ralph Josselin's diary. But with the onset of the permanent decline of fertility in the nineteenth century, it appears that couples used a variety of methods, probably less frequency of coitus combined with some type of birth control. *Coitus interruptus,* condoms, diaphragms ("womb veils"), and sponges to absorb semen were used, as was douching, not only with water but also with such harsh chemicals as prussic acid and sulfuric acid as spermicides. Before the spate of anti-abortion laws in the 1860s, abortifacients were frequently advertised in newspapers.[14] Whatever methods or combinations of methods were used, the birth rate, particularly among white Americans, declined substantially over the nineteenth century.

Mortality

Not only were the birth rates high before the demographic transition, but so also were death rates. One way to measure change over time is the rising life expectancy, partially shown in the table below.

Table 5
Life Expectancy at Birth[15]

Group / Location	Years	Male	Female	Back Projection[16]
England	1550-1599			36.8
England	1650-1699			33.9
England	1750-1799			36.5
United States	1850	36.5	38.5	
United States	1900	48.2	51.1	

Life expectancy was so low, not because most people died in their thirties but because child mortality was so high. In the period before the demographic transition in Europe, about one-quarter of children died before age ten, and half of children died before they married. The Josselin family was thus fairly typical, with three of their ten children dying within their first decade and another two dying before they married. Ralph Josselin kept a diary so that we have good records for the births of his children. Other families are not so fortunate. Studying the parish registers of north Shropshire in England, R.E. Jones estimated that from 1561 to 1700 about one-third of infant burials were not recorded in parish registers and this rose to almost half of infant burials in the eighteenth century. Because many of these infants died before baptism,

---

[14] Wells, 96-7; Paul A. David and Warren C. Sanderson, "Rudimentary Contraceptive Methods and the American Transition to Marital Fertility Control, 1855-1915," in *Long-Term Factors in American Economic Growth,* ed. Stanley L. Engerman and Robert E. Gallman (Chicago: University of Chicago Press, 1986), 207-79.

[15] Wrigley and Schofield, *Population History,* 252, and *Life Expectancy by Age, 1850-2004,* http://www.infoplease.com/ipa/A0005140.html.

[16] Analysis based on data in which the total population is inferred from known fertility and mortality and estimated migration.

Jones estimates that about 10 percent had no record for birth or death in the registers, a significant omission for genealogists reconstructing families.[17] Between the high infant morality and the living standards in pre-Industrial Revolution Europe, Thomas Hobbes's characterization of life as "nasty, brutish, and short" seems apt.[18]

By the mid-nineteenth century, childhood mortality (death before the age of five) began dropping in England, although infant mortality did not begin to decline before 1900.[19] The United States was similar in that infant mortality remained high in the mid-nineteenth century but was almost halved by 1920 to 8.6 percent. By 1950 it had dropped still further to 2.9 percent. The decline was so great by the late twentieth century that Robert V. Wells noted, "A white girl baby today has a greater chance to live to sixty than her counterpart born in 1870 did of surviving to her first birthday."[20] The connection between the declining death and birth rates now becomes clear. Couples before the demographic revolution had to bear twice as many children as twentieth-century couples to have the same number of children survive to bear children of their own.

Migration

The demographic transition also helps researchers to understand migration. As the number of deaths declined before the number of births decreased, the population growth disrupted the relative stability of earlier populations. As capitalism changed markets for agricultural goods and home crafts, increased numbers of children could not be absorbed into struggling local economies. Some children, at least, needed to seek their fortunes elsewhere. In regions where urban areas were growing rapidly because of industrialization, young men and women moved to nearby cities. Where such opportunities were not close by, they moved longer distances, often to other countries. In the late nineteenth century, when transoceanic travel was inexpensive and international boundaries were relatively open, migration to find jobs was especially robust. It is not surprising that the demographic transition in Europe and the large migration movements from Europe to the Americas coincided in the nineteenth and early twentieth centuries.

While population growth was one important push factor in emigration, destinations of migrants were determined by a variety of considerations, including economic opportunities, trade routes, and relatives and friends already established in new areas. International migrants were ambitious, but by and large they were not individualists blazing new trails; they generally followed the paths of previous wealthier emigrants. Both general histories of migration and local histories are sources for tracing settlers back to their overseas origins.

---

[17] R.E. Jones, "Infant Mortality in Rural North Shropshire, 1561-1810," *Population Studies* 30, no. 2 (1976): 305-318. On the unreliability of Anglican parish registers at the end of the eighteenth and beginning of the nineteenth centuries, see E.A. Wrigley, R.S. Davies, J.E. Oeppen, and R.S. Schofield, *English Population History from Family Reconstitution, 1580-1837* (Cambridge: Cambridge University Press, 1997), 73-118.

[18] Thomas Hobbes, *Leviathan, or the Matter, Forme, and Power of a Commonwealth, Ecclesiasticall and Civill* (1651), ed. Richard E. Flathman and David Johnston (New York: W. W. Norton & Company, 1997), 70.

[19] Robert Woods, *Demography of Victorian England and Wales* (Cambridge: Cambridge University Press, 2000), 247-52.

[20] Jones, "Infant Mortality," 314; R.V. Wells, *Revolutions in America*, 224, 222 (quote).

A Genealogist's Toolbox

A genealogist's toolbox should be well stocked with knowledge and skills, and among these should be a general understanding of not only demographic changes but also of population changes in the time and place where research is being conducted. Knowing what to expect in terms of birth, marriage, death, and migration patterns helps the researcher to not only narrow the search for specific dates but also to broaden the search to find entire families.

> A genealogist's toolbox should be well stocked with knowledge and skills, and among these should be a general understanding of not only demographic changes but also of population changes in the time and place where research is being conducted.

This essay has sketched only the broad outlines of demographic change and provides a few examples of changes in specific areas. Wise genealogists should research the demographic history of the regions in which they are working, just as they learn the region's general history and geography. Search library catalogs using terms such as demography, population history, mortality history, and fertility history, and combine such search terms with the country or state where research is ongoing. Many demographic studies are reported in scholarly journals, so searches of article indexes such as *America: History and Life* and *Historical Abstracts* will also be useful.

Appended to this essay are several works that may provide specific information or references to other works about historical demography.

Demography also highlights the necessity of searching for entire families, not simply those individuals who will appear on pedigree charts. The high death rate before the demographic transition means that half of individuals born would not be connected to their families if family historians research only their own ancestors. Moreover, between 10 and 15 percent of couples today are infertile, probably the same as in the past. Full-family research will connect these couples to their families of origin; they have no descendants to make those connections.

Historical demography is an important but often overlooked resource for family historians. Knowledge of it will help in conducting research and in understanding the nature of our ancestors' lives: women who spent much of their married lives pregnant and parents who experienced deaths of some of their infants, for example. Family historians neglect history at the peril of failure; history may not remove every roadblock, but it is an essential tool for every astute genealogist.

For Further Study

United States

Bean, Lee L., Geraldine P. Mineau, and Douglas L. Anderton. *Fertility Change on the American Frontier: Adaptation and Innovation.* Berkeley: University of California Press, 1990.
Analysis of nineteenth-century population in Utah.

Billington, Ray Allen and Martin Ridge. *Western Expansion: A History of the American Frontier,* 5th ed. New York: Macmillan, 1982.
A classic dealing with westward expansion from the eastern coast, containing many useful maps.

David, Paul A. and Warren C. Sanderson. "Rudimentary Contraceptive Methods and the American Transition to Marital Fertility Control, 1855-1915," in *Long-Term Factors in American Economic Growth,* ed. Stanley L. Engerman and Robert E. Gallman. Chicago: University of Chicago Press, 1986.

Fischer, David Hackett. *Albion's Seed: Four British Folkways in America.* New York: Oxford University Press, 1989.
Classic study of the folkways of those who settled in Massachusetts, the Delaware Valley, the Chesapeake, and the backcountry.

Gerhan, David R., comp. *Bibliography of American Demographic History.* Westport, Conn.: Greenwood Press, 1995.
Contains many bibliographic references to marriage and fertility, health and death, migration, and family structures.

Haines, Michael R. "Long-Term Marriage Patterns in the United States from Colonial Times to the Present." *History of the Family* 1, no. 1 (1996): 15-39.
Contains chart of changing average marriages from 1880 to 1990.

Klein, Herbert S. *A Population History of the United States.* New York: Cambridge University Press, 2004.
A chronological overview of changes in birth rates, death rates, and migration.

Vinovskis, Maris A., ed. *Studies in American Historical Demography.* New York: Academic Press, 1979.
Reprints a number of articles on a variety of subjects, including premarital pregnancy, family size and fertility control among Quakers, age at marriage and family limitation, and death in early Massachusetts.

Wells, Robert V. *Revolutions in Americans' Lives: A Demographic Perspective on the History of Americans, Their Families, and Their Society.* Westport, Conn.: Greenwood Press, 1985.
A chronological history of changes in birth rates and death rates and how these changed families and the country. Also includes discussion of immigration and migration.

Europe

Chesnais, Jean-Claude. *The Demographic Transition: Stages, Patterns, and Economic Implications, A Longitudinal Study of Sixty-Seven Countries Covering the Period 1720-1984.* Trans. Elizabeth and Philip Kreager. Oxford: Clarendon Press, 1992.
Contains many charts and graphs dealing with changes in births, deaths, and migration over time for a variety of countries; has short bibliography for various countries.

Haines, Michael R. "Western Fertility in Mid-Transition: Fertility and Nuptiality in the United States and Selected Nations at the Turn of the Century." *Journal of Family History* 15 no. 1 (1990): 23-48.
Contains information on total fertility rate (number of children born if woman was typical of her time and place and bore children to the end of her child-bearing years).

Hajnal, John. "European Marriage Patterns in Perspective." *Population in History, Essays in Historical Demography,* ed. D. V. Glass and D. E. C. Eversley, 101-146. London: Edward Arnold, 1965.
Classic statement of differences that distinguished northern European marriage patterns from other agricultural regions: late marriage ages for women as well as men and significant numbers of women not marrying.

Laslett, Peter. *The World We Have Lost, Further Explored.* London: Methuen, 1983.
One of the more readable studies of changes in birth, death, and migration rates in England.

Lee, Ronald. "The Demographic Transition: Three Centuries of Fundamental Change." *Journal of Economic Perspectives* 17 (Fall 2003): 167-190.
While this article uses demographic history to predict the future, its usefulness lies in its providing the general outlines of changes in mortality and fertility in the past.

Tilly, Charles, ed. *Historical Studies of Changing Fertility.* Princeton: Princeton University Press, 1978.
Articles about Europe in general and individual countries (also Massachusetts).

Wrigley, E. A. and R. S. Scholfield. *The Population History of England, 1541-1871: A Reconstruction*. London: Edward Arnold Ltd., 1981.
> A detailed study of changes in factors shaping the population in England. Statistically sophisticated but containing useful information for genealogists.

Wrigley, E. A., R. S. Davies, J. E. Oeppen, and R. S. Schofield. *English Population History from Family Reconstitution, 1580-1837*. Cambridge: Cambridge University Press, 1997.
> Continuing study of English communities, although it does not sufficiently take into account migration, understating marriage age, life expectancy, and birth intervals.

Woods, Robert. *The Demography of Victorian England and Wales*. New York: Cambridge University Press, 2000.
> In-depth study of the demography of England and Wales in the last two-thirds of the nineteenth century. It compares that era to other periods and makes comparisons to other countries.

6

Migration Methodology

Karen Clifford, AG, FUGA

When an individual or group begins in one place and moves to a new location, it is known as "migration." General movements of population are also termed migrations. There are many genealogical problems that can be solved by applying either a study of migration patterns or developing a migration theory, including those enumerated below:

- A family appears to have missing children, but those children cannot be found in local records.
- Daughters have married and/or left home somewhere between points X and Y. Where are the records found?
- A specific locality in a state is needed in order to focus on local original records.
- The pedigree cannot be extended when the ancestors came from another unknown locality.
- The family under study left no records of their origins.

Some reasons an ancestor may not have kept records, written a diary, or recorded his own migration story was often due to the time he spent securing the basics of life. He may have been maintaining the land he acquired through gift, purchase, or squatting. A major cause for migration was often economic. How does one fill in the gaps left vacant by uncommunicative ancestors and at the same time locate more sources of information to guide ongoing research?

While migration often went hand in hand with land ownership and economics, other reasons motivated migrations, including wars, political or religious upheavals, and other factors. Small, less discernible factors also played a key role in the movement of those ancestors who appear to have "beamed down" from another planet, which might be locality, family, or individual based and may not be recognized until the family is found in other records. A focus on migration methodologies may help solve these mysteries.

Did Migration Occur?

First, check to see if the family really migrated at all! In many cases, they lived within a different city, county, or state jurisdiction a short distance from their last known residence. Since a picture is often worth a thousand words, the most effective solution may be to locate a map of the locality of the ancestor at the time he lived there. Electronic programs exist that make this task easier. For the United States, this author's favorite is an electronic mapping program called *Animap* (Animated Mapping Program).[1] Other time-specific historical maps made during the different time periods the ancestor lived in a specific area may also be found through the help of the Internet, such as:

- Google searches of university card catalogs for map collections.
- Cyndi's List, http://www.cyndislist.com. Click on Maps and Geography.
- Federal, state, historical, and public libraries via their card catalog searches, such as the Library of Congress, the Library of Virginia, the Allen County Public Library, and local city and county libraries.

Study Map Clues

Once you are able to visualize the area, study the clues these historical maps provide. Are roads or paths identified? Are physical obstacles revealed, including mountains, rivers, waterfalls, or thick forests? Are country, ethnic, or state boundary problems indicated?

Study Compiled Historical Records

When the physical obstacles are not large enough or not visual, as in communication barriers, religious differences, or ethnic clashes, it is necessary to study local, county, regional, and state general, religious, and sometimes occupational histories to determine the obstacles.

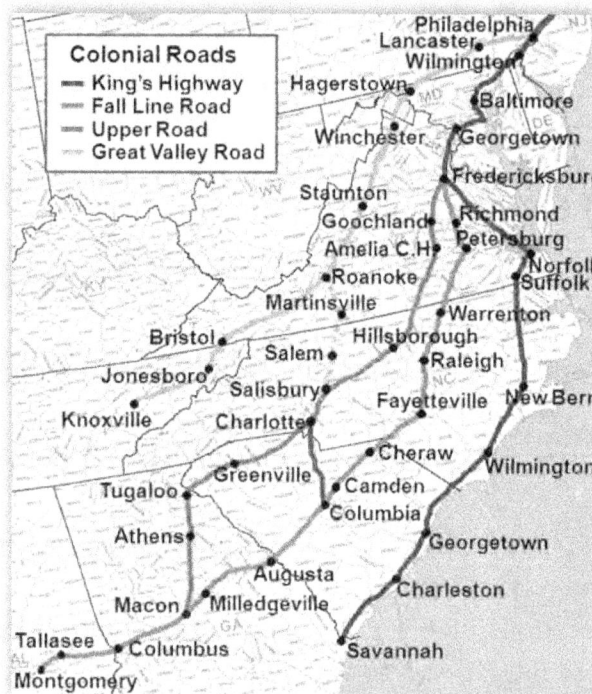

"Colonial Roads," courtesy of the FamilySearch Research Wiki. Used by permission.

These same sources often indicate if boundaries were a problem. Undiscovered boundary disputes can block research because the researcher will not be searching original records in the

---

[1] Available from http://www.Goldbug.com.

correct jurisdiction. Watch for localities that at one time had a territorial status, with their own jurisdictions and types of records. Histories may mention foreign sovereigns and the involvement of citizens in bank fraud, land schemes, and enterprise systems.

Nearly every state was involved in some form of land dispute, either because of poor mapping at the time of colonization, inadequate equipment for surveying, or insufficient government descriptions of the land mass. Some boundary disputes became great barriers to movements or created records in places unknown to most clerks who work in today's courthouses. Or, the records might be in a different state or county altogether.

Migration Detours[2]

Be aware of migration detours. If two countries claimed the same land during the time the ancestor lived there, the ancestor's records might be located in a foreign country. Records that involved settlers in Florida are kept in Cuba; those pertaining to early New Mexico settlers are found in Spain.

Records may also be written in a foreign language, even if they are located in the United States. In Louisiana, records may be found in French, Spanish, or Latin. The latter was more often used because of religion rather than because of land ownership by a foreign country.

Records may belong to an individual or a company rather than a nation. Methods for obtaining those records require different processes than those used when visiting a courthouse. Consider the records of the North Carolina proprietor, Lord Granville. The records he created and maintained of the individuals who purchased land from him in the area north of Albemarle Sound are private papers, not state or county courthouse records. They are found in Great Britain.

The ancestor may be listed in the records of two different countries or counties, or other jurisdictions with administration over that locality. The methodology to find clues for migration requires searching records of both localities. Even if the ancestor was found in one set of records, don't ignore the other set. Many New Yorkers marched straight west into Canada and stayed a season on their way to Michigan or other Midwestern areas. Births, marriages, and deaths occurred along the way. The only way to know if a record exists is to look in both countries.

Sometimes individuals were recorded erroneously to meet census quotas, to prove certain issues, or to give one side an upper hand. Therefore, if you find two people of the same name, follow both of them to determine if they truly existed as two individuals or as only one person. A thorough search of county and local histories will often provide you with these types of clues. If that doesn't work, read the newspapers of the time period to see what was reported by the local editors.

---

[2] For further reading, see the following chapters of Kory L. Meyerink, ed., *Printed Sources: A Guide to Published Genealogical Records* (Salt Lake City: Ancestry, 1998): Carol Mehr Schiffman, "Geographic Tools," 100-144 [covers many maps, finding aids, and resources which are in print for helping with migration studies]; Loretto Dennis Szucs, "Ethnic Sources," 147-173; David T. Thackery, "Military Sources," 469-498; Meyerink, "Family Histories and Genealogies," 575-625; Meyerink, "County and Local Histories," 626-669; Meyerink, "Biographies," 671-707; and Meyerink, "Genealogical Periodicals," 709-751.

After you have determined migration probably occurred, obtain historical maps with the locality names spelled as they were during the specific time period. Then study the histories of the jurisdiction to focus on locality names and the barriers or potential problems involved in migration study. At that point, you can develop a step-by-step process for studying the migration of a particular family.

Determining an Ancestor's Migration Trail

Begin with family stories and traditions recorded in journals, diaries, letters, and other family papers, and remain open to other records that may prove helpful. When searching for the original immigrant, watch for unusual record sources, such as ethnic insurance, church records, or vaccination papers, that may contain the names of the ancestor's town of origin in the Old Country. The focus of this essay is United States internal migration, but sometimes the records of immigration also give clues to migration.

Focus on what has been proven and then move back in time. Learn the names of major migration trails and the chronology of those trails in the areas of your ancestor's movements. Your

Learn the names of major migration trails and the chronology of those trails in the areas of your ancestor's movements.

ancestor may not have traveled that entire route, but this familiarity with the development of various regions along the route can lead to otherwise-overlooked records. Be aware that when the United States was still unformed, travelers sometimes needed a passport to travel through an area possessed by a Native American tribe or another nation. Those passports often listed the last residence of the traveler. Clues might be given along a migration route in addition to those at the end or beginning of the migration trail.

Be aware of records that might contain locality clues, and use those records first that are more likely to contain information about migration. Such records include federal and state census records; federal, state, and private land records; probate records, including administration records; vital records; county histories; and military records. Tax records might also be helpful, but they do not always provide information on migration. While certain records, such as newspapers, are abundant with migration clues, they might not be as easy to search.

Newspapers advertised legal notices of business moves, forwarded mail, and unclaimed mail. Legal notices, such as insolvent debtors or forced land sales, are a good indication that economic downturn was a cause for migration. Notice of a graduation or marriage could suggest a move for educational opportunities or marriage prospects. Some newspapers gave notification of an immigrant's original home,[3] of runaway servants, of farewell parties for those planning to move

---

[3] Ruth-Ann M. Harris and B. Emer O'Keeffe, eds., *The Search for Missing Friends: Irish Immigrant Advertisements Placed in the Boston Pilot, 1831-1920*, 8 vols. (Boston: New England Historic Genealogical Society, 1989-1997).

(or for those who moved and came back to visit), or of obituaries listing relatives from other towns. Individuals setting up a new business in another town might have advertised such a move.

This being the case, it is important to record the results of all original records in which your ancestors or their children might have appeared and left migration clues. Most ancestors who migrated were young adults when they moved. Therefore, by tracing the birthplaces of the children through census and vital records, you can determine their migration pattern.

Use church, county, and town records in your searches. (If the ancestor lived in New England, town records are more effective; or if in a European town, parish records.) Record all places mentioned, including those of friends and neighbors who associated with the ancestor's family. It is often helpful to locate the ancestor's friends and neighbors who have already been researched by others in compiled pedigree databases, such as Family Tree, http://www.family search.org or Public Member Trees, http://www.ancestry.com. Study the migration of these people to see if the ancestor under investigation traveled the same paths.

Look for evidence of military service. Most men enlisted close to home. The enlistment papers often identify the home residence, as do the records made when the soldier mustered out or received a pension. Read all the declarations, and record all places and years in the records. Use the easier compiled indexes and guides to military pensions and bounty lands, such as those provided by Virgil White and through databases on the Internet, before ordering the original records. Indexes save time and help lead you to associate papers that could provide even more information. Some original military records are also available online in digital format.

Trace tracts of land, for they often yield original residences as well as clues to land sales transacted by powers of attorney. If the ancestor lived on land that was originally given for military service or received public domain lands or a land grant, other records may provide evidence of a former residence that were preliminary to the actual final papers. Learn about these records in instruction books, such as the *Researcher's Guide to American Genealogy* by Val Greenwood.[4]

Use Internet search engines to expedite record searches, and include variant name spellings for both the ancestor and the places in which he lived. Location names changed, just as the spelling of given names and surnames did. Without the proper spelling of these identifiers, search engines may miss finding those sources online.

Read the general, ethnic, and occupational histories of the county and state for migration information on the ancestor and his neighbors or associates. The majority of migrants took one or two generations to migrate in incremental steps from the "hub" of their ancestral roots. Sometimes customs, occupations, and languages may be discovered. One example is that of Jost Hite, an immigrant Alsatian who settled in the Shenandoah Valley with his three sons-in-law, Jacob Chrisman, George Bowman, and Paul Froman. In 1734, Jost was granted 100,000 acres of land. He resold the land to other Germans in small family farms of 100 to 500 acres each, as recorded in records of Frederick and Orange Counties, Virginia.

---

4 Val D. Greenwood, *The Researcher's Guide to American Genealogy,* 3rd ed. (Baltimore: Genealogical Publishing Company, 2000).

Migration tends to increase as industry develops and transportation improves, providing people greater flexibility in moving from place to place. For example, while most people might have moved south and west from Virginia, many others went northeast to the city of Baltimore where culture, education, and other alliances might be made.[5] Study records pertaining to large migration movements that may contain the name of the ancestor being studied, such as the opening of the canals in New York, Pennsylvania, Ohio, New Jersey, Indiana, and Illinois; the opening of the railroads across the West; the wagon train trails; occupational migrations involving mining or gold fever; company movements involving the ancestor or other neighbors of the ancestor; or a foreign country that invited people to come and settle its frontiers.

> **Migration tends to increase as industry develops and transportation improves, providing people greater flexibility in moving from place to place.**

Knowledge of business ventures in new areas is very fruitful to the study of migration. Several men often started an economic enterprise together. They might have been the charter members who became so by investing in the company. But when the group settled the new place, relatively few of the company members actually made the original journey. Instead, they waited until things were a bit more settled and sent out others to represent themselves. Then a chain migration occurred, with other family members following within a short period or a generation of time. Business minutes often recorded the names of original settlers, as in the case of the original settlers of New England.[6] But don't forget that some did not follow the masses.

Study the records of an ethnic group or special emigration group to which the ancestor might have belonged—for example, Germans to America, Scotch-Irish to Virginia, and Mormons to Utah. In each case, migration was initiated by an agent who had oversight of organizing companies to travel together. Some set aside financial funds as a means of helping others arrive (such as an emigration fund). People of the same ethnic origins tended to emigrate together and settle in the same neighborhoods in the United States. Many settlers, or their first-generation descendants, formed clubs or other organizations to maintain their customs and origins. Histories written about or by these organizations may list information about the early immigrants, with the names of the places they came from in the Old Country.

People immigrated to America for two main reasons: to flee from persecution (often the movement of families) and to seek greater economic opportunities (often the movement of un-

---

[5] David Hackett Fisher and James C. Kelly, *Bound Away: Virginia and the Westward Movement* (Charlottesville, Va.: University Press of Virginia, 2000).

[6] Robert Charles Anderson, ed., "Focus on Massachusetts Bay Freemen, Becoming a Freeman," *Great Migration Newsletter,* Volumes 1-15 (1990-2006) (Boston: Great Migration Study Project, New England Historic Genealogical Society, 2007), 307.

attached young men). If the movement involved a family, all members of the family should be sought, since any one of them could provide clues about the others. Likewise, emigration from abroad and internal migration at home could have included entire neighborhoods led by a pastor or other leader. History may provide the clue.

After studying the records commonly known to contain clues to migration, it is important to record all clues chronologically, placing historical events beside the ancestral events. In doing so, it is possible to determine if record groups involving events in the life of the ancestor have been overlooked, un-analyzed, or destroyed. If overlooked, they should be found. If un-analyzed, they should be studied. If destroyed, substitute records might be found.

Take, for example, the work of Robert Charles Anderson in "Secrets of the Great Migration Study Project: Squeezing More Out of the Early New England Records of the Great Migration Series."[7] In this paper, which he presented at the 2004 Federation of Genealogical Societies/Austin Genealogical Society conference in Austin, Texas, he briefly outlined how he put together his monumental work, the Great Migration series. His methodology for compiling the series provided unusual and unexpected insights into the lives of the early immigrants of New England between 1620 and 1640. In most cases, these insights could not have been obtained by studying just the family of direct interest to a given researcher. Mr. Anderson set up criteria for the information he gathered to make it easier to analyze. In the way of records, he first looked for migration. He wanted to know each person's last known residence in a desire to understand what caused the move to New England. He discovered that a modest number of people (maybe five or six) had different residences in New England from those with whom they traveled. He also discovered that a small minority of immigrants returned to England during the Cromwell era or moved to a different colony. This scenario reflects the likely case of ancestors anyone might study. A small number will go against the flow of others.

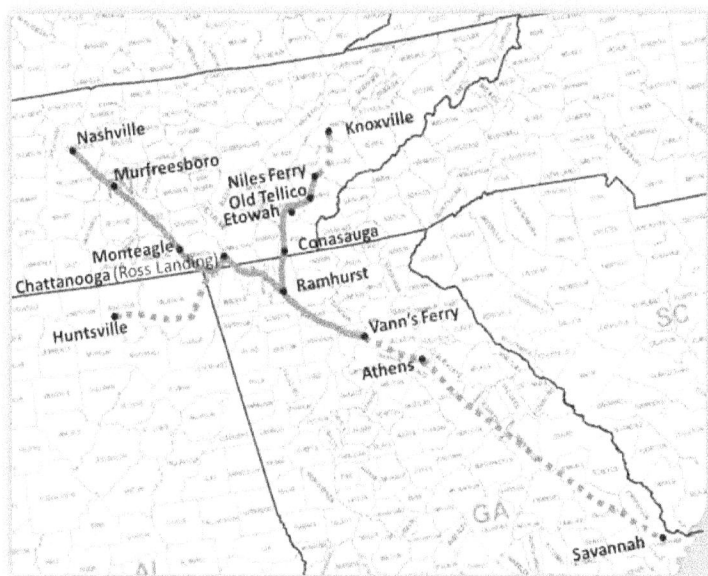

"Georgia Road," courtesy of the FamilySearch Research Wiki. Used by permission.

Anderson then focused on land, tax, court, town, probate, and estate records, adding this information to his list of potential conclusions. Next, he reviewed compiled genealogies. Finally he compared the associations of the individuals. Could certain immigrants have been closely

---

7 Robert C. Anderson, "Secrets of the Great Migration Study Project: Squeezing More out of the Early New England Records" (paper presented at the 2004 Federation of Genealogical Societies/Texas State Genealogical Society/Austin Genealogical Society conference in Austin, Texas).

related to each other, or might they have traveled together? Understanding these associations could make the origins of an ancestor much easier to uncover.

The study of migration is helpful to the family historian. It may enable the researcher to extend family lines by following the common migration movements of other groups who settled in the area of interest, and it can do even more.

The simple fact that people very seldom traveled alone causes links by association to occur. The fact that they usually followed fixed routes set by others helps make migration studies useful. Even if an ancestor did not settle in the same locality as other members of his family or with former neighbors, he probably traveled with them along similar paths, which could lead the researcher to other areas to research and new sources to study.

For Further Study

Anderson, Robert Charles, ed. "Focus on Massachusetts Bay Freemen, Becoming a Freeman." *Great Migration Newsletter,* Volumes 1-15 (1990-2006). Boston: Great Migration Study Project, New England Historic Genealogical Society, 2007.

Anderson, Robert Charles. "Secrets of the Great Migration Study Project: Squeezing More out of the Early New England Records" (paper presented at the 2004 Federation of Genealogical Societies/Texas State Genealogical Society/Austin Genealogical Society conference in Austin, Texas).

Eichholz, Alice. *Red Book: American State, County, and Town Sources,* 3rd ed. Provo, Utah: Ancestry, 2004.

Fisher, David Hackett and James C. Kelly. *Bound Away: Virginia and the Westward Movement.* Charlottesville, Va.: University Press of Virginia, 2000.

The Handybook for Genealogists. 11th ed. Logan, Utah: Everton Publishers, 2006.

Harris, Ruth-Ann M. and B. Emer O'Keeffe, eds. *The Search for Missing Friends; Irish Immigrant Advertisements Placed in the Boston Pilot, 1831-1860,* 8 vols. Boston: New England Historic Genealogical Society, 1989-1997.

Meyerink, Kory, ed. *Printed Sources: A Guide to Published Genealogical Resources.* Salt Lake City: Ancestry, 1998.

7

Strategies for Tracing Female Lines

Judith Eccles Wight, AG

One of the more difficult research problems that genealogists face is tracing their female ancestors. In most countries, women had few legal rights so they seldom left a paper trail. The problem is further complicated with married women who assumed the surnames of their husbands. Unless maiden surnames and other details are known, it is difficult, but not impossible, to identify the families of female ancestors. To begin, start with basic research strategies. These include the following:

Contact All Known Family Members

There is nothing more discouraging than to spend hours of work, not to mention money, researching an ancestor only to find that someone already has the information. The Internet is a fertile field for finding others who may be unknown to you but who are related to the same family.

An unknown and distantly related cousin who was found on the Internet provided the maiden surname of a woman who married a brother (the cousin's direct-line ancestor) of my 4th great grandfather. The information was not easy to come by, but he had more of a vested interest in finding her than did I.

Research the Extended Family

Somewhere within the extended family (grandparents, parents, siblings of the parents, children of the parents, cousins, grandchildren, etc.), a record may exist that will solve a particular genealogical brick wall.

A woman researched her Irish family that immigrated to Canada in the mid-1800s. She found a family in a Canadian census that she thought was hers, based on the names of a couple of children and approximate years of birth. She knew her ancestor and his brother eventually came to the United States and settled in two different counties in Kansas. A biographical sketch of the grandchild of the brother gave the name of the Irish-born grandfather, the maiden name of the Irish-born grandmother, and other details about them, including all of their children and a married sister who remained in Ireland. It also named the place where the immigrant generation settled in Canada and identified the family's place of origin in Ireland. The family she found in the Canadian census proved not to be her ancestor's.

Research Members of the Community

Focus research on those people from the female ancestor's community who originated from the same country or state of origin as the ancestor. Ancestors often settled with people they knew from their homeland. Some of these people may have been related to each other. If the maiden surname of an ancestor is unknown, it is all the more important to learn about the people who resided in the same community as she did and who were born in the same state or country as she was. This may not be as feasible if the family settled in a large city.

> Focus research on those people from the female ancestor's community who originated from the same country or state of origin as the ancestor.

Check Compiled Sources

Study local histories, published biographies, the *Genealogical Research Directory*[1] (published annually), and other such sources. Local genealogical organizations sometimes keep files of families their members are researching. Many libraries have a local history section. Staff and volunteers may have collected material, such as obituaries, for the people in the area.

Check the Internet early, and then keep checking the Internet. Individuals, organizations, and archives are putting new resources online constantly. Genealogical periodicals often publish compiled family histories or information abstracted from local record sources. Subscribers to these periodicals publish queries for family lines they are researching.

When using research done by others, consider how well the information is documented. Undocumented records may result in tracing the wrong ancestor or searching in the wrong area.

Pay Attention to Unusual Given Names

Surnames were often used as given names. My grandfather was named David Richmond Eccles. Richmond was his Scottish-born mother's maiden surname. This practice can be documented in many other families.

---

[1] *Genealogical Research Directory: National and International*, 25 vols. (Sydney, N.S.W.: K.A. Johnson and M.R. Sainty, 1981-2007).

Learn About Foreign Naming Practices and Patterns

Many couples named their children by following naming patterns from their homeland. Learn the naming patterns of the country from which your ancestor came, and see if her family followed a naming pattern that could provide a clue to her relations.

My Scottish Richmond family followed the Scottish naming pattern. The oldest daughter, Isabella Frazer Richmond, was named after the mother's mother, Isobell Frazer. The second child, John Richmond, was named after the father's father. The third child and second daughter, Margaret Kay Richmond, was named after the father's mother, Margaret Kay.

Identify Unknown People in the Ancestor's Records

In addition to the genealogical details listed in records, it is important to look for other clues. Who were the witnesses, the sponsors, and the informants in vital or civil registration records and church records? They were often related to the ancestor in question. Who was the court-appointed guardian to minor children? That person could have been related to the family. A piece of property was sold to the husband for a paltry sum of money. The person selling the property most likely was related. Who gave depositions in a military pension record? These people knew the solider and could well have been related by blood or by marriage.

The Irish place of origin for Thomas Flanagan of Manchester, New Hampshire, was discovered using this strategy. In the newspaper account of his funeral was a list of people who attended the service, including several people who lived in Massachusetts. It was determined that the father of some of the married women who came from Massachusetts was an unknown brother of Thomas. The naturalization record of that brother listed the county of origin in Ireland, where the family was eventually located in a Catholic parish record. Although this example is a success story for finding an elusive Irish male ancestor, the same research strategy may result in locating a woman.

> **Who were the witnesses, the sponsors, and the informants in vital or civil registration records and church records? They were often related to the ancestor in question.**

Use a Broad Spectrum of Records

It is also essential to scrutinize a broad spectrum of records. One never knows where information will be found pertaining to female ancestors. For married women, it is especially important to research the men in their lives, including husbands, sons, and if known, brothers and fathers, as they are the ones who usually left a paper trail.

The list that follows identifies some sources of information for female ancestors. It is hoped that this list will stimulate researchers to think of other records that might also be searched.

- Home sources, such as family Bibles, letters, diaries, journals, pictures, baby books, birthday books, and so forth.
- Civil or vital records of birth, marriage, and death.
- Church records of birth/baptism, marriage, and death/burial.
- Church-related sources such as congregational censuses, visiting books kept by ministers, financial accounts, membership lists, Sunday School rolls, and records of church society organizations.
- Probate records, including wills, administrations, inventories, accounts, etc.
- Guardianship records.
- Federal and state census returns. Pre-1880 census returns do not list relationships, but relatives often lived near each other. Later censuses do not always list relationships of other people living with the family, who nonetheless may have been related. The 1925 census of Iowa lists the names of the parents, including the mother's maiden surname, of each person enumerated.

Elizabeth Snedden Ellis.
Photo in possession of the author.

- City directories. Note people living at the same address (unless it is a tenement, hotel, or similar type dwelling).
- Newspapers. In addition to obituaries, newspapers contain marriage and funeral reports, details about criminal activities, names of people from the area who served in a war, ads placed by people who were seeking lost relatives, and so on.
- Cemetery records. People buried in the same or neighboring plots often were related.
- Funeral homes/undertakers' records.
- Land records including deeds, leases, and mortgages. This is one of the best sources for finding female ancestors. Relatives of the wife may have sold property to her husband, or she may have inherited property from family members. A deed involving my 4th great grandfather identified the maiden surname of his wife, as well as the names and residences of her living siblings.
- Military records, including pensions.
- Society and fraternal organizations.
- Membership records. Organizations such as the Masons and the Colonial Dames contain genealogical information. Records of the Grand Army of the Republic are particularly rich in details about the soldier and may also include information about his wife, parents, and children. The maiden surnames of both the wife and the mother of one soldier were found in a GAR record that was viewed.

- Insurance policies.
- School and alumni records.
- Employment records. For women, check records of religious orders (nuns), schools (women trained there as well as worked in schools), and other occupations that might have kept employee records. Employment records for men may also contain information about their wives or daughters. Pension records of some members of the Royal Irish Constabulary listed names and ages of children as well as where older children lived.
- Bank records. The Emigrant Savings Bank in New York City kept details of their customers, including the name of the account owner, address, occupation, next of kin, and other information. Ancestry.com contains some of the Emigrant Savings Bank records.
- Institution records, such as for poor houses, orphanages, hospitals, and asylums.

Is it impossible to trace female lines? Sometimes. Much depends on the time period, the place where the women lived, and what records survive. By following the research strategies discussed in this article and accessing a wide variety of records, however, identifying the lineages of female ancestors can happen more frequently with very successful results.

For Further Study

Carmack, Sharon DeBartolo. *A Genealogist's Guide to Discovering Your Female Ancestors: Special Strategies for Uncovering Hard-to-Find Information About Your Female Lineage.* Cincinnati: Betterway Books, 1998.

Neill, Michael John. "Female Ancestors: After the Marriage." *Ancestry Daily News,* 13 October 2004.

"Reassembling Female Lives." *National Genealogical Society Quarterly* 8, no. 2 (2000): 165-228.

Schaeffer, Christina Kassabian. *The Hidden Half of the Family: A Sourcebook for Women's Genealogy.* Baltimore: Genealogical Publishing Company, 1999.

Casting the Net Wide: Searching Horizontal Kin and Neighbors

Amy Harris, Ph.D., AG

Excellent genealogists quickly realize that good research does not only go deep, it goes wide. Many clients and others are interested in "how far back" a particular line has been traced, but an excellent genealogist cannot afford to think or research this way. Instead, they recognize the importance of searching broadly—for lateral kin and in multiple records.[1] They also practice long-scope research that considers *all* family members and throughout their *entire* life cycle. When genealogists search broadly both in terms of kinship and chronology, they increase the likelihood of identifying the correct ancestral candidates and of discovering information about previous generations.

Searching for complete family groupings (i.e. all the siblings of an ancestor, or all the children of an ancestral couple) is absolutely essential to professional research methodology. The records about one ancestor never contain all the clues

> By researching siblings, cousins, and neighbors, advanced researchers are able to build stronger cases for pursuing particular candidates for earlier ancestors.

---

[1] For a particularly good example of this type of research used by a historian see Laurel Thatcher Ulrich, *A Midwife's Tale: The Life of Martha Ballard, Based on Her Diary, 1785-1812* (New York City: Vintage, 1991).

77

pertaining to previous generations. By researching siblings, cousins, and neighbors, advanced researchers are able to build stronger cases for pursing particular candidates for earlier ancestors. Also, as research moves beyond the middle of the nineteenth century and records become less consistent and less informative, corroborating evidence from multiple sources becomes standard procedure. This method conforms with the "systematic and exhaustive" genealogical proof standard and that "every deduction is clearly reasoned and persuasively explained."[2]

Daniel Browett Harris and Mary Ann Parkinson Family, c 1910, Utah. Photo in possession of author.

Searching Broadly – Kinship

Kin—particularly horizontal kin, such as siblings and cousins—are important to any genealogical research project. Sibling relationships last longer than marriage and parenthood; therefore siblings are found in genealogical documents throughout the life course. As children, siblings might be christened on the same day, attend the same school, or be apprenticed to the same employer (often a sibling of their parents). Adult siblings frequently resided together or near each other, witnessed each other's marriages and property transactions, helped raise and employ each other's children, and executed parents' and each other's wills.

The importance of searching for extended kin is best demonstrated by a short case study. Like many immigrant families, the Focareto/Fogareto families of Cleveland and Chicago pose

---

[2] Donn Devine, "Evidence Analysis" in Elizabeth Shown Mills, ed., *Professional Genealogy: A Manual for Researchers, Writers, Editors, Lecturers, and Librarians* (Baltimore: Genealogical Publishing Company, 2001), 330.

research problems. The surname was spelled a variety of ways in original records, a problem compounded by indexers' and transcribers' various renderings of the surname. There are several strategies for finding more information on these families, but the easiest is often to think very broadly about the family during the preliminary stages of research. For example, searching for the ancestors of Nicola Focareto (born 1850 in Italy and died 1935 in Ohio) in the *International Genealogical Index* (IGI)* yielded no results. However, searching for his brother Pasquale Fogareto (born 1859 in Italy and died 1945 in Illinois) yielded a submitted record for his parents: Luigi Focareta and Maria Elena Linfante.[3] While an IGI entry is not definitive proof of this connection, it provides clues for further research and indicates that there is another researcher who may have additional source information.

Thinking of kinship broadly and paying attention to neighbors also helps to find all the children belonging to a couple. Additionally, because married women in America and many European countries change their names at marriage, they can be difficult to track. Searching broadly among known kin and neighbors can help trace women throughout their life course.

To return to the Focareto family, consider the path taken to find the marriage of Nicola's daughter, Carmela. Nicola's son, Pasquale Focareto, died in Cleveland, Ohio, in 1952. A transcription of his obituary listed his brother Anthony and listed his sisters by their married names: Adliene Peluso, Carmels Christophor, and Mary Rossi.[4] The transcription contained what appeared to be spelling errors in the names, and its anglicization of apparently Italian surnames meant finding marriage records for these three women could be difficult. Mary/Maria Focareto and her husband, Anthony Rossi/Ross, were relatively easy to find in census and marriage records. Finding "Adliene" and "Carmels," however, proved fruitless. Were those poor transcriptions of "Adeline" and "Carmela"? Or had their names undergone some other unrecognizable transformation? A glance at the neighborhood where Mary Rossi lived in 1930, however, gave further clues to her sisters' names.

Mary and Anthony Rossi (appeared as Ross in the census) lived on East 176th Street in Cleveland. Across the street (but on the next page in the census) lived the Michael and Carmela Christopher family, and next door to the Christophers was the Dominic and Lena Plosi family (complete with the "Fernazzi" children from Lena's previous marriage to Ralph Farinacci).[5] Simply scanning the neighborhood on a census sheet provided possible names for the Focareto sisters, their husbands, and other surname variations. In 1920, the families

* The International Genealogical Index (IGI) is no longer available under that title. However, most records from the IGI can be accessed at FamilySearch.org.

3 Pascale Antonio Focareta entry, *International Genealogical Index* (Salt Lake City: Family History Library), http://www.familysearch.org.

4 Cleveland Public Library, Cleveland Necrology File (from local newspapers), Pasquale Focareto, ID number 0502141, 6 October 1952, *Cleveland Press;* Cleveland Necrology File, Reel #109, http://dxsrv4.cpl.org/WebZ/Authorize?sessionid=0&next=/html/obit_start.html&dbchoice=1:dbname=necr&b.

5 Anthony Ross household, 1930 U.S. Census, Cleveland, Cuyahoga, Ohio, enumeration district 819, sheet 17B, dwelling 7, family 11; Michael Christopher household, 1930 U.S. Census, Cleveland, Cuyahoga, Ohio, enumeration district 819, sheet 18A, dwelling 16, family 21; Dominic Plosi household, 1930 U.S. Census, Cleveland, Cuyahoga, Ohio, enumeration district 819, sheet 18A, dwelling 17, family 22; National Archives T626, Ancestry.com *1930 United States Federal Census* [database online], Provo, Utah: Ancestry.com Operations Inc., 2002.

still lived next door to one another on East 176ᵗʰ Street, but their names had changed again; they appeared as Micha and Carry Christopho and Dominico and Lina Pelosi.[6] The Anthony and Mary Ross family had moved to another Cleveland neighborhood, but their names remained the same.[7]

Name in 1972 Obituary Transcription	Name in 1930 Census	Name in 1920 Census
Adliene Peluso	Lena and Dominic Plosi	Lina and Dominico Pelosi and Fernazzis (step-children of Dominico)
Carmels Christophor	Carmela and Michael Christopher	Carry and Michael Christopho
Mary Rossi	Mary and Anthony Ross	Mary and Anthony Ross

The 1910 census provided more clues but also raised more questions. No Michael and Carry/Carmela Christopher/Christopho family readily appeared. However, Carry's brothers, Pasquale (written Patsy) and Anthony (Tony) Focareto were neighbors on East 123ʳᵈ Street in Cleveland (a street in the neighborhood of East 176ᵗʰ Street), and next door to them were two Christophoro families. One was headed by Dominick and Maria, and one was headed by Angelo and Carry.[8] Three blocks away on East 126ᵗʰ Street was the Raphael and Adelina Farnacia family.[9] And one street over on Coltman Road was the Tony and Mary Rosso Family.[10]

Pursuing the family in the 1900 census gave further clues. Nicola Focareto's children, Antonio, Anna M., and Pasquale, all lived with their parents. Also living in the household was a boarder: Antonio Rossi.[11] Living next door to the Focareto family was the Luigi Christoforo family, including his two sons, Domenico and Arcangelo, and his daughter-in-law, Carmela.[12]

---

[6] Dominico Pelosi household, 1920 U.S. Census, Cleveland, Cuyahoga, Ohio, enumeration district 503, sheet 6A, dwelling 106, family 121; Micha Christopho household, 1920 U.S. Census, Cleveland, Cuyahoga, Ohio, enumeration district 503, sheet 6A; National Archives T625-1373, Ancestry.com *1920 United States Federal Census* [database online], Provo, Utah: Ancestry.com Operations Inc., 2002.

[7] Anthony Ross household, 1920 U.S. Census, Cleveland, Cuyahoga, Ohio, enumeration district 392, sheet 7B, dwelling 50, family 126, National Archives T625-1370, Ancestry.com *1920 United States Federal Census* [database online], Provo, Utah: Ancestry.com Operations Inc., 2002.

[8] Angelo Christoforo household, 1920 U.S. Census, Cleveland, Cuyahoga, Ohio, enumeration district 393, sheet 19A, dwelling 142, family 351, National Archives T624-1176, Ancestry.com *1910 United States Federal Census* [database online], Provo, Utah: Ancestry.com Operations Inc., 2002.

[9] Raphael Farnacia household, 1920 U.S. Census, Cleveland, Cuyahoga, Ohio, enumeration district 393, sheet 3A, dwelling 29, family 50, National Archives T624-1176, Ancestry.com *1910 United States Federal Census* [database online], Provo, Utah: Ancestry.com Operations Inc., 2002.

[10] Tony Rosso household, 1910 U.S. Census, Cleveland, Cuyahoga, Ohio, enumeration district 393, sheet 20B, dwelling 159, family 390, National Archives T624-1176, Ancestry.com *1910 United States Federal Census* [database online], Provo, Utah: Ancestry.com Operations Inc., 2002.

[11] Nicola Focareto household, 1900 U.S. Census, Cleveland, Cuyahoga, Ohio, enumeration district 105, sheet 9A, dwelling 81, family 161, National Archives T623-1255, Ancestry.com *1900 United States Federal Census* [database online], Provo, Utah: Ancestry.com Operations Inc., 2002.

[12] Luigi Christoforo household, 1900 U.S. Census, Cleveland, Cuyahoga, Ohio, enumeration district 105, sheet 9A, dwelling 82, family 162, National Archives T623-1255, Ancestry.com *1900 United States Federal Census* [database online], Provo, Utah: Ancestry.com Operations Inc., 2002.

Taking all of the various spellings into account made it easier to search for Anna Maria Focareto's marriage to Antonio Rossi. The index listed them as Mary Focareto and Tony Ross.[13] That perhaps would not have been such a leap of research, but finding Carry/Carmela Focareto's marriage to Michael or Angelo Christopher/Christoforo would prove more challenging. Using all the various spellings and renderings of the names and surnames of these women and searching all available censuses revealed enough clues so that when the marriage index offered an entry for Carmela Focareta's marriage to Arcangelo Dichristofano, there was proof this was the same person enumerated as Michael Christopher in the 1930 census.[14] At some point, he must have decided to go by Michael—the biblical Archangel's name. Tracking all family members through all available censuses clarified Carmela's marriage information and provided clues about her siblings and family of origin.

Name in 1920 Census	Name in 1910 Census	Name in 1900 Census	Name in Marriage Index
Lina and Dominico Pelosi with Fernazzis (step-children of Dominico)	Adelina and Raphael Farnacia	Adelina and Raffaela Farinacci	Lena Farinacio and Domenick Pelosi
Carry and Michael Christopho	Carry and Angelo Christophoro	Carmela and Arcangelo Christoforo	Carmela Focareta and Arcangelo Dichristofano
Mary and Anthony Ross	Mary and Tony Rosso	Anna M. Focareto and Antonio Rossi	Mary Focareto and Tony Ross

Searching laterally is also essential to finding earlier ancestors. As stated earlier, searching for Nicola's brother separately found possible parents. Additionally, the search detailed above would allow a researcher to extend the pedigrees for the Rossi, DiChristofano, Pelosi, and Focareto families. For example, searching broadly proved that the Mary Ross found in the 1930 census was the same as the Anna M. Focareto found in the 1900 census. This meant that when searching for her birth—in 1884 in Pennsylvania—the researcher would know to look for all variations of Maria/Mary and not just Ann/Anna. Therefore, a birth entry for Maria Focareto in Pittsburgh on 24 December 1884 appeared to be a good candidate.[15] The birth record itself listed her parents as Nicola Focareto and Lucia Diorio Focareto—providing for the first time a maiden name for Lucia Focareto and thereby revealing evidence necessary to extend the pedigree.

---

13 Probate Court of Cuyahoga County, Ohio, *Historical Marriage License Index, 1810–April 1998*, vol. 51, page 74, http://probate.cuyahogacounty.us/ml.

14 Probate Court of Cuyahoga County, Ohio, *Historical Marriage License Index, 1810–April 1998*, vol. 34, page 334, http://probate.cuyahogacounty.us/ml.

15 Allegheny County, Pennsylvania Orphan's Court, Delayed Birth Record Dockets no. 73-74, filed 1948-1949 (Salt Lake City: Filmed by the Genealogical Society of Utah, 1971), FHL US/CAN film 894,791.

A Note on Single Men and Women

If Carmela Focareto's marriage posed special problems that were solved by searching for all of her siblings and looking for records created throughout her and their lives, unmarried women and men can be beneficial to genealogical research. Single adults without children tended to leave goods and land to and invest educational and occupational resources in their nieces and nephews. And women who never married did not change their surnames, making finding them more straightforward. Additionally, records about single women often contain information about their siblings, parents, nieces and nephews, illegitimate children, and grandparents. For example, a 1775 probate for the recently deceased Anne Cox, a never-married woman, listed two of her sisters: Mary Haynes (widow) and Martha Walker.[16] The letters of administration stated that Anne was a spinster from Longford within the parish of St. Catherine, Gloucester, Gloucestershire, England. Another Cox sibling, Thomas, brought the probate dispute that generated the letters of administration. Looking at the original dispute paper reveals that Martha Walker's husband was Richard Walker and that they and Mary Haynes also lived in Longford.[17] Therefore, by looking for unmarried Anne Cox, several additional pieces of information were revealed: two sisters' married names; one of their husband's names; and knowledge that her two sisters and a brother lived past 1775, that one of her brothers-in-law predeceased her, and that her sisters and brother-in-law lived in Longford in 1775.

Records about and by single men and women also contain clues about previous and later generations. For example, the will of Frances Mary Travell (written 1764, probated 1768) lists the names of two brothers, a sister-in-law, a sister, a niece, and three maternal aunts.[18] Searching for wills from those people reveals two additional sisters, more nieces and grandnieces, two nephews, two illegitimate nephews, and another brother. In fact, only by looking at all the wills for every family member could the illegitimate nephews' names, birth, death, and occupation information be identified.

Searching Broadly – Chronology and Methodology

The previous examples illustrate that searching for records covering the entire lifecycle pays dividends for genealogical research. Those examples were based on already knowing some additional information, such as siblings' names. Sometimes at the beginning of a research project, however, other family members' names may not be known. In that case, searching broadly in a chronological fashion can not only give clues about an ancestor's progenitors but also provide information about collateral kin and neighbors. For example, a gravestone for Singleton Ferguson in a rural United States cemetery lists not only his 1895 death but also his 1840 birth in

---

[16] Anne Cox, Letters of Administration, 6 March 1775, Gloucester Diocese (Gloucestershire Archives, GDRO Wills 1775-30).

[17] Gloucester Diocese, Testamentary Cause, Anne Cox, 11 February 1775 (Gloucestershire Archives, GDRO B4/2/C120).

[18] France Mary Travell, Will, written 31 August 1764, proved 16 January 1768, Prerogative Court of Canterbury (Gloucestershire Archives, Bowly Family of Cirencester Collection, D495/F6).

Gilcruse [Gilcrux], Cumberland, England.[19] These specific clues about Ferguson's origins open possibilities for searching for his siblings, neighbors, and parents in Cumberland.

The example of Singleton Ferguson's grave marker also emphasizes the point that all available records about an event should be searched. Therefore, even a church or civil record of a death should not stop an excellent genealogist from looking for a gravestone or monumental inscription. As the Focareto example demonstrated, searching for ancestors in all available records is essential to gathering clues and proving links to kin and ancestors.

Conclusion

Searching across time and kinship is one mark of an excellent genealogist. Beginning researchers often feel the lure of pushing lines back in time and forget that tracking ancestors and their lateral kin throughout their lifetimes and in multiple records reveals a treasure trove of information that simplifies research on previous generations and builds a methodologically sound foundation for claiming the connection to those previous generations.

---

[19] Tintic Cemetery (Tintic, Juab County, Utah), Singleton Ferguson marker, personally read, digital photo 24 July 2009. Photo in author's possession. Utah death records began in 1898, so the headstone may be the only place this information is preserved.

9

Researching Minorities in the United States

Jimmy B. Parker, AG, FUGA

The concept of "minorities research" is an interesting one. What is it, anyway? What about a person or group sets them apart as a minority? Every individual, family, ethnic group, religion, etc. may qualify as a minority under certain conditions. What constitutes a minority may vary with locality, time period, and attitude. And even if a person or group is considered a minority, how does that affect research? Are the records different for that group? Does the research methodology change because of that minority status?

Perhaps the simplest definition of a minority is being different from the "mainstream" or "majority" of a population in a locality. In that sense, an individual whose skin color is different from the majority of his neighbors might be considered a minority. Or someone of a particular religion may be considered a minority if his religion is different than that of his neighbors. Or someone from a different country, or who speaks a different language than his neighbors, may be considered a minority.

These differences may or may not determine what records must be searched, or how they are searched, to find the ancestry of that person. The best approach is to begin research on such an ancestor in the same way you would for anyone else in that locality and time period. When a difference is identified, that is the time to ask if that should make a difference in your research methods and to look for records specific to that minority.

All of our ancestors were unique (in fact, all of *us* are unique!). That uniqueness may be a great asset as you try to identify an ancestor. So how do we identify our ancestor's uniqueness? Here are some suggestions.

Study Historical Background

As is true in all genealogical projects, it is important to gather as much family information as possible from older family members, including any ethnic, religious, or cultural ties. Family traditions are important clues, although they may have been distorted over time.

It is important to gather as much family information as possible from older family members, including any ethnic, religious, or cultural ties.

It is also important to study the local history of the neighborhoods, towns, counties, and other localities where ancestors lived. Local histories often provide information about minorities in the area.

Once possible minority groups are identified, it is then important to study the history of those groups. For example, you might study a history of the Irish in Philadelphia or Huguenot immigration to the United States. Some people have traditions of American Indian ancestry. Many people came to America as indentured servants or as slaves. Studying this historical background can help you identify where your ancestors lived and when they lived there, where they migrated, any records that may be unique to that minority, any attitudes or teachings of the minority group that may affect the records, and other information to help you understand your family's history.

If the minority involves a language other than that spoken by most residents of the locality, it may be important to learn that language, or at least enough of it to be able to read the records. Sometimes the original records may be written in that language. Members of that minority may have tried to retain their culture by publishing newspapers or magazines in their language.

How Does Being a Minority Affect Records and Research?

For most minorities in the United States, some unique records and resources are available. These include histories, newspapers, and periodicals (such as the *Swedish-American Historical Quarterly*). In addition, various local and national societies have been organized to gather, preserve, and share the cultural contributions and histories of one or more minority groups. Some examples are the Balch Institute for Ethnic Studies in Philadelphia and the American Historical Society of Germans from Russia in Lincoln, Nebraska. Many such organizations have libraries, archives, Web sites, and publications.

Sometimes traditions affected whether or not a minority was included in a type of record. For example, the Society of Friends discouraged their members from serving in military units, thereby making it unlikely to find military records for Quakers, although there were exceptions.

Many libraries have cataloged their holdings in a way that highlights their research materials regarding minorities. The Family History Library in Salt Lake City has a subject heading under many localities such as "Tennessee—Minorities." Other libraries use similar subject headings. A subject search in the catalogs of many libraries will also reveal their holdings for a specific minority, such as "Afro-Americans," American Loyalists," "Italians—New York," or "Melungeons."

Handbooks on how to research specific groups (such as Czech, German, Hispanic, Indian, Irish, Polish, etc.) have been written. Some examples are included in the very limited bibliography at the end of this article.

Examples

Many examples could be given of minority groups in the United States. The country's population is made up of people from all over the world who, when they first came to the United States, were undoubtedly in the minority. So in that sense, all of our ancestors, at one time or another, were probably classified as minorities.

There is a basic set of records most genealogists use to trace their ancestors—vital records, church records, census records, probate records, and so on. In some cases, the records for groups classified as minorities are strikingly different from that basic set, especially for an ethnic group or a religion. Those differences may require an adjustment in research methodology for those minorities.

American Indian

Many records exist for the American Indian unique to that ethnic group. Records kept by the various levels of the Bureau of Indian Affairs, such as allotment records and individual Indian history cards, are distinctive records for the native population. Other records for the Indians bear names familiar to most genealogists, such as census rolls, heirship papers, school records, and others. But even those records are different enough in how they were kept or the information they contain that they require a modified methodology in finding and using them. Individual tribes also created and maintain records such as enrollment records, tribal court records, records of their tribal police force, etc.

A description of many records unique to American Indians can be found in the FamilySearch Wiki being developed by a community

Photo courtesy of the Library of Congress.

of contributors (see https://wiki.familysearch.org/en/Indians_of_the_United_States_and_Their_Records).

European Immigrants to the United States

From the 17th through the 19th centuries, immigrants poured into the American colonies and the United States from most of the European countries. Those immigrants brought with them their languages, traditions, and religions. Many of them felt more comfortable settling together with others from similar cultural backgrounds. For example, groups of Scandinavians settled together in the Upper Midwest and in Utah; Germans settled in Pennsylvania, Texas, and Iowa; the Dutch settled in New York; the Basques settled in Nevada and Idaho; and the French settled in Louisiana, to name only a few examples.

Each of these groups, at least for a time, tried to maintain their language, their religion, and other aspects of their culture. Eventually, through intermarriage and intermingling with others, the uniqueness of their groups dispersed, and with that dispersal, the uniqueness of their culture and records became less noticeable.

Chinese Immigrants to the United States

Early Chinese immigrants to the United States were, for the most part, well-received and accepted. Many of them were merchants, fishermen, artisans, hotel and restaurant owners, and businessmen.

The California Gold Rush in the mid-1800s brought a great influx of "common laborers" from China to work in the gold fields and in related fields in and around San Francisco. Many of these laborers congregated in neighborhoods, which came to be known as the "Chinatown" of the city where each was located.

In the 1860s, nearly ten thousand Chinese were laborers on the transcontinental railroad, particularly on the western leg of the Central Pacific Railroad. By 1880, approximately 20 percent of the Chinese in the United States were engaged in mining, another 20 percent worked in agriculture, about 15 percent worked in manufacturing, 15 percent were employed as domestic servants, and 10 percent worked as laundry workers. The remainder was involved in other professions, many in tasks no one else seemed to want to do.

Some of the workers in the United States began to resent the Chinese workers, whom they felt were taking away jobs from them. As a result, the Chinese Exclusion Act was passed in 1882. This act severely curtailed Chinese immigration and also created records of great interest to genealogists, including questionnaires regarding individual and family information. For a more detailed description of some of the records of Chinese immigration, see the National Archives Web site, http://www.archives.gov/locations/finding-aids/chinese-immigration.html.

The Society of Friends (Quakers)

Members of the Society of Friends (often referred to as Quakers) began emigrating from England, Wales, and Germany in the late 1600s, many settling near Philadelphia. By 1700, they had gained considerable influence in most of the New England and middle-Atlantic colonies. Quaker migration to the southern colonies, especially North Carolina, continued until the Revolutionary War, when the strength of the Society began to decline. Many Quakers left the southern states and migrated primarily to Ohio, Indiana, Illinois, and Canada.

The minutes of Monthly Meetings (the name of their local congregation) of the Society of Friends contain references to migrations, disciplinary actions, and vital events. Original marriage records, usually in the possession of the family, often contain signatures of all who witnessed the marriage.

Many of the records of Quaker Monthly Meetings have been gathered in the Friends Historical Library at Swarthmore College in Pennsylvania. Most have been microfilmed and many have also been abstracted, indexed, and published as the *Encyclopedia of American Quaker Genealogy*, a five-volume set compiled by William Wade Hinshaw, with a sixth volume having been compiled after Mr. Hinshaw's death by Willard Heiss. Additional information regarding the holdings of the Friends Historical Library is available online at http://www.swarthmore.edu/x6673.xml.

United Empire Loyalists

When the American colonists determined it was necessary to break their connection with the "mother country" of England, not all were in favor of doing so. In fact, some historians love to point out that it was a determined few who were responsible for carrying out that separation. While those "patriots" (or "rebels," depending upon which side of the conflict you favored) may have been in the minority at the beginning of the American Revolution, the resulting surrender of Lord Cornwallis changed things. Those who thought they were remaining loyal to their government suddenly found themselves as outcasts. They were labeled as "United Empire Loyalists" and were forced out of the new United States of America.

Many of these Loyalists went to New Brunswick, Nova Scotia, and Ontario in Canada and to the British West Indies. A few even returned to England. The British government tried to make provisions to reward their loyalty by granting land set aside for that purpose. Records of their claims and subsequent grants of property were created. One series of records of particular interest is the American Loyalist Claims Records of the Exchequer and Audit Department in the Public Record Office in London (their reference number A.O. 13). This set of records is arranged by state and is indexed. Many histories of the Loyalists are also available, as are collections of records in the provinces of Canada where they settled.

For Further Study

African American Genealogical Sourcebook. Detroit: Gale Research, 1995.

Blessing, Patrick Joseph. *The Irish in America: A Guide to the Literature and Manuscript Collection.* Washington, D.C.: Catholic University of America Press, 1992.

Colletta, John Philip. *Finding Italian Roots: The Complete Guide for Americans.* Baltimore: Genealogical Publishing Company, 1993.

Hispanic American Genealogical Sourcebook. New York: Gale Research, 1995.

Native American Genealogical Sourcebook. Detroit: Gale Research, 1995.

Smith, Jessie C., ed. *Ethnic Genealogy: A Research Guide.* Westport, Conn.: Greenwood Press, 1983.

Thernstrom, Stephen, ed. *Harvard Encyclopedia of American Ethnic Groups.* Cambridge, Mass.: Harvard University Press, 1980.

Tracing Immigrant Origins Research Outline. Salt Lake City: Family History Library, 1992.

10

Big City Research

James W. Petty, AG, CG

Big city research is, by nature, a study of ancestry in large population centers using genealogical and historical records and organizing research using logical and scientific approaches, or methods of research, called methodologies. It is about thinking outside the box of traditional genealogy and discovering new and interesting records, of which there is great abundance in the big cities. Research in the metropolitan centers of all countries requires recognizing standard or traditional research concepts and then expanding on them in order to separate and define specific individuals and families in a large population base. For the purposes of this essay, the focus will be on big city research methodologies largely from the view of United States genealogy. However, while specific records and genealogical research differ from country to country, the principles of big city research are applicable wherever in the world research is conducted. These principles include: find, quantify, document, and combine data to identify individuals and families.

Genealogical methodology refers to the historical and scientific approach to genealogy research. True scientific methodology is built on a cause and effect concept; it's about patterns. Genealogical methodology is more of a historical cause and consequence formula, built upon documentation and evidence. While mankind is constantly changing and impacting the world around it, genealogy research can be associated with a scientific approach because patterns in human interaction are repeated again and again and can be used to seek out clues and new information about ancestors. When more people congregate in confined areas (cities), there is a greater need to coordinate the needs and problems of that populace. Historical events inform the researcher of causes that stimulate human interaction and the creation of records, and that information can influence how people and their consequent relationships are interpreted.

The Definition and Special Nature of Big Cities

There is no specific definition for "Big City," except that for genealogists, it is any city where ancestors lived that seems too big for traditional genealogy methods (meaning a basic search of the principal record sources, such as census, vital records, deeds, probate, and court minutes) to solve ancestral questions. These large municipalities began as small communities and should be treated as such by researchers during their early period of history. For instance, in 1790, New York City had a population of 33,000 inhabitants; big for its time but equivalent to the size of a small town in America today. Research in New York City in 1790 would likely involve a basic approach to finding genealogy information. There were few census records and no civil vital records to speak of. Much of Manhattan Island was farm land, so land and probate records played an important role. A century later in 1890 (before it combined with four other counties to create its present-day metropolis), New York City reached the one million mark in population. Simply finding and identifying an ancestor in that chaos of humanity and records is a daunting challenge. Times and records changed over that period of time, requiring the researcher to adjust his approach to finding family members.

> **For genealogists, a big city is any city where ancestors lived that seems too big for traditional genealogy methods.**

Big city research is very different from traditional genealogy research; and to be successful, the genealogist must understand the special nature of big cities and know how to use the available records and applicable methodologies. Big cities, like small towns, represent collections of people and records; but unlike its smaller counterpart, the metropolis reflects the problems and benefits that large population centers provide for the genealogist: multiplicity of cultures and languages, ethnicities and traditions, governmental jurisdictions and records, records, records, and of course, lots of people.

There isn't a standardized set of records relative to all big cities. Specific record types found in large communities can also be found in rural and small-town America. But because of the density of the population and its written resources, it is the approach to the research process or how the methodologies are used that differentiates big city research from other forms of genealogical study. Therefore, this essay on genealogy research in metropolitan areas will not focus on defining records but will explore methodologies that must be utilized in order to discover information in this expanded laboratory of human interaction.

The researcher needs to be knowledgeable about the history of the community he is studying in order to understand possible reasons for an ancestor being there and what impressed him or her to stay or move on. Every metropolitan community began as a small entity before growing into a dominant city. Each big city achieved its position because of certain factors but not all for the same reason. In some cases it was the center for government in a state or colony, such as Boston, Atlanta, or Phoenix; but not all big cities were capitals or seats of government. Some grew because they were prominent shipping and immigration ports, such as New York City, New Orleans, and Philadelphia. Some developed due to commerce and industry, like Pittsburg and Chicago. Others had special reasons, such as religion in Salt Lake City, the Gold Rush in San Francisco, and the Lights of Hollywood in Los Angeles.

In addition to the factors of growth, genealogists have to deal with losses in big cities. Chicago was destroyed by fire in 1871; San Francisco was devastated by earthquake and fire in 1906; Atlanta was bombarded into silence by the siege of Union Army soldiers in 1864. In each of these cities, the loss of historical records presents special challenges to researchers trying to dig their way into the ancestral past. The researcher must be open to the unique ways that individual large communities deal with record loss and must be willing to seek out alternative record sources.

Varieties of People and Cultures

Big cities owe their heritage to their history and the special needs and issues of their inhabitants. Immigration has always been the primary influence on the growth of big cities. Each metropolitan area was a melting pot for a variety of races and cultures. America has been known since its inception as an independent country and a symbol of hope for repressed people of any country. Very often when ethnic families began their trek to America, it was with just the few possessions they could carry; consequently they settled in the ports and cities where they arrived. Many found new opportunities and then called for their extended families and friends to join them in this new home.

> **Immigration has always been the primary influence on the growth of big cities.**

Some immigrants were able to travel to prepared destinations. Russians and Swedes flocked to the North Central States as cultural groups. French Huguenots arrived in coordinated settlements all along the eastern seaboard of America. Mormons from the British Isles, Scandinavia, and other European countries gave up all they had to find new hope in the American West, while Jews fled the oppressive gulags and socialist tyranny of Russia and Germany. The Irish fled hunger and religious discrimination to find their place in this great expansive land. While many spread across the countryside, a vast number joined family and comrades in the swelling centers of humanity known to us today as big cities. Researchers must be fully aware of the historical and social background of these locations as they search for their individual ancestors.

Government

The very nature of population centers has driven many cities to adopt their own specialized civil and record keeping systems. Charlottesville, Virginia, in 1762 became the first of many "independent cities" established with county-level government authority, separate from the county in which they resided; endowed with the rights to record vital records, deeds, probate, and other authority normally held by county government. While many of these independent cities of Virginia may not merit the genealogical classification of "big cities," they demonstrate the importance to genealogists of being aware of government jurisdiction in the place where they have undertaken research. Many other metropolitan communities across the country have taken similar steps in order to manage their people and industries. In 1898, New York County, New York, united with the neighboring counties of Kings, Queens, Bronx, and Richmond (Staten Island) to establish the first true metropolis in America, known as New York City. As a governmental authority, it manages vital records and court proceedings, but it still operates with separate county governments to handle property, probate, naturalization, and other community governmental services.

Archives and Repositories

Record preservation is an enormous chore for any governmental or social entity. In the current day of digitization and computer archiving, it would seem to be an ideal situation for big cities to conserve the space taken up by paper files and even by microfilm. But microfilming and digitization doesn't necessarily solve the problem. City and county offices still have to maintain paper records and provide access to information to the public. Some records can be sealed and warehoused, but many others, such as books, registers, and case files, have to be where they can be brought out into the open. And this doesn't apply to governmental records only. Business records have to be maintained, as do school records, church registers, hospital files, public and private libraries, cemetery sexton records, architectural and highway plans, and the list goes on and on. Some private record sources have seen their way into historical societies and museums or into university archives to be studied by historians and students. Some archives have published extensive inventories of their holdings, summarizing descriptions of the collections and indexing the items by department, category, and topic.

For example, in Ohio, the state archives has divided the entire state into districts, with each district directed by a university archives program, where records can be cared for, preserved, catalogued, and made available to the public. Researchers must become familiar with the archival system of their area of interest in order to thoroughly pursue the possibilities.

One of the most fearsome and yet most exciting aspects of the research is the great number of resources available and the diversity of the records.

Different Types of Records

Big city research is intimidating simply because of the size of the project and the number of people involved. One of the most fearsome and yet most exciting aspects of the research is the great number of resources available and the diversity of the records. The nature of population is that the more people there are, the more names there are, and the more difficult it is to identify an individual. In a small nineteenth-century town, the local postmaster was likely to know everyone in the community. In a large city, the postmaster would be lucky if he was familiar with everyone in a given high-rise apartment building. Consequently, the higher the number of people, the greater the need for records to identify the individual. In a big city setting, every type of court record can be found, along with property, probate, and vital records. Business licenses, medical registers, school enrollments, police blotters, and every sort of record documenting human activity can be found. A researcher only needs to use his imagination to discover clues in unusual resources.

Methodologies

Genealogy requires research patterns known as methodologies. No set of records is unique to any single research plan. The goal is to achieve discovery of ancestry in various records according to patterns of human activity. In a smaller population center, it can be relatively simple to identify ancestors in a standard selection of record sources and proceed in research from generation to generation, because so few families and individuals are involved in the scope of the research. However, in a large city there may be so many names to consider and so many record types that the traditional methodology has to give way to select and specific approaches of study.

Using a traditional approach, a basic census search in areas of small populations can identify a family and associate them with extended family members as well as with neighbors and associates. Vital record searches can identify marriages, deaths, and later births of family members. Two or three cemeteries should find family groups of the surname. Probate records will likely provide wills or estate information to identify family members. There may be individual congregations for Protestant, Catholic, Jewish, and other religions that can all be searched (if need be) to identify the religious participation of the family being researched.

In contrast, a metropolitan area may have dozens or scores of sources for vital records. Instead of six or eight religious congregations, there may be numerous congregations of each denomination, with their associated social organizations, as well as cemeteries; and most of the cemeteries will be located outside of the city boundaries. Individual neighborhoods and even each block may have been the source for social activities and groups. In such population centers, only a relatively few people owned real estate, and rentals or leases dominated the housing market. Ethnic groups and families often were drawn together sharing common bonds in a strange new world.

Tackling a research project in a big city environment requires extensive studies in each aspect of the traditional research approach. Different methodologies must be utilized to deal with the numerous individuals and resources that abound in the metro community. The following are recommended approaches for dealing with genealogical research in big cities:

1. Find the Person

The primary search in genealogy research is to find and accurately identify people. In a big city, there may be many persons with names in common with one another and other attributes also held in common, complicating the identification process. Once a principal ancestral personality has been identified, the genealogist can begin building on that foundation; determining associates, family memberships, relationships, and personal attributes such as occupation, military service, and other clues that will help flesh out the man or woman in a genealogical picture.

A researcher should always work from the known to the unknown. If one starts with imaginary information, the results will reflect that beginning . . . imaginary. People have been known to claim a relationship to names randomly found in telephone books; or to historical figures simply because they bore the same surname, with no other evidence to substantiate their findings. Amateur researchers have also claimed connections to places or castles solely on the basis that it bore their surname. The vast majority of claims along these lines never work out. This concept is magnified in big city investigation because so many people, with names in common, enter, stay, or migrate through such communities without any apparent connection with one another. Therefore, finding the correct person always requires research into original records of the big city and combining information from more than one resource to distinguish the right individual.

Censuses and Directories. In a big city setting, census records and city directories are utilized together to locate specific names and to separate specific individuals based on name, age, associations, relationships, occupations, birthplace, and addresses. Censuses play a vital role in all geographic areas of genealogical study. These lists of inhabitants, taken on a periodic timetable, create a type of social outline upon which other research studies can be based. In big city research, censuses not only identify individuals but also outline ethnic communities within the city and illustrate social order. In addition to the standard federal censuses taken every ten years, some places participated in state

1870 U.S. Census, Ward 14, New York City, New York, New York, ED 6 page 195B (first enumeration).

enumerations, which were usually recorded on years ending in 5 (1855, 1865, etc.). Descriptions of state censuses can be found on the Internet including the completeness of the counties in each state in different years. Most state censuses have been microfilmed by the Family History Library of The Church of Jesus Christ of Latter-day Saints and are available on microfilm through their library system. Many of the state censuses are also being digitized and made available online.

In addition to federal and state censuses, it is important to note that in 1870 a special re-enumeration was taken for three major cities in the United States (New York, Philadelphia, and Indianapolis). In 1880 St. Louis was enumerated a second time. Censuses are the means by which the number of representatives for each state to the United States Congress are determined. In 1870, the officials of those cities claimed that the censuses in their major cities were very incomplete, and a second enumeration was ordered for those communities. These second enumerations were often very different from the first enumerations in their content and listing of citizens. These additional census recordings appear on Internet census sites. Researchers should make certain that information from both censuses is gathered (where possible) for a complete evaluation.

Example of 1870 Census—First and Second Enumerations

Following the Civil War, Robert H. Johnson, a freed African American, migrated from Virginia to New York City, where he married and began his family. His death certificate identified him as the son of Lawson Johnson. The 1870 census of New York City, first enumeration (ward 14, election district 6), New York County, New York, page 195 (dated July 1, 1870),[1] shows:

Johnston, Robert		Age 27, Male, Black, Occupation: Porter, Birthplace: Virginina.
"	Henrietta	Age 24, Female, Black, Occupation: Keeping House, Birthplace: New York.
"	Robt.	Age 1, (born Feb. 20), Male, Black, Birthplace: New York.
"	Lawson	Age 24, Male, Black, Occupation: Work, Birthplace: Virginia.

The 1870 census of New York City, second enumeration (ward 14, election district 8), New York County, New York, page 598B (dated January 11, 1871),[2] shows:

Johnson, Robt.		Age 29, Male, Colored, Occupation: Porter, Birthplace: Virginia.
"	Henrietta	Age 28, Female, Colored, Occupation: Keeping House, Birthplace: New York.
"	Robt.	Age 1, Male, Colored, Birthplace: New York.
"	Lawson	Age 14, Male, Colored, Occupation: Doctor's Boy, Birthplace: Virginia.

---

[1] 1870 U.S. Census, Ward 14, New York City, New York, New York, enumeration district 6, page 195B, family 638, lines 1-4; National Archives M593_992, Ancestry.com *1870 United States Federal Census* [database online], Provo, Utah: Ancestry.com Operations Inc., 2009.

[2] 1870 U.S. Census, Ward 14, New York City, New York, New York, enumeration district 8, (2nd Enum), page 598B, lines 23-26; National Archives M593-1032, Ancestry.com *1870 United States Federal Census* [database online], Provo, Utah: Ancestry.com Operations Inc., 2009.

This is clearly the same family, even though the surname is slightly different, ages vary, and the family is located in a different election district. But it shows that in a six-month period, the Robert Johnson family may have moved across the street. The age differences provide clues for tracing the family back in other records.

The Internet has had a profound change on census research in big cities. Prior to the digitization of National Archives (NARA) microfilm of U.S. Federal Census records, searching such records was often a tedious and boring undertaking. The few published indexes that existed, primarily for 1920 and earlier censuses, limited researchers to a single version of spellings and name

1870 U.S. Census, Ward 14, New York City, New York, New York, ED 8 page 598B (second enumeration).

variations. In big cities, spellings and name variations can be expected to an unnerving extent. Census takers often did not speak or understand the languages of the people they interviewed, and modern-day indexers often misread census entries and record strange interpretations of what they see. But with Internet transcriptions of the original records, many different methods can be applied to identify a specific name. Soundex searches can produce possibilities; wild card variations, where only the first three or four letters of a name are used, can be examined; and entries can be searched by surname only or by given name only. Combined with city directories, census searches can be made based on address and street names; and also by the names of known neighbors.

Another type of "census record" commonly associated with cities are directories. City directories are essential in big city research. These were created not for interactive communication of the citizens as modern day telephone books do, but rather to assist businesses in the community in identifying people in the market place. As this type of record became established, residents of the cities began to recognize the advantages of these "people finders" and also saw the usefulness of them as guides to the businesses listed therein. Directories are like annual census returns. With information collected and published about the same time each year, early city directories would generally identify the names of heads of households (husbands and widows) and other members of the household over legal age, along with the descriptive name of their occupation, the address of their residence, and possibly the address of their workplace. Widows were often identified with the name of their deceased husband. Sometimes specific names of business companies were also stated in the entries.

City directories provided descriptions of city streets (Jones Street, beginning at 235 White Ave. and ending at 898 Walpole). These also identified specific street addresses where other streets intersected. Maps were often included, making it possible for users to identify the exact location of an address. Political boundaries (ward and district numbers) were also shown on maps, and as the population grew, the maps reflected the changes in ward and district boundaries. As the value of directories grew in the public perception, other services and industries were identified in each annual publication, including descriptions and addresses of churches and their officials, hospitals, civil government offices, schools, social clubs and fraternal groups, and much more. For a genealogist, these details in a city is of immense importance, because every place of social interaction created records, and having the means to graphically identify where a person lived in relation to churches, cemeteries, schools, businesses, hospitals, and other facilities provides tremendous opportunities for successful research.

Residential movement in cities was constant. Combining census and directory information allows a researcher to track names and addresses from directory listings and to find individuals in federal censuses (where indexed items may be too misinterpreted to recognize) or in non-indexed state censuses.

Example of City Directory Use: Carl H. Schenk of Buffalo, Erie County, New York

Carl H. Schenk appeared in the 1900 census of Buffalo, Erie County, New York, with his wife Catherine and children, living in the home of his father-in-law, Frederick Siewert, at 80 Adams Street.[3] Carl had married in 1887 or 1888. A few entries away on the same page of the census was the listing for Mrs. Caroline Schenk, a sixty-year-old widow, living at 90 Adams Street. Caroline Schenk was the mother of fourteen children, five of whom were still living in 1900. It would appear that Caroline Schenk could have been the mother of Carl, but based on census information there were discrepancies. Caroline was shown to have emigrated from Germany in 1855, whereas Carl immigrated to America in 1869. Neither Caroline nor Carl appeared in the 1880 census of Buffalo, New York, nor did they appear anywhere else in the state. Schenk was not an uncommon name, and neither was the given name Carl (or Charles).

City directories for Buffalo, New York, were studied for the time period of 1899 back to 1880. In 1899, Carl H. Schenk appeared in the city directory as an iron molder working for the

---

[3] 1900 U.S. Census, Ward 8, Buffalo, Erie, New York, enumeration district 61, page 12A, dwelling 146, family 262; National Archives T623_1026, Ancestry.com *1900 United States Federal Census* [database online], Provo, Utah: Ancestry.com Operations Inc., 2004.

| 50 | A. Allegheny; B. Birmingham; D. Duquesne; E. B. East Birmingham; E. P. East Pittsb'gh; | [C] | L. Lawrenceville; M. Manchester; S. P. South Pittsburgh; T. Temperanceville, &c. |

Cavanaugh Peter, shoemaker, bds Nicholson's Diamond
Cavanaugh Thomas, lab, Penna av n Chatham
Cavanaugh John, prin. Western Academy,109 Fourth, h Pitt township
Cavenaugh Peter, lab, Enoch n DeVilliers
Cavender Patrick, blacksmith, Keating's ay ab Granville
Cavener John, lab, Pitt tp n Soho
Caveney Peter, grocery, 149 Fifth
Cavens Elizabeth, widow Peter, r 90 Ross
Cavett Adaline widow Lewis, Brown's ay near Bank lane, A
Cavett Thomas, engineer, 5 Water
Cavinan Thomas, lab, r 72 Chatham
Cavner Wm., lab, Second n Lock No 1
Cavitt John, engineer, cor Steubenville pike and Alexander, T
Cavvett Wm., engineer, n Sawmill run, W P
Cawley John, carp, Brown's ay n Leacock, A
Cawley Owen, lab, Try n Penna av
Cazchiras Edward, lab, 45 Spring ay
Ceaser Leopold, printer, r 52 Virgin ay
Cegraih Chas, lab, Chestnut n Canal, A
Cehill Edward, teamster, Bridge n Walnut, T
Cella Louis, tavern, Fifth opp Court House
Celler John, cooper, Sidney n Harmony, E B
Celler Michael, eating saloon, 57 Fifth, h Fifth opp Court House
Cellighen John, baker, Isabella n Anderson,A
Cener Toney, glass blower, Carson n Oliver.B
Centner Mrs., widow Jos., Gist cor St Patrick ay
Central Board of Education, 2d floor, 110 Smithfield
Central High School, 3d floor 110 Smithfield
Central Hall, Dispatch building, 69 Fifth
Central Presbyterian Church, Smithfield near Sixth
Cerpan E. P., Penna av n E P
Cesar Lewis, tobacconist, 238 Ohio, A
Cha George, cigar maker, Diamond ay n Wood
Chaco Wm., (col) riverman, East lane n river, A
Chadwick Rachel, widow Wm, Ohio n Chestnut, A
Chadwick Chas, of Chadwick & Sons, bds 211 Penn
Chadwick I. W., of Chadwick & Sons, 211 Penn
Chadwick Jos, sawyer, Market n Chestnut, M
Chadwick & Sons, paper and rag warehouse, 149 & 151 Wood
Chaeky Jas, blacksmith, Beaver n Fayette, M
Chala Dominic, apple vender, Webster above Washington
Chalfant Chas, carp, Allegheny st n Penn
Chalfant James A., steamboat mate, Hay's court, r 57 High
Chalfant Jno, carp, Spring ay n Allegheny st
Chalfant John W., of Spang, Chalfant & Co., bds Monongahela House
Chalman Luke, coal merchant, Basin ay near Washington

Challender David, glass blower, Harmony n Sidney, E B
Chalmer George, coach maker, Gist n St Patrick's ay
Chalmer John, saddler, Allen n A V R R, L
Chalmers George B, machinist, Pitt tp
Chalmers John, carp, 32 Ridge
Chalmers Jas, pattern maker, 36 Pride, 8th Ward
Chambers A. jr., clerk, Carson S. P
Chambers Alex., of A. & D. H. Chambers,Carson ab Oliver, B
Chambers Alex., carp, Resaca n Benton ay, A
Chambers Anthony, carp, Avery, A
Chambers A. & D. H., glass manufacturers, warehouse 117 Water
Chambers A. & D. H., grocers and dry goods, cor Oliver and Carson, S P
Chambers A. & D. H., glass works cor Bingham and Oliver, S P
Chambers A. J., painter, cor Neville and Perry, B
Chambers Archibald, carp, Resaca, A
Chambers Chas A., patent agent, Federal, h Duncan n Centre av
Chambers D. H., of A. & D. H. Chambers, First n Smithfield
Chambers David M., carp, 140 Fulton
Chambers Francis, brakeman, bds Penn near Clymer
Chambers Frank, lab, bds 700 Liberty
Chambers Henry, stone mason,bds 700 Lib'ty
Chambers Hugh, boiler, Chestnut ay n Fifth, S P
Chambers Hugh, lab, Chestnut ay n Fourth, S P
Chambers James, carp, 74 Logan
Chambers James, gent, 179 First
Chambers J. B., carp, 36 Pride
Chambers John, s b clerk, 21 Marbury
Chambers Joseph, clerk, Strawberry ay near Beaver, A
Chambers Joseph, lab, 11 Milligan's block Liberty n Carson
Chambers Joseph, helper, bds 46 Carson, Mon Boro
Chambers Joseph B., lab, bds court on Centre bt Coal and Bingham, B
Chambers Martha,widow John, Monterey near Benton ay, A
Chambers Mrs., widow Wm., cor Peach ay & Webster
Chambers Matthew, manager Chamber's glass works, Carson n McKee, B
Chambers Robert, helper, bds 46 Carson, Mon Boro
Chambers Sarah, 46 Carson, Mon Boro
Chambers Sarah, B H, Federal n Benton ay, A
Chambers Wm., carp, 30 N Com, A
Chambers Wm., of Moore & Chambers, 30 Montgomery av, A
Chambers Wm., clerk, 21 Marbury
Chamberlin Chas, of Johnston & Co., Centre av
Chamberlin Lewis J., dentist, 130 Smithfield, h Pike n South, L

1861 City Directory of Pittsburgh, Pennsylvania, page 50.

Buffalo Scale Company.[4] He lived at 80 Adams Street. Caroline Schenk was listed as the widow of William Schenk and was living at 90 Adams Street. This information remained consistent each year back to 1888 when Carl would have married Catherine Siewert. Prior to 1887, Carl Schenk was listed as a molder, living at 90 Adams Street, as was the widow Caroline Schenk.[5] In 1884, Caroline Schenk's name was replaced by William Schenk, stonemason at 90 Adams.[6] Carl Schenk and William Schenk were listed there as early as 1882.[7] Neither William, Caroline, nor Carl Schenk was listed in 1880.

This detailed information suggests that William Schenk may have been the father of Carl H. Schenk, but Caroline, because of her early immigration date, may not have been his mother. William Schenk may have immigrated to America in 1869 with children from a previous wife and remarried to Caroline after his arrival. Implied in the directories is William's death about 1885. With the information from the city directories, it is possible to formulate possible family groups and develop a plan for further searches.

---

[4] *Buffalo (New York) City Directory of 1899* (Woodbridge, Conn.: Research Publications, 1980-1984), FHL US/CAN film 1,376,637.
[5] *Buffalo (New York) City Directory of 1886* (Woodbridge, Conn.: Research Publications, 1980-1984), FHL US/CAN film 1,376,625.
[6] *Buffalo (New York) City Directory of 1884* (Woodbridge, Conn.: Research Publications, 1980-1984), FHL US/CAN film 1,376,623.
[7] *Buffalo (New York) City Directory of 1882* (Woodbridge, Conn.: Research Publications, 1980-1984), FHL US/CAN film 1,376,622.

Additional Resources. In the "Find the Person" stage of a project, if the census and directory approach is insufficient, a number of alternative resources should be considered. Vital records indexes can be searched for births, marriages, and deaths in the big city environment. Probate indexes, deed indexes, naturalization indexes, and indexes for any major document groups can help pinpoint individuals. Information from these indexes must be combined with other data found in continuing research in order to accurately identify the proper people.

2. Establish Life and Death

The methodology for searching vital and related records takes place after locating individuals and family members. Those initial searches establish names, locations, and approximate dates of birth, marriage, and death for which specific records can be sought.

Vital Records. Vital records (births, marriages, and deaths) are of primary interest in genealogical study. Other resources assist in identifying people, but the ultimate goal is to determine births, marriages, deaths, and the places and relationships associated with those events. In big cities, vital record events were often recorded earlier than in other communities or counties in their respective states. For instance, New York State began recording birth and death records on a general basis in 1880. Marriage records were not recorded on a standardized basis in the counties until 1908. In New York City, however, municipal records of births began in the 1840s, and similar records of deaths began in 1795. Some marriage records were kept by the city as early as the 1820s. In Pennsylvania, where birth and death records began to be kept in counties on a general basis about 1893 and marriages about 1885, the city of Philadelphia began recording deaths and burials prior to 1810 and official births, marriages, and deaths in 1860. In Louisiana where state registration officially began in 1914, and counties and smaller communities began recording births and deaths in the late 1870s, New Orleans began recording vital record events on a municipal basis in 1819.

In searching for vital records in large cities, a researcher must be aware of many other record sources that also provide such information. Vital records were not recorded simply to know who was born and who died, or these records would have been kept much earlier. Vital registration was utilized to manage social, medical, and economic responsibilities created by expanding populations in these communities. Statistics of births, marriages, and deaths provided the justification for funding and the consequent taxing to support social programs to care for the poor and indolent. Big cities were hothouses for the problems of society. These problems, however unsavory they may have been to the ideals of public perception, were still a fact of life and to the genealogist a fact of record. Poverty, crime, prostitution, illness, and the management of the populace that were

> **In searching for vital records in large cities, a researcher must be aware of many other record sources that also provide such information.**

linked to these conditions became the major issues in cities where people of this class congregated in search of support and gain. During the 1800s, medical discoveries ignited the imaginations of people to better care for the downtrodden in their environs, and programs were devised and put into motion to account for the weak, homeless, and ne'er-do-wells who often filled the streets and alleyways of the Gotham in which they resided. Records were kept of all these "expenses to society" and may still exist today. The researcher must consider why records were created and then search beyond the popular records of census, vital, and probate to learn what records are available, where they are located, and how to access them.

The records created to account for these people are a treasure for genealogists and historians. Almshouses served as both home and hospital for many of the underclass people in cities. These were county homes that evolved with the growth of the populace. The records of patients/residents provided information about birth, death, and family members, making it possible for doctors, nurses, and government administrators to communicate as needed. Such records also contained details about patients escaping (elopements) and other personal details pertaining to their incarceration. These facilities also kept a record of burials in local cemeteries. In New York City, many of the poor and diseased, following their deaths, were sent to the burial ground at Ward's Island Potter's Field, where over a thirty-year period between 1850 and 1880, over a million bodies were buried. These were not just poor persons but also all classes of immigrants who contracted illnesses during their migration to America.

For example, Lars Larsen, a Danish immigrant, came to America with his wife and five children, as well as servants, arriving at Castle Garden in the Port of New York on 30 July 1866. During the trip across the Atlantic on the Bark *Cavour,* his wife Sidse contracted cholera, as did her baby son. They died and were buried at sea. Upon arrival at New York, Lars and three of his four remaining children were ill and were sent to Ward's Island for medical care. Nine days after their arrival, on 8 August 1866, his little daughter Marie Karen Larsen, weakened by cholera, died of dysentery and typhoid; and three weeks later on 3 September, Lars Larsen passed away due to the same illness.[8] They were buried in the mass burial ground trenches on the island. The three remaining children survived and walked on to Utah prior to the completion of the transcontinental railroad in 1869. They had not known of the death of their sister, and family members wondered about her for over a century until the death certificates for Karen and her father Lars were discovered in the New York City death records.

Medical Records. Medical registers kept by municipal health departments also provide information invaluable to genealogy researchers. In many cases, finding such records can be difficult, as they are not standard research fare. Modern hospitals often restrict medical records, releasing only birth and death information to civil authorities; but early records may have been gathered and stored in city archives, or in collections of historical societies and specialty museums. Nineteenth-century medical care was very different from modern health care. There was

---

[8] Work Projects Administration for the City of New York, Manhattan Death Certificates, 1866 (New York, New York: Work Projects Administration, 1942), FHL US/CAN film 1,324,506.

little or no understanding of chemical medications, and people who could afford good medical care received it in their homes. Hospitals in the 1800s were asylums for the poor and insane and often quickened the death of many patients. But they were also training grounds for research doctors looking for new cures for the many illnesses that existed. Records of such hospitals provide names of patients with birth and death information, in many cases preceding public vital records of the same.

The goals of medical specialists in the nineteenth century were to alleviate pain and keep contagious disease to a minimum, in order to protect society in general. An example of this care can be found in Philadelphia, Pennsylvania, where municipal medical registers for the almshouse includes a volume known as the Prostitutes Register, 1863.[9] This is not, in fact, a register of prostitutes but rather is a medical record of women who were examined for venereal disease. This register of almshouse inmates lists names, ages, birthplaces, length of time resident in Philadelphia, reason for entering United States if an immigrant, literacy, marital status, number of children, ages, present location, and whether or not legitimate. Again records were seeking cause and consequences to better manage the needs of the people of the community.

Church and Religious Registers. Next to civil vital records, church and religious registers are the best-recognized sources for birth, death, and marriage information. However, these resources require knowing the religious preference, as well as the congregation the individual may have attended. As mentioned in the discussion on directories, maps and addresses become important in searching these types of records.

Criminal Records. Crime was a source for vital records. Police files were filled with details about individuals who ran afoul of the law. Reformatories and prisons in big cities were often filled up, and records were created with the purpose of determining who the inmates were, in order to identify them and describe their physical features, so they could be located after their initial release, if needed.

Additional Resources. Divorce records, which are often associated with marriages in the vital records category, are actually court proceedings disbanding a relationship. Divorces are conducted in courts of chancery or equity, where property rights are resolved. Divorce information can provide data regarding the marriage of a couple that predates existing marriage records. It also provides an ending date previous to a new marriage.

While hospitals, asylums, almshouses, prisons, and potter's fields painted an apparent canvas of the underbelly of society, newspapers, church and synagogue registers, funeral home files, and burial notices served as the social register for a higher class of big city ancestry. Newspapers often published notices of marriages and deaths. Many different newspapers existed in large cities; it was the major form of public communication and advertising. In big cities, there were

---

[9] Alms House (Philadelphia, Pennsylvania), Spruce and Pine Streets, 10th and 11th Streets, Prostitutes Register, 1863 (Salt Lake City: Filmed by the Genealogical Society of Utah, 1975), FHL US/CAN film 972,953 item 1.

newspapers for every culture and society. Many of these early newspapers are now being digitized, indexed, and published online.

3. Follow the Money

The goal in this approach to research is to find relationships through property ownership. Vital record information is rare in this type of search but may come into play when examining records relating to marriage relationships or pertaining to death and probate matters.

Land and Property Records. Property ownership has always been one of the defining rights of American society. In large cities, this is also recognized as the means by which individuals were able to accumulate wealth. Originally most people in a city owned, leased, or rented their own homes. As cities began to grow in population and size, land became more valuable and the community began to grow up instead of out. The acquisition of properties by landlords and businesses limited the ability of a majority of the populace to rise above the laboring class of society.

These communities depended heavily upon deeds and other real estate records that set the bounds and titles of their growing municipalities. These property records are less likely to provide vital record information; instead they provide details about the social interaction and relationships of people. This is as true in a metropolitan area as in a rural countryside. Families passed property on to other family members, either by deed or by probate. Family businesses often went from father to son, or to other family members, and the associated real estate titles were transferred by deed. Upon death, probate courts became involved, distributing property among the heirs of the owners.

Probate Records. Probate proceedings in big city research have their own special attributes. In other settings, probate is thought of as the means to distribute land. However, while buildings and real estate play an important role in estate settlements, in big cities many of the inhabitants who possessed property may not have owned land. Their estates may have consisted of personal goods, the tools of the trade, the furnishings of the home, and accumulated wealth. Many people died without immediate family around them, and their heirs became a more distant circle of family, as well as friends and associates. This is especially important when dealing with immigrant estates, as extended family members may have settled elsewhere in the United States or Canada, or may still have been in the Old Country. Probate records should be studied, as they may identify family members and origins.

Chancery Court Records. Records of the Chancery Court (also known as Equity Court in some places) are a valuable source for property ownership information. It was in this court that debt, contracts, and other issues involving property ownership were contested. For genealogical purposes, property ownership disputes may have been due to the death of an individual, wherein debts were left behind which had to be resolved and settled by the heirs of the estate, thereby identifying family members and relationships. Divorce proceedings were generally attached to this court because of division of property.

In the course of settling an estate, evidence of bank accounts was often provided. This is especially important in big city research because there were often dozens (if not more) of banks, where customers kept their liquid assets. Each bank kept register lists about its clientele, with data about their personal history as well as their financial standing, so the bank could manage its association with each person in the event of loan failures, bank failure, and death or estate settlements.

4. Identify Religion and Society Memberships

Men and women are social creatures and depend on interaction with other human beings. Individuals and families arriving in the great cities of America needed the association of other people, whether to promote business, participate in clubs, share common interests, or worship in unity with friends and family. And again, whenever activities took place, records were created.

Church Records. Big cities typically have dozens, if not hundreds, of religious groups and societies seeking to meet the spiritual needs of the faithful. The more populous the city, the more likely it is that many faiths, denominations, congregations, and holy orders will be represented. Over the centuries, congregations have come and gone. Some have passed their registers of holy ordinances on to succeeding generations of priests, rabbis, and pastors, while others have merged with other religious entities and their records now sit forgotten on shelves and in closets. Nevertheless, the records of religious organizations remain one of the most important sources researchers can utilize in their search for ancestry and family.

> **Big cities typically have dozens, if not hundreds, of religious groups and societies seeking to meet the spiritual needs of the faithful.**

Through the centuries in Europe, the church has played a major role in government. In many aspects, the church was the government, and its records served as the vital records of the nation where it ruled. Consequently, the tradition of keeping records of birth/baptism, marriage, and death/burial was already part of their several practices by the time they came to America. Non-Christian religious groups, such as Jews, Buddhists, Hindus, and the multitude of cultural religious organizations, may not have had the same tradition of record keeping, but arrival in a new land as a diverse and scattered community of people may have led to records which would retain memories and connections with their citizens elsewhere in America.

Directories provide lists of churches and synagogues in each major city, along with information about location, cemeteries and current leaders. With this information, searches can be made to locate and obtain access to the records of these groups. In large cities, there are often registers or directories of Christian churches by denomination. Many such records are available on microfilm through the Family History Library system. Catholic records are generally accessible through arch-diocesan archives, which provide research services of their registers. Religious historical organizations such as the Presbyterian Historical Society, in Philadelphia, collect and care for records of their faith from throughout the United States. The Internet now provides tremendous assistance in identifying and locating religious records anywhere in the United States and other countries. Other historical and genealogical societies have also gathered church records in order to preserve them and make information available to the public. For genealogists in the big city, it is a matter of spending the time to find records in question and then searching them for their families.

Fraternal and Multi-Interest Society Records. Churches were not the only organizations that drew people together. Clubs and societies existed for all kinds of special interests. Former military personnel participated in veterans associations; the International Order of Odd Fellows, the Knights of Columbus, Woodmen of the World, the International Order of Eagles, the Shiners, and many other like-minded organizations held regular meetings, provided service to the downtrodden, marched in public parades, and created records. Members of the Masonic Lodge and Eastern Star met at their temples, conducted their services, pledged to contribute to the greater good, and created records. German immigrants gathered with their families in German associations, as did the Irish, the Scots, and the Lithuanians. Immigrant groups such as the Polish, the Italians, the Swedes, the Danes, the Greeks, and the Armenians gathered together and remembered their old homes, celebrated their new homes, shared their traditions, and made records.

Organizations, clubs, and associations that existed in the times of ancestors can be identified in the city directories of the day. Today, records of those associations may still exist in the archives of the various groups, or in historical societies. To find existing societies, researchers can visit Gale's Directory Library, http://www.galecengage.com, online. Gale's has long provided information about existing organizations, societies, and associations, with updated information about each society's address and contact information.

5. Follow Ancestors Across the Ocean

Many of the great cities have achieved their status because of their positions as primary ports of trade and immigration. These cities, located all along the Atlantic and Pacific seaboards and also up the Mississippi River, have attained their recognition because they have become the centers of industry and importation. Every port along a coastline is capable of receiving goods, but certain ports evolve because of the location and their availability to buyers as well as to sellers. Each of the major port cities along the Atlantic Seaboard, i.e. Boston, New York, Philadelphia, Baltimore, Norfolk, Charleston, Mobile, and New Orleans, is attached to the mouth of a major river or waterway leading back into the interior of America. Each of these cities grew into a hub of activity for the region of the country around it. New York City, at the mouth of the Hudson River, was a focal point for all of New England. On the opposite end of the Erie Canal, at the confluence of two of the Great Lakes, Buffalo, New York, became one of the major cities leading to the Midwest. With the advent of the Erie Canal, followed by the development of railroads, New York City became the hub of America. This same development took place in other cities as well.

The importance of this concept is that along with all of the importation of goods and services to these central ports, there was also a huge influx of immigrant population. The ships that brought goods to American shores also brought millions of travelers; immigrants looking for new opportunities, refugees seeking a place of hope, or pilgrims looking for religious liberties. While many of these pioneers pushed on beyond their ports of entry to settle in the interior regions of America, for many others, arrival in America was their target, and the port became their home. The growth of these cities and the expansion of business from both importation and population growth resulted in a greater demand for labor and jobs. The growth of the labor force was not a one way road, either. While immigrant groups provided bodies that companies could draw from, thousands of Americans from the interior of the country flocked to these cities as places of work opportunity.

Shipping and Passenger Records. Immigration lists applied not only to passengers arriving on the great shipping lines crossing the oceans but also to sailors and staff who manned those and all ships. Many seamen worked their way to America and continued to work their way wherever they went after arriving in this country. Up through the early nineteenth century, British warships dominated the seas. At ports and on the high seas, British press gangs accosted private citizens and sailors, capturing and confining them to work on British ships. As a result, legislation passed in 1796 provided the registration of sailors at ports up and down the East Coast, in an effort to protect them from British or foreign impressments. These records, known as the Seamans' Protection Certificate Applications, were kept at the custom houses of each port, and registration often continued up through the 1860s. A number of these records from different ports have been published.

Original passenger lists and crew lists are available through the collections of the National Archives. Records were kept at every port of entry as people prepared to leave their ships, and as they disembarked their names were marked against those lists. Many U.S. passenger lists are available on microfilm, and many are now digitized on the Internet. These computer versions have also been indexed and can often be found in connection with pictures of the ships on which the immigrants arrived.

Prior to the late nineteenth century, these lists provided only very basic detail about each person, such as his name, age, occupation, and country of origin. In the late 1800s, passenger records began listing details such as birthplaces, next of kin in the Old Country, and relatives or sponsors in America, along with personal descriptions. In many cases, the sponsor or family member was located in the major port city, providing researchers with clues to extended family members leading to other resources for study in that metropolitan area.

Naturalization and Passport Records. Sometime after arrival in a given port, the new residents had the opportunity to apply for U.S. citizenship. These records of naturalization provide researchers with details regarding the origins of an immigrant that can link them with family members both in America and in the mother country. As with passenger lists, the records began as simple registrations and oaths, providing little more than names and the countries of origin. As more people flooded into America, the need to manage immigrants required the adding of details to naturalization records, such as birth information, dates of arrival, and the names of the ships on which immigrants arrived. The popular tradition that immigrants with difficult-to-pronounce names changed their names at the port of entry is not always true. Immigration ports were often manned by people of many cultures, able to understand and record the native names of the arrivals. However, in twentieth-century records, it is not uncommon to find individuals indicating a change of name between the time of arrival and the date of citizenship.

Many people traveled in the other direction, as well, using U.S. ports for embarkation to sail to Europe and elsewhere. Often these included former immigrants returning to their original homelands to encourage family and friends to join them in America. For U.S. citizens traveling out of America, it was required that a passport be obtained, verifying their American citizenship at foreign ports, and allowing them to return to the United States at the end of their trip. This document detailed birth information and data about their residency. For former immigrants to America, it served as protection from foreign government officials who might have detained these individuals for military service or other residential obligations. In big city research, passport records should be searched for all persons within a known family and also for the surname in question, in case other relatives who came to America might have traveled abroad after their arrival here. These records help to identify places of origin, family relationships, and other details regarding arrival and citizenship.

Banking Records. Banking records may also come into play in the immigration approach to research. Immigrant banks were established in a number of large cities, particularly those in seaboard ports, where immigrants could establish a financial base, and where accounts could be created to provide funds for family members who were intending to emigrate.

Immigrant Societies. Immigrants banded together upon arrival in the cities where they settled. Societies were formed to assist new arrivals and to encourage those intending to come. French Huguenots in the early 1700s organized in London after fleeing the troubled lands along the French and German borders and came to America in shiploads, arriving at centers of French settlement such as New York, Richmond, Charleston, and New Orleans. The records of their associations in London and in each major city in America reflect the trials and successes of settling in this new land.

Jewish organizations sprang up in cities like Philadelphia and spread to other American centers of Judaism. The Hebrew Immigrant Aid Society monitored the immigrant arrivals in Philadelphia, Baltimore, and to some extent in New York City as well and provided assistance and support to many of the Jewish families arriving in America during the latter half of the nineteenth century.

6. Follow Ethnic Trails

Immigrants coming to America were strangers in a strange land. Everything was new and different; government and laws were both less confining and more difficult to understand. The culture of the American community was foreign to them and was composed of many nationalities. Neighborhoods in the city could be made up of natives from Germany, Russia, Ireland, Italy, England, Scandinavia, and China. Life was a mixture of language and culture.

Communities within the major cities flourished as people of common heritage drew together in neighborhoods. Such designations as "Chinatown" and "Little Italy" are in every big city composed of ethnic groups. Their culture was illustrated in their businesses, their churches, and their cemeteries. Many of these groups had their own native language newspapers, providing accounts of Lithuanian life in Chicago or German news from the fatherland. Newspapers helped ethnic communities stay together while the individuals sought to become more American. Many different ethnic associations also established financial support through insurance groups, thereby allowing new arrivals the means to acquire a type of social protection while getting established in a new home.

Slavery. Although slavery would be a significant concern in southern big cities, such as Norfolk, Charleston, Atlanta, Mobile, and New Orleans, it was a major issue in the north as well. Cities such as New York City, Philadelphia, and Providence were prominent centers of the slave trade up through 1800 and permitted slavery through mid-nineteenth century, until shortly before the Civil War began in 1861. Anti-slavery movements in the 1780s resulted in states' legislations enacting the graduated abolition of slavery but not an outright end to the practice. Slaves born after the enactment of such laws were to be freed upon reaching the age of 28. In some cases, their families were required to live with or near the slave owners until that slave reached the required age. Philadelphia in 1790 was a city of 18,000 inhabitants (a big city in that day), of which 1,400 were slaves. By 1840, the Philadelphia slave population was down to 64. Census statistics did not provide a classification for slaves in northern states after 1840.

In the larger cities, slaves did not work on farms and fields but were usually one or two to a home and worked alongside their owners in their various workplaces and trades. Records for slaves in big cities, as in other places across the United States, can be found in property records, deeds, probate records, and church registers. However, a notable resource for information on African Americans in a time of slavery was in insurance records. Note Jerry M. Hynson's description of the Baltimore Life Insurance Company:

> The Baltimore Life Insurance Company was among the first to actively sell life insurance in the United States . . . the Baltimore Life possessed a virtual monopoly on slave life insurance until the end of the 1840s. . . . The Baltimore Life was most likely the first life institution in the United States to underwrite the lives of slaves . . . they insured a handful of slaves almost every year during the 1830s and 1840s . . . the popularity of slave policies . . . began increasing rapidly during the 1850s; by the eve of the Civil War, approximately half of all policies sold by the company were on slave risks. The vast majority of these slaves were being insured through their Richmond agency, which now dealt almost exclusively in slave policies.[10]

Photo courtesy of the Library of Congress.

While most of these slaves may not have resided in metropolitan areas, some did, and any information describing African American identities in this time period is valuable.

Banking also played a role in the lives of former slaves. In 1865, following the Civil War, the federal government instituted a central bank known as the Freedman's Savings and Trust Company in Washington, D.C. This bank had branches in many of the large cities in the eastern United States. It enabled former slaves to create bank accounts and aimed to support them as they began life in a free so-

---

[10] Jerry M. Hynson, *Baltimore Life Insurance Company Abstracts of Records* (Westminster, Md.: Heritage Books, 2004).

ciety.[11] These bank records provide valuable information about identity and family relationships. The information contained in many of the registers is as follows: account number, name of depositor, date of entry, place born, place brought up, residence, age, complexion, name of employer or occupation, wife or husband, children, father, mother, brothers and sisters, remarks, and signature. The early books sometimes also contain the name of the former master or mistress and the name of the plantation. In many entries, not all of the requested data are given. Copies of death certificates have been pinned to some of the entries.

7. Trace Crime and Punishment

Nobody likes to think of his ancestor as a bad person, much less as a criminal. Nevertheless, it seems to be the sad nature of some men to take advantage of other people, or to solve problems by fighting. Society has managed to keep its jails and prisons full, and many of these incarcerated men and women of previous days were our ancestors.

Census records are an important tool in this methodology. If an ancestor was incarcerated at the time of a state or federal census, he and all of the inmates will be listed in the census. However, census records are a "hit and miss" record for inmates, because people were usually imprisoned for relatively short periods of time. Most crimes were for theft, assault, or social injustice. More serious crimes resulted in more serious punishments. Perhaps a more valuable source for identifying people in the criminal system would be newspapers, where matters of crime were the bread and butter of the journalism field.

Criminal court records provide initial information identifying the people entering this judicial aspect of society. Court minutes and case files detail individuals and their crimes. Upon conviction, many of these individuals were imprisoned, where records were created to identify and track them. It was recognized that prisoners, upon release, might return to criminal activity, so details about their birth, physical description, residence, and family were often recorded to aid law enforcement.

Conclusion

Big city genealogy research is about organization and thinking outside of the box of traditional genealogy methods. The methodologies for big city research allow the genealogist to approach the records on the basis of patterns, with the goal of discovering specific

> Big city genealogy research is about organization and thinking outside of the box of traditional genealogy methods.

information. It is still a huge search because of the volume of records that exist for large populations. But by limiting the topic or event for research and specifying the time period involved, the records can be studied in a successful manner. In big city research, it isn't about not having enough information, it is about using the many available collections of documents to best advantage.

---

[11] Freedman's Savings and Trust Company (Washington, D.C.), *Registers of Signatures of Depositors, 1865-1874* (Washington, D.C.: National Archives Records Administration, Central Plains Region, 1969) (Microfilm Publication Number M816).

11

An Introduction to Medieval Research

John M. Kitzmiller, II, AG, FSA(Scot), FSH(Eng)

Tracing one's ancestry back to kings and queens, knights and lords can be a fascinating and exciting endeavor in genealogy. An individual is the sum of all of his ancestry, and these links can provide the security of identity to many—no matter what level of society in which their ancestors participated. An overview of this type of research would not only be interesting but useful in the search for a potential connection back into history.

A definition of the time periods involved and the discussion of both old and new sources that are available are the starting points. Technically, the medieval time period began around the fifth century and is generally divided into three periods: Early Middle Ages (fifth – tenth centuries); High Middle Ages (eleventh – thirteenth centuries); and Late Middle Ages (thirteenth – fifteenth centuries). Can one *really* connect his ancestry from the 1500s back through these time periods? Yes, but only with great caution. Where would obstacles occur, and how can one overcome these obstacles? This research process begins with a basic understanding

All photos in this chapter courtesy of the author.

of the principles of immigrant origins research, the culture of the times, and the key records of the manors. This essay seeks to introduce these foundations.

First, Where Am I?

What is meant by this phrase? Does the family's pedigree chart show a noble or royal lineage? Can it be trusted? How does one know if the pedigree is correct, or not? A prominent genealogist once said that he kept a special file that was labeled "Royal ancestors I used to have"! This comment refers to the ever-changing connections to royal ancestry, especially when another person by the same name is found in the same place. Generally the genealogy from someone back to the immigrant tends to be correct, and the genealogy from certain known individuals in Europe back to royalty also tends to be correct. The connector (often called the "gateway" ancestor) is the point where most of these extended pedigrees fail. There are several sources that are often overlooked for heraldic clues, such as silverware, tombstones (especially in New England), bookplates, watches, and other household items.

Second, What Do I Do?

Search for sources that may establish the correctness of the proposed ancestry. Be careful in using early, published genealogies and histories, which have a tendency to be inaccurate when it comes to a connection to the landed gentry. Another factor that complicates matters is that only a small percentage of these key immigrants to North America appear in the known surviving ship lists. Find the current status of colonial royal lines using an index to articles such as PERSI (the Periodical Source Index). These indexes point to periodicals, such as the *New England Historical and Genealogical Register, The Genealogist,* and *The American Genealogist,* that routinely publish this type of data.

Another venue includes published articles and books with compiled royal/noble lines from colonial immigrants with solid documentation, such as those by genealogists Paul C. Reed, Leslie Mahler, Gary Boyd Roberts, and many others. Following up on the bibliographies of such genealogists provides a great learning experience on potential royal and nobility sources.

Bridging Documents

Another issue in researching medieval ancestral lines is the availability of record sources for the time periods in question. Using England as an example, parish registers (christenings, burials, and marriages) officially started in the year 1538, but many did not begin until the 1600s. So, how can they be utilized to document the "bridge" between an American family and English nobility?

Generally, when seeking the origins of any immigrant, one must work from the country of destination to the country

> Generally, when seeking the origins of any immigrant, one must work from the country of destination to the country of origin.

of origin. It's not enough to know they came from England. The question actually should be: "Where did they come from *exactly*?" Most immigration problems are solved from the records of the country of destination. So, from an American perspective, this would mean recognizing that the majority of immigrants to New England arrived between the early 1630s and the 1650s, most having come from England. However, this also means that they were born about 1580 to 1610, at a time when many parishes in England had not yet begun keeping records. This makes it very difficult to connect with certainty an American immigrant of this time period to a christening record in England.

Knowing only that an immigrant came from England will work (for connecting to nobility) if there is a national index to these records and if the ancestor in question was really of the landed level of society. However, that is seldom the case, and there is no true national index.

What alternative sources could help one bridge this oceanic gap? If the locality in England is known, local histories could provide a clue. Visitations are an important link between "historical" families and those who were in the peerage. Gazetteers are also useful, in that they often provide the name of the landowner at the time of printing. Why is this important? If an ancestor lived on a manor or an estate, for instance, any mention of him would be found in landowners' papers, such as rentals. Many other sources are available to bridge the gap between "historical" families and noble or royal families.

Medieval Families

Understanding records of the medieval time period and what information can be derived from them is very important. The major record types useful in medieval research are those that deal with the ownership and transfer of land. Land tenure, or how land is held

> The major record types useful in medieval research are those that deal with the ownership and transfer of land.

(from the crown or other feudal superiors), is an important facet of research. The explanation of this is quite simple—a major source of revenue to the crown and all those in the feudal system was the taxation on land or services. Records of individuals involved in the payment of taxes and the identification of the next taxpayer generate considerable classes of records.

Lists of individuals that fit the above definitions were maintained for centuries. Since land and land ownership are so crucial for successfully tracing medieval families, it is important to understand the basics of land ownership in a culture far removed from 21st century America. Understanding these concepts makes it possible to work effectively with the records that derived from this culture.

Medieval Land Tenure
Norman Land Tenure

The Normans introduced a new type of land tenure (ownership) based upon the feudal system. The main concept was that *all* land was held of or from the crown. Tenants who held land directly from the crown were termed *mesne* tenants. These usually were of the higher-ranking nobility, such as earls, dukes, and some barons. Other terms that were more often used in the records were tenant-in-chief or tenant-in-capite.

Most tenants-in-chief did not actually make personal use of the lands by living upon them. Many of these tenants owned large parts of shires or counties, so they would farm out their rights in return for payment, which was usually made in terms of service or money. What these feudal lords owed their tenants was protection and justice to those who held from them.

Demesne tenants were the lords who actually held and used lands personally. In this hierarchy of ownership, the demesne tenant would hold land directly from his *mesne* lord.

The lowest category of landholder was the actual tenant of the manor, which will be discussed under manorial records. Most of the tenants of the feudal system lived on a manor. A manor usually consisted of the lord of the manor's home or castle, his tenants' dwellings, and enough tillable acreage to support them all.

Three Types of Land Tenure

All land was held directly either by freehold, copyhold, or leasehold. Of the several kinds of freehold tenure, knight service or fee (chivalry) was the most important form. A lord who held land via knight's service would provide a certain number of knights at predetermined times each year. A knight's service included a fully equipped knight, a squire, and their retinue. Land could be held by one, two, six, or ten knights' fees, and that "fee" was the annual rent or payment required to continue holding the land. Later, this knight's service was translated into money payments.

Another freehold land tenure was called *frank almoign*. These lands were held by some spiritual service to the king, usually by saying a predetermined number of prayers for his soul.

The third form of freehold tenure was called *serjeantry*. This term means service in Latin and always referred to service to the king.

Freehold tenure was not subject to the customs of the manor or the will of the lord of the manor. The conveyance of freehold property was without restriction. Usually this type of tenure was conveyed by *livery of seisin* that was recorded on a deed of conveyance. This conveyance may be called an indenture of *feoffment*, and the purchaser had to pay an entry fee called a *relief.*

A freeholder could lease his land (hence, Leasehold tenure, below). Leases were usually contracted for the term of one year. The occupier entered property via a deed of grant (or release). The freeholder would hold an interest in this land (reversion), and the reversion was an *hereditament* and could be conveyed without *livery of seisin*. The conveyance of *entailed freeholds* was a bit more difficult. This meant the inheritance could be restricted to specified heirs and that the owner was unable to sell it until the entail was no longer in force. What this usually meant was that there were no other male heirs.

Copyhold tenure was the more common method of manorial tenants' land tenure. Originally this was a tenure dependent upon the lord's will and the customs of the manor. The conditions of the tenure demanded some type of service in return for the copyhold, which was later changed to a monetary payment. A tenant's title was written on

the manor court rolls, of which he received a copy (hence the term, copyhold). The conveyance of copyhold tenure required the tenant to surrender title to the lord of the manor. The new tenant was admitted on payment of a fine, which was not abolished until 1922!

Leasehold tenure was based on a lease that was usually for a fixed number of years. It could be held by a specified number of *lives*, which was recorded in the lease. If one of the *lives* died, a new individual could be inserted.

Medieval Record Sets

To understand medieval records, it is first important to understand what a *manor* was. Manors could consist of a single parish, a township, or an estate. An estate could consist of one or several manors, and a group of estates would comprise an *honour* or *fee*. The rights or privileges of the lord of the manor were many. The first right was that of *Sac* and *Soc* and was a legal jurisdiction claimed by the lord. This was the right to hold a court and the right to receive profits and services from the manor. The second major right was that of *tenancy at will*, where a tenure was granted by the lord.

There are three major groups of records associated with a manor, which are estreats, court baron records, and court leet records.

> There are three major groups of records associated with a manor, which are estreats, court baron records, and court leet records.

Estreats

Estreats are the recording of legal proceedings. They are found on the manor court rolls.

Court Baron

The court baron was a manorial court that enforced the customs of the manor. It concerned the property of the lord of the manor and so was a private jurisdiction. There was usually a jury that originally consisted of at least two freeholders. The jurisdiction of the court and its associated records were concerned with escheats, surrenders and transfers of land, dower administration, and management of the commons and wastes. The court also kept track of the rights of the lord and the tenants.

Court Leet

In the above context, the court leet was also considered a manorial court. Its jurisdiction was the extension of the royal authority at a local level. This court and its records were concerned with minor offences and also with the maintenance of roads, bridges, etc. Every male above 12 (or 16) was required to attend, and they met twice a year.

This court was responsible for the *view of frankpledge*. Frankpledge is a Saxon term that denotes the fact that each individual in a tithing was responsible for the actions of all. The manor court rolls have lists of those who were accountable. The actual record of the court leet is almost a standardized form. The roll starts with a list of freeholders, followed by the "List of the Homage," who originally were freeholders but later were made up of copyholders and leaseholders. The "List of the Jury" consisted of copyholders and leaseholders.

Locations of English Manor Records

The gathering of English manor records occurred at the national, county, and local levels. At the national level, the main collection is located at the Public Record Office, and the catalog can be accessed via the Manorial Documents Register online. *The Historical Manuscripts Commissions* has a comprehensive list to surviving manorial records.

At the county level, some manor records (or a copy) have been deposited in local County Record Offices (CRO). The County Record Office Guides have lists of these records, many of which have been published. *The Victoria County Histories* frequently follows the descent of manors in a specific county. Some local records are still in possession of the current landowner, and many of these have been identified by Historical Manuscripts Commissions.

For Further Study

Camp, A.J. *Wills and Their Whereabouts.* Bridge Place: Phillimore and Co., 1963.

FitzHugh, T. *A Dictionary of Genealogy.* Totowa, New Jersey: Barnes and Noble Books, 1985.

Hone, N.J. *The Manor and Manorial Records.* London: Methuen & Co., 1912.

John, E. *Land Tenure in Early England.* Leicester: Leicester University Press, 1964.

Latham, R.E. *Revised Medieval Latin Word-List.* London: Oxford University Press, 1965.

Martin, C.T. *The Record Interpreter.* London: Stevens and Sons, 1910.

Milsom, S.F.C. *The Legal Framework of English Feudalism.* Cambridge: Cambridge University Press, 1976.

Nelson, Glade I. and John M. Kitzmiller. "Medieval Genealogy." *Printed Sources: A Guide to Published Genealogical Records.* Salt Lake City: Ancestry, 1998.

Sanders, I.J. *English Baronies, A Study of Their Origin and Descent 1086-1327.* Oxford: Clarendon Press, 1960.

Smith, R.M. *Land, Kinship, and Life-Cycle.* London: Cambridge University Press, 1984.

12

Timelines: Essential to the Genealogist's Toolbox

Joy Price, AG

When a person inquires, "How do I learn about my family tree?" he is usually given a pedigree chart, a family group record, and an explanation of how to fill in the blanks. "I don't want charts. My interest is to know more about those on my family tree," might be the discouraged reply. Since most ancestors did not keep journals or write their own personal histories, digging is necessary to discover their stories. Entering information into organizational and analytical forms could seem like a waste of time to a newcomer, or like busywork to researchers who enjoy and would prefer digging into records. However, organization saves hours of frustration. If data is not organized and recorded onto forms, research time and effort are often duplicated, or worse, the data may become lost. George O. Zabriskie stated,

> Genealogical information . . . with enrichment material, is of no value slumberingly at rest in our work papers. . . . To locate and gather this information and then fail to put it to work in our permanent family records is like planning to build a new house but stopping all action after assembling all necessary plans and materials.[1]

In addition to pedigree charts, family group records, and research calendars, time-

Summarizing and chronologically listing life's events stimulates interest and creates a device for analysis.

---

[1] George O. Zabriskie, *Climb Your Family Tree Systematically* (Salt Lake City: Parliament Press, 1969), 222.

lines are essential to a genealogist's toolbox. Summarizing and chronologically listing life's events stimulates interest and creates a device for analysis.

Timelines, Chronologies, and Narrative Reports

A family group record is a skeletal, chronological form for names, dates, and places. The intent of timelines and chronologies is to allow for more informative listings than the vital data listed on the basic charts, adding "flesh" to the skeleton. Chronologies may be in sentence format or brief biographies, such as:

1. Dennis Davis was born on 5 February 1791 in Anne Arundel County, Maryland, to Robert and Ann (Collins) Davis.
2. He married Joanna Thomas (1791-1836) around 1811, possibly in Caldwell County, Kentucky.
3. He died on 20 February 1879 and was buried in Black Oak, Caldwell, Missouri.

Comparatively, timelines are usually structured in column format to more easily visualize, recognize, and analyze the life events of an individual or members of a family. They show the data in a graphic view—a new perspective. As sequential calendars, timelines chart a summary of known facts, hypothesized events, or clues about an individual's life, in order of occurrence. They arrange the events chronologically in the life of a particular person or a span of time in the existence of a family. As explained by Karen Clifford, "They reduce the critical elements necessary for family history—events, times, and places—to an understandable conclusion."[2] These timelines are sometimes called summaries, lifelines, calendars, chronology tables, or research chronologies.

Specific Functions

Timelines help researchers become better acquainted with an ancestor's life, identify an ancestor's relationships and associates, organize the information and place it in proper sequence, evaluate the accuracy of data and sources, place the events of an ancestor's life into historical context, and summarize information for family history publications. As an evaluative and analytical tool, timelines can reveal relationships and point out inconsistencies, providing the researcher with new ideas for future research.

Timelines can reveal relationships and point out inconsistencies, providing the researcher with new ideas for future research.

providing the researcher with new ideas for future research.

---

[2] Karen Clifford, *The Complete Beginner's Guide to Genealogy, the Internet, and Your Genealogy Computer Program* (Baltimore: Genealogical Publishing Company, 2001), 4-6, 8-14.

Timelines for an Individual

Multiple advantages exist in recording life event data chronologically for an individual. These timelines can include, but are not limited to, dates and places of births of children, deaths of parents, census information, childhood, school, residences, marriage, occupational and military events, land purchases, and family activities. Beverly DeLong Whitaker promises, "You will be surprised at how helpful it can be. . . . A timeline becomes a marvelous study tool, providing you with data to evaluate from a different perspective."[3]

Timelines can incorporate various features and be customized to fit the researcher's needs. When beginning research for an ancestor, timelines can consist of a simple penciled horizontal line, with known facts supplied with dates above the line and events and places written below the line, as in the following example.

Illustration 1
Simple Horizontal Timeline

1798	1827	1828-1835	1837	1847	1848-1851	1853
Birth to Lumen & Permelia Clark Wells, Vermont	(age 29) Married Louisa Gill Antwerp, New York	Births 4 children in Antwerp, New York	Land purchase Geauga Co., Ohio	Death of wife, Louisa married Hannah Miller Platte Co., Missouri	Births 4 children Franklin Co., Indiana	Death (age 55) in Cedar Grove, Indiana

While evaluating data on a pedigree, an experienced researcher may envision a simple timeline in his mind. Physically recording this visual image may be the preliminary step to recording events, and the researcher can add to it as more information is acquired. Effective timelines often use vertical columns, with the dates listed down the left-hand side of the page and the events next to the corresponding dates on the right, as in the illustration below. Note that if a separate column is not made for locations, they can be typed in bold letters within the event column.

---

[3] Beverly DeLong Whitaker, *Beyond Pedigrees: Organizing and Enhancing Your Work* (Salt Lake City: Ancestry, 1993), 7.

Illustration 2
Timeline for Rinaman Family in Western Pennsylvania

Date	Name	Event	Locality	Source
ca. 1767 (birth)	Christopher Rineyman	1850 census (age 83) (4 Rinamans - listed below)	Allegheny Co., Pine Twp.	Doc 3
ca. 1774 (birth)	Cathrine Rinaman	Death record (age 83) June 1857	Allegheny Co., Pittsburgh (Infirmary)	Doc 10
ca. 1779 (birth)	William Rineyman (wife - Lucy?, age 60)	1850 census (age 71) (+Thomas J. - listed below)	Allegheny Co., Pine Twp.	Doc 3
Sep 1786 (birth)	John Reineman	Birth to parents Christopher & Ursula	Westmoreland County Church - Weber	Doc 1
Sep 1788	Christopher & Ursula Rinaman	Witnesses at christening for Sarah Brucks	Westmoreland County Church - Weber	Doc 1
ca. 1798 birth	Elizabeth Rineyman	1850 census (age 52) in Christopher household - possibly daughter?)	Allegheny Co., Pine Twp.	Doc 1
1803 Doc date	Christopher Binneman William Binneman (Rinaman?)	Residents of Pine Township (north of Pittsburgh)	Allegheny County history	Doc 11
ca. 1803 (birth)	John Rineyman	1850 census (age 47) listed/Mary A. + 9 children	Allegheny Co., Pine Twp.	Doc 3
Mar 1809	Wilhelm (?Kineman)	Birth to parents Peter/Susanna Kineman?	Allegheny County Church - Weber	Doc 2

Timelines can be customized to fit the needs of a particular individual or research project. The following individual timeline often works well for researching an individual.

Illustration 3
Sample Timeline for an Individual

Ancestor_____   Page _____
Researcher _____   ID # _____
Birth Date _____   Birthplace_____
Spouse _____   Parents _____

Date	Age	Name	Event*	Locality	Comments and Analysis	Type of Source (citation on research calendar)

* Events can include birth, marriage, death, baptism, burial, births of children, illnesses, land purchases, migration, church service, military service, civic service, schooling, probate proceedings, local and national historical events, etc.

Timelines for a Family

Timelines for related persons and associates can be merged together, with the names of each person signified in bold type, color-coded, or placed in a separate column. This style of timeline will probably consist of more than one page and provide an addendum to a narrative or a collection of biographies. Timelines developed for an entire family are effective because they:

- Enhance the mental "big" picture of their lives.
- Validate family relationships previously difficult to prove.
- Illustrate how lives fit together.
- Show how the events of one family member correlate to those of another.
- Identify family members or associates living nearby.
- Organize and help to document the data.
- Illuminate discrepancies and planning research.

When creating a family timeline, it is helpful to record each person's age next to each major event. Recording the birth dates and birthplaces of the person's children, in addition to listing the family's census entry of each decade, provides the researcher with hints about when the family migrated from one place to another.

Family timelines can also reveal missing puzzle pieces about the family, such as occupations, the family's religion or military affiliation, the migration routes they followed, and why and with whom they traveled. Discrepancies or erroneous conclusions might become obvious, such as distinguishing the same name for persons living nearby at the same time, ruling out the wrong parents because of ages, spotting a child who doesn't belong, or identifying a missing child. As explained by Roseann R. Hogan, Ph.D.:

> I have used [a family timeline] to determine research strategies by linking families and to solve problems that probably would not have been solved if not for the way in which the data was presented. Seeing the context of my findings and what the data was telling me has often resulted in an "at long last" experience as the solution finally jumps off the page.... I use my archives/library research time much more effectively ... link the myriad clues and make connections, eliminate rival hypotheses, and eventually establish a relationship that could not be documented otherwise. Thus, another important use of the chronology is facilitating the development of data for establishing a relationship based on a preponderance of evidence.[4]

Tips for Designing Timelines

Whether a timeline is of an individual or a family, it is practical to design it with a word processor, database manager, or graphic design computer software program. When created electronically, it can easily be updated as new information is acquired. The layout can be adjusted to accommodate the additional data, which can be transferred and inserted into the timeline. One advantage in using a computer is the ability to search the timeline by keyword. This is especially helpful when the timeline includes multiple families or generations of ancestors and descendants.

The timeline can either be (1) prepared first as an outline, then researching the details and using it to produce a biography or family history; (2) created from a printed biography or family narrative as a charted chronological summary or an addendum; or (3) developed as a cooperative effort of both methods. The last option includes benefits for evaluating results and planning future research. When supplemented with family activities and historical events, timelines attract interest. When writing a life story for possible publication, a timeline can direct future research.

For family timelines, categories become the column headings for dates and events, with other possible columns for places, names, ages, the origin of the information, and comments. Fill-in-the-blank forms with these headings could also include source citations or cross-references, using a document number to correspond with the documentation on an attached research calendar.

Timelines should illustrate and explain research by cross-referencing either a research calendar or a family narrative with matching citation superscript numbers. Documentation for each event should be included on the timeline to verify the resources used. Complete source citations, analysis, hypotheses, discrepancies, inaccuracies, explanations as to why records are not available, and future research strategies, however, are usually better noted on an accompanying research calendar than on the timeline itself.

---

[4] Roseann R. Hogan, "Chronology: Keeping it All Together," *Ancestry Magazine* 15, no. 2 (1997), http://www.ancestry.com/learn/library/article.aspx?article=1672.

Historical Events Impacted Their Lives

Only the "begats" (the names, dates, and places) are indicated on pedigree charts. Although essential, this doesn't present a complete overview of the unique, "real" person or family story, which is composed of many other significant events. Transcending genealogy (the acquisition of vital data) is family history, the research of additional records that add substance and flesh out an ancestor's life story.

> Historical data should be added to both individual and family timelines, placing them within a larger historical context.

Our ancestors did not live in a vacuum. Historical events impacted their lives, occupations, migrations, and decisions. Historical data should be added to both individual and family timelines, placing them within a larger historical context. How did battles for independence or religious beliefs affect them? Was the family part of a migrating group? Did they survive a famine, widespread illness, or occupational hazard? Were boundary lines changed where they resided, requiring the researcher to look elsewhere for a pertinent record? What disaster explains the unavailability of a record? According to Loretto Dennis Szucs,

> Local histories of the area in which your family lived make the most fascinating reading; it's almost like setting a stage and dropping the ancestor into place. The customs and surroundings take on new meaning, and so does the life of the individual . . . Once you have the historical background in your mind, you will better understand the kinds of records that may have been created in the times and places where your people were present. Creating a historical time line with a parallel time line for an individual is an excellent way to put things into perspective.[5]

In order to obtain local historical information about the town, county, or state in which an ancestor lived, use local histories, periodicals, newspapers, and manuscript collections. Historical timelines for each state are included in the *Handybook for Genealogists*. Encyclopedias and many Web sites provide dates and places of historical events that took place throughout the world.

Adding historical content to timelines also provides more interest to an ancestor's living descendants. Wouldn't it be more enjoyable and understandable to young students when memorizing historical data if they could relate it to someone in their family? If children were taught the stories and timelines of their ancestors, would the study of history and geography be more interesting and important to them?

---

[5] Loretto Dennis Szucs, *Family History Made Easy* (Salt Lake City: Ancestry, 1998), 122.

For Further Study

Clifford, Karen. *The Complete Beginner's Guide to Genealogy, the Internet, and Your Genealogy Computer Program.* Baltimore: Genealogical Publishing Company, 2001.

Croom, Emily Anne. *The Sleuth Book for Genealogists.* Cincinnati, Ohio: Betterway Books, 2000.

The Handybook for Genealogists. 11th ed. Logan, Utah: Everton Publishers, 2006.

Hogan, Roseann R. "Chronology: Keeping it All Together." *Ancestry Magazine* 15, no. 2 (1997). http://www.ancestry.com/learn/library/article.aspx?article=1672 (accessed 14 October 2009).

Knuthson, Chuck. "Timelines: A Chronology of Life Events." *NGS News Magazine* 34, no. 3 (2008): 38-42.

Microsoft. "Create a Timeline Using Microsoft Office Excel." http://www.microsoft.com/Education/createtimeline.mspx?pf=true (accessed 4 September 2009).

Millenia Corporation. "Legacy Family Tree." http://www.legacyfamilytree.com (accessed 4 September 2009).

"OurTimeLines." http://www.ourtimelines.com (accessed 4 September 2009).

Progeny Software, Inc. "Genelines Timeline Charting Tool." http://www.progenygenealogy.com/genelines.html (accessed 4 September 2009).

RootsMagic, Inc. "Personal Historian." http://www.personalhistorian.com (accessed 4 September 2009).

Szucs, Loretto Dennis and Sandra Hargreaves Luebking, eds. *The Source: A Guidebook of American Genealogy,* 2nd ed. Salt Lake City: Ancestry, 1997.

Szucs, Loretto Dennis. *Family History Made Easy.* Salt Lake City: Ancestry, 1998.

Whitaker, Beverly DeLong. *Beyond Pedigrees: Organizing and Enhancing Your Work.* Salt Lake City: Ancestry, 1993.

Zabriskie, George Olin. *Climb Your Family Tree Systematically.* Salt Lake City: Parliament Press, 1969.

13

Using DNA to Find Immigrant Origins

Nathan W. Murphy, MA, AG

Using DNA evidence to solve colonial American immigration problems is one of the most exciting applications of this new tool to the field of genealogy. Even after family members have made serious attempts for decades, many Americans still come up empty-handed when it comes to tracing their colonial immigrants' exact European places of origin. This essay will examine England as a case study to explain how to use living people's DNA to identify the overseas origins of colonial Americans. Similar methodologies will also produce revealing results in other time periods and places.

Researchers interested in soundly accomplishing this task will benefit from taking an inter-disciplinary approach by combining evidence gleaned from genealogical, genetic, and surname studies. Genealogical skills will be required to accurately document pedigrees in the countries of origin and destination and track down qualified living descendants of historical figures to participate. An adequate understanding of Y-chromosome DNA testing (which is not as complicated as it may sound) will be needed to interpret participants' results. Knowledge of surnames and their frequencies, distributions, and meanings will also help researchers select the most appropriate immigrants to study.

The first step in this process is to select an appropriate colonial immigrant for a project. The immigrant acts as a nexus connecting the Old World to the New. What qualifies an ancestor as an appropriate colonial immigrant? First, the immigrant must be male. The immigrant must have qualified living male patrilineal descendants who are well documented. Many families "daughtered-out," meaning they produced no sons to inherit Y-chromosomes. In other families, "non-paternity events" such as illegitimacies or adoptions disrupted the biological transferal of Y-chromosomes from father to son. Families where such instances are known or suspected should be avoided for this type of project (see figure 1).

Figure 1
The Basics of Y-chromosome DNA Testing:
A Pedigree, Genetic Signatures, and Interpretation Tools

William Baines

Henry Baines

Patrilineal ancestry

Agnes Shield

William Baines

Francis Allen

Sybil Allen

Eleanor Rawlins

- Y-chromosome DNA tests identify the genetic signatures of living men and their direct patrilineal ancestry.

- Immigrant origin DNA tests should be refined to 37 or more markers to allow clear interpretations.

- Genetic match at 37 markers = no more than five mismatches in alleles at a distance of no more than one or two steps. For example, the genetic signatures below (table created by World Families Network and used by permission) identify two matching signatures that mismatch in one allele (576), at a distance of one step.

- According to FTDNA Tip™, the probability that the two participants share a common ancestor within the past 12 generations is 97.14%.

393	390	19	391	385a	385b	426	388	439	389I1	392	389I2	458	459a	459b	455	454	447	437	448	449	464a	464b	464c	464d	460	GATA H4	YCAII a	YCAII b	456	607	576	570	CDYa	CDYb	442	438
13	24	14	11	10	14	12	12	14	12	13	28	18	9	10	11	11	26	15	18	29	14	14	15	17	11	11	19	23	15	14	18	17	35	37	12	12
13	24	14	11	10	14	12	12	14	12	13	28	18	9	10	11	11	26	15	18	29	14	14	15	17	11	11	19	23	15	14	17	17	35	37	12	12

By networking with other genealogists, the process of finding an immigrant's living descendants in the United States is often relatively straightforward. It can be accomplished by making a few Internet searches at Ancestry Community message boards, GenForum message boards, RootsWeb mailing lists, or WorldConnect; then sending out a couple of e-mails and making a telephone call or two ("Ancestry Community Message Boards," Ancestry, http://www.ancestry.com/community; "GenForum Message Boards," Genealogy, http://genforum.genealogy.com; "Mailing Lists," RootsWeb, http://lists.rootsweb.com; "WorldConnect," RootsWeb, http://worldconnect.rootsweb.com). If compiled sources lack documentation, they should be verified. It is best to test descendants of at least two sons of an immigrant as a measure to safeguard against unsuspected "non-paternity events." Results become clearer as more descendants are tested. They make it possible to "calculate the likely sequence which was carried by the immigrant ancestor."[1]

DNA testing involves some expense. Standard DNA tests often cost between $200 and $300, and it is often necessary to purchase approximately eight or ten to produce satisfactorily clear results for an immigrant origins DNA project. Some people will volunteer to pay for their own kits, while others will require incentives, such as free tests, for motivation. An immigrant for whom a family organization or one-name study has been established is ideal, as the estimated cost of $1,500 to $2,000 required to purchase DNA testing kits can be divided among members interested in following the project's progress. In comparison to the cost of hiring a professional genealogist to tackle immigrant origin problems and relying only on traditional genealogical research techniques, DNA projects usually produce quicker results for less money.

Other considerations include surname origins. Some surnames are better suited for immigrant origin DNA projects than others. Did the surname originate in a country where the majority of the population used patronymics until modern times, such as Denmark, Norway, Sweden, or Wales? If so, the steps listed in this essay cannot be accomplished, as Y-chromosomes are most easily traced when following fixed inherited surnames, and when surnames change every generation, Y-chromosomes and surnames do not align. During the past millennium, most European countries have used fixed inherited surnames, and colonial immigrants from these regions provide ideal candidates for immigrant origin DNA projects.

How common is the surname? Is it monogenetic (i.e. does everyone with a specific surname descend from one common ancestor who bore that name)? In England, for example, like most of Europe, surnames are classified into four broad categories, based on their origins. Most surnames that derive from patronymics (patronyms) or occupations (metonyms) are polygenetic and can be quite common. They were coined independently in different regions of England. They usually require larger numbers of participants to produce revealing DNA studies. Surnames derived from a person's physical description or nickname, or minor place-names, such as hamlets, villages, or landscape features (toponyms), are often less common and some are monogenetic. Foreign surnames in England are also often monogenetic. In monogenetic studies, the DNA of all male descendants should match, the exception being those who result from "non-paternity events."[2]

Proof that a surname is monogenetic is one of the most interesting genealogical facts that DNA surname studies expose. Most surname dictionaries identify surname classifications. Two free online examples can be found at Ancestry and Spatial Literacy. Studying immigrants

---

[1] "Solving Great Migration Problems with DNA Data," *Federation of Genealogical Societies Conference Syllabus* (2006).

[2] "Family Facts," Ancestry, http://www.ancestry.com/learn/facts; "Surname Profiler: Surnames as a Quantitative Resource," http://www.spatial-literacy.org/UCLnames/default.aspx; "Register of One-Name Studies," Guild of One-Name Studies, http://www.one-name/org/register.shtml; Patrick Hanks and Flavia Hodges, *A Dictionary of Surnames* (Oxford: Oxford University Press, 1988), xvi-xxiv.

with less-common surnames produces more convincing results and requires less genealogical research and funding to accomplish. Surnames registered with the Guild of One-Name Studies are usually less common and have great potential for immigrant origin DNA projects.

Proof that a surname is monogenetic is one of the most interesting genealogical facts that DNA surname studies expose.

After an appropriate colonial immigrant is selected, it is time to develop a Web site for the project. Web sites for over 5,000 DNA surname projects already exist, and immigrant origin DNA projects easily assimilate into these pre-existing studies. The Web sites of testing companies such as Family Tree DNA and Relative Genetics, for example, provide lists and contact details for project administrators. The World Families Network also maintains such a list.[3]

If a Web site has not been created, there are other options. For those who lack the computer skills to build a site, the World Families Network has made an agreement with Family Tree DNA, the largest testing company, to build free Web sites for groups that order testing kits through Family Tree DNA. The sites are ready made, fully functional, and easily edited by a simple Web-editing program that resembles a word processor.[4] For tips on how to decide which testing company is right for your project, consult the works by Chris Pomeroy, Megan Smolenyak, and Ann Turner in the selected bibliography at the end of this essay.

Because prices change, it is best to review each company's Web site for updates. Building a Web site; creating listings at Family Tree DNA, Relative Genetics, or the World Families Network; and placing online posts at surname message boards, such as Ancestry Community, GenForum, and RootsWeb are excellent ways to advertise new DNA projects.

After a site is launched and the immigrant's DNA signature is established, it is time to start looking for genetic matches in the Old World. A good way to start is by identifying surname concentrations in the nation of origin at the emigrant's time of departure. In England, there are many indexes that can be used to create seventeenth- and eighteenth-century surname distribution maps, including the International Genealogical Index, British Isles Vital Records Index, Boyd's Marriage Index, and the National Burial Index. All except the British Isles Vital Records Index are available online, although a fee or subscription is required to view two of them. Using these sources, it is possible to identify a region or regions in England where the surname occurred most frequently. This analysis will also provide an indication of how common the surname was at that particular time. Genealogists should remember to check for phonetic

---

[3] "Family Tree DNA Projects," Family Tree DNA, http://www.familytreedna.com/surname.asp; "Project Search," Relative Genetics, http://www.relativegenetics.com/genomics/search/surname.html?promo=00RLG; "Search of Surname DNA Project List," World Families Network, http://www.worldfamilies.net/search/search.php.
[4] World Families Network, http://worldfamilies.net.

variants. These clusters can be easily placed on a map using commercial software such as *Gen-Map UK*.[5]

Employing parish and probate records, descendants of families that remained in England can be tracked down into the early nineteenth century. From there it is possible to quickly follow descendants down into the early twentieth century using census records. Ancestry maintains the complete English census collection on its Web site and has indexed everyone counted between 1841 and 1901. Ancestry also offers a free online tool, "Distribution of Families in England and Wales in 1891," which plots the distribution of surnames on a map based on the 1891 census. Another free online resource, "Surname Profiler: Surnames as a Quantitative Resource," provides the same feature for 1881 using the 1881 census as a source and 1998 using that year's electoral rolls. Next, online telephone directories such as British Telecom might pinpoint descendants still living in the area where the surname occurred at the turn of the twentieth century. Directories also provide contact information.[6]

Another approach is to network with genealogists who descend from these English families in order to locate qualified descendants who wish to participate in the project. The Web site GenesReunited and the annually updated publication *Genealogical Research Directory*[7] are excellent ways to locate English-descended genealogists. If the immigrant's surname is fortunate enough to be counted among the 7,000 registered with the Guild of One-Name Studies, one-namers can provide great assistance to immigrant origin DNA projects. Curiously, many of the genealogists included in these lists live in Australia today, where family history is a popular hobby. Thus, Australia, in addition to England itself, is a prime recruiting ground for representatives of families of English descent.[8]

It is ideal to recruit multiple qualified descendants from each surname cluster. This will enable you to determine if most individuals in the cluster are monogenetic. It is important to test each cluster in order to be thorough, as not everyone with the same surname in England descends from one common ancestor. Many surnames have multiple places of origin; and illegitimacy was common. Some clusters, located at great distances from each other, will turn out to be related. As relationships (or the lack of relationships) are sorted out between clusters, the genetic evidence needed to pinpoint a colonial immigrant's origin will be acquired. It will then be possible to isolate which DNA sequences from regional clusters match the American immigrant's genetic signature. These matches act as a "Genealogical Positioning System," quoting

---

[5] International Genealogical Index, Family Search, http://www.familysearch.org; British Isles Vital Records Index, CD-ROM, available for purchase at Distribution Services, The Church of Jesus Christ of Latter-day Saints, http://www.ldscatalog.com; Boyd's Marriage Index, British Origins, http://www.britishorigins.com; National Burial Index, Family History Online, http://www.familyhistoryonline.co.uk; Archer Software, *GenMap UK*, http://www.archersoftware.co.uk.

[6] "Distribution of Families in England and Wales in 1891," Ancestry, http://www.ancestry.com/learn/facts/Fact.aspx?fid=6&ln=; "Surname Profiler," The Phone Book, British Telecom, http://www.bt.com.

[7] *Genealogical Research Directory: National and International*, 25 vols. (Sydney, N.S.W.: K.A. Johnson and M.R. Sainty, 1981-2007).

[8] Genes Reunited, http://www.genesreunited.com; *Genealogical Research Directory: National and International*, 25 vols. (Sydney, N.S.W.: K.A. Johnson and M.R. Sainty, 1981-2007).

Relative Genetics, to guide researchers in the right direction and pursue related families. After families in the matching cluster are reconstructed, the immigrant's connection often becomes apparent, and the mystery of his origin is solved.

Case Studies
The Stepp–Stapp DNA Project

Abraham Stapp (ca 1650–ca 1714) and his brother Joshua Stapp (ca 1655–ca 1695) settled in colonial Virginia. Historical documents in Virginia provide no indication of their overseas origins, though several pieces of evidence suggest they were English. Descendants decided to organize a DNA surname project and constructed an exemplary Web site, http://www. steppfamily.com. The project recruited multiple qualified American descendants of each brother to be tested and the DNA of all of these participants matched. Studies were also completed to determine the distribution of this surname in England at the time these brothers emigrated (figure 2). Three principal clusters were identified: one in Cornwall, another in the region northwest of London, and a third along the Lincolnshire-Yorkshire border. Armed with a genetic signature for their colonial American immigrants, the project proceeded to recruit descendants from these English clusters. To date, participants from two of the three clusters have been genetically tested and a match has been found in the cluster along the Lincolnshire-Yorkshire border, as noted in figure 2.

This project discovered a very promising lead and is well underway to pinpointing the exact birthplace of the American immigrants. In order to complete a "reasonably exhaustive search," an element of the Genealogical Proof Standard, the project would benefit from ruling out the third cluster as a match. In addition, refining the Lincolnshire sample to a higher resolution in order to glean a more precise estimate of how long ago participants shared a common ancestor, continuing to recruit participants of documented English descent, and focusing genealogical investigations on reconstructing families along the Lincolnshire-Yorkshire border, would be beneficial.

The Maybury DNA Project

The Maybury DNA Project, http://www.mayburyfamily.org/dnareport.html, is a notable example of what can be accomplished by testing a large number of individuals who share a less-common surname. To date, 63 participants have joined the study. The project has recruited Mabary, Maberry, Mabra, Mabrey, Mabry, Mayberry, and Maybury men with documented descents from families in England, colonial Massachusetts, colonial Pennsylvania, colonial Virginia, and counties Londonderry and Kerry, Ireland. The amazing find is that 93 percent of the participants, excluding a family of Germanic origin, are genetic matches. The 7 percent that do not match should match according to the paper trail. Non-paternity events likely account for these differences.

Because many of the results have been refined to 37 markers, it has been possible to estimate that they share a common ancestor who most likely lived in southeast England in the 1500s. DNA has revealed that the family's descendants scattered throughout Britain's former posses-

Figure 2
Surname Distribution Map for the Stepp/Stapp Surname in Early Modern England

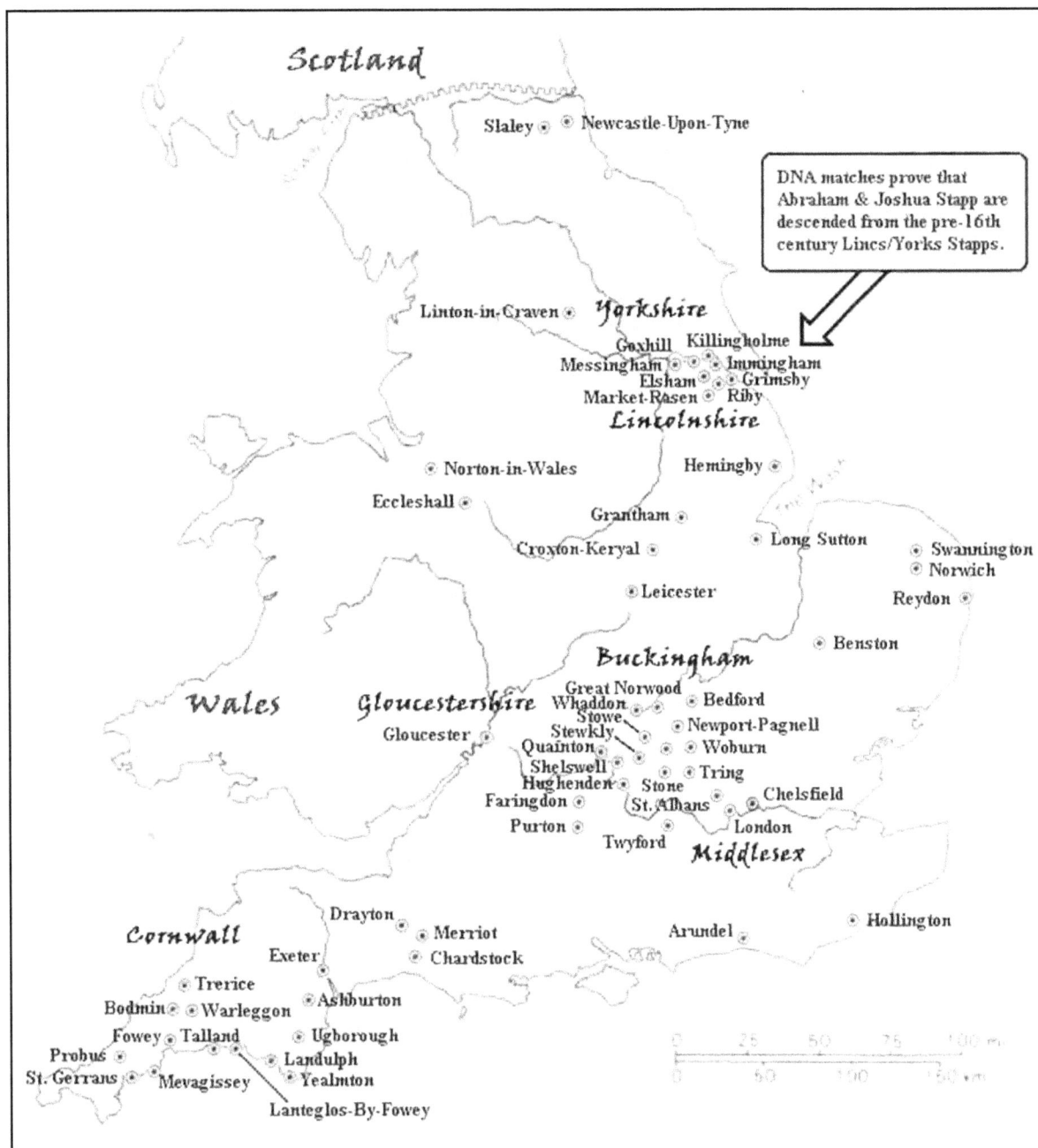

Created by the Stepp/Stapp DNA Project, http://www.steppfamily.com. Used by permission.

sions, including Australia, Canada, Ireland, and the United States. An interesting observation is that the first Maybury on record in England was an iron maker, and descendants continued this trade for several hundred years both in the Old and New Worlds. Because some of the American and Australian immigrants descend from individuals who lived in Ireland for a few generations, it is not possible to thoroughly re-create a sketch of their branches, due to incomplete records. Nevertheless, this project has jumped over that hurdle by determining that Mayburys of Irish descent genetically match Mayburys who lived in England before branches of the family left for Ireland. The project leader suspects that the earliest Maybury originated in France, where the surname is spelled *Mabire*. If the surname is of foreign origin, this could account for its monogenetic nature. It will be interesting to see how this family's DNA compares with Mabire families in France.

A Mayberry family from what is now Germany settled in Bedford County, Virginia, during the Revolutionary War era. As expected, descendants of this family do not genetically match the English family. Because the surname "Mayberry" does not exist in Germany, genealogists have assumed, probably rightly so, that it was anglicized in colonial America. They have not been successful in de-scrambling the original spelling, but hopefully one day in the future, as more individuals are tested, DNA matches will reveal this vital immigration information. This DNA project has reached an advanced stage of development, wherein it is possible for almost any American male by this surname to be tested and immediately learn if his ancestors lived in England or Germany.

Summary

With such endless new possibilities in sight, it is hard to argue with Family Tree DNA's slogan that "genealogy by genetics is the greatest addition to genealogy since the creation of the family tree!"

Review steps in setting up a DNA project:
1. Identify an appropriate colonial immigrant and determine if qualified descendants are alive today.
2. Raise $1,500 to $2,000 to cover testing costs.
3. Develop a Web site for the DNA project and advertise it.
4. Pinpoint concentrations of the immigrant's surname in the Old World at the time of departure.
5. Track down qualified descendants from each cluster.
6. Recruit at least two participants for the DNA project who descend from the colonial immigrant and multiple participants who descend from each cluster.
7. Compare the international samples and determine which results match and which do not.
8. Focus genealogical activities on reconstructing families from clusters that match American samples until the immigrant's exact relationship is determined.

For Further Study

American Genealogy. Provo, Utah: Ancestry, 2006.

Ancestry. "Ancestry Community Message Boards." http://www.ancestry.com/community.

Ancestry. "Distribution of Families in England and Wales in 1891." http://www.ancestry.com/learn/facts/Fact.aspx?fid=6&ln=.

Ancestry. "Family Facts." http://www.ancestry.com/learn/facts.

Anderson, Robert Charles. "Solving Great Migration Problems with DNA Data." *Federation of Genealogical Societies Conference Syllabus* (2006): 98-99.

Archer Software. "GenMap UK." http://www.archersoftware.co.uk/.

British Origins. "Boyd's Marriage Index." http://www.britishorigins.com.

Family History Online. "National Burial Index." http://www.familyhistoryonline.co.uk.

Family Tree DNA. "Family Tree DNA Projects." http://www.familytreedna.com/surname.asp.

"Genealogy and Genetics: A Theme Issue of the National Genealogical Society Quarterly." *NGS Quarterly* 93, no. 4 (Dec 2005).

Genealogy. "GenForum Message Boards." http://genforum.genealogy.com.

"Genes Reunited." http://www.genesreunited.com.

Guild of One-Name Studies. "Register of One-Name Studies." http://www.one-name.org/register.shtml.

Hanks, Patrick and Flavia Hodges. *A Dictionary of Surnames.* Oxford: Oxford University Press, 1988.

Johnson, Keith and Malcolm R. Sainty. *Genealogical Research Directory: National and International,* 25 vols. Sydney, N.S.W.: K.A. Johnson and M.R. Sainty, 1981-2007.

The Phone Book, British Telecom. http://www.bt.com.

Pomeroy, Chris. "Divided by the Pond: Why Genetic Drift Means U.S. Results Can't Pinpoint the Origin of a British Surname." *Eastman's Online Genealogy Newsletter.* 23 September 2009. http://www.eogn.com.

Pomeroy, Chris. *DNA and Family History: How Genetic Testing Can Advance Your Genealogical Research.* Kew, United Kingdom: The National Archives, 2004.

Relative Genetics. "Project Search." http://www.relativegenetics.com/genomics/search/surname.html?promo=00RLG.

RootsWeb. "Mailing Lists." http://lists.rootsweb.com.

RootsWeb. "WorldConnect." http://worldconnect.rootsweb.com.

Smolenyak, Megan Smolenyak and Ann Turner. *Tracing Your Roots with DNA.* United States: Rodale Press, 2004.

"Surname Profiler: Surnames as a Quantitative Resource." http://www.spatial-literacy.org/UCL names/default.aspx.

Szucs, Loretto Dennis, Kory L. Meyerink, and Marian L. Smith. "Immigration Records." In *The Source: A Guidebook of American Genealogy,* edited by Loretto Dennis Szucs and Sandra Hargreaves Luebking, 441-520. Salt Lake City: Ancestry, 1997.

World Families Network. "Search of Surname DNA Project List." http://www.worldfamilies.net/search/search.php.

14

Child-Naming Patterns: A Tool to Assist with Family Reconstitution

Richard Woodruff Price, MA, AG

A major focus of work for the genealogist is the study of names, including their meaning and relationships to others. The task of assigning a given or Christian name to a child is simple but originates from cultural, historical, and familial customs. The choice of a name usually came from the parents.

Names identify individuals. The name also "defines an individual's position in his family and in society at large; it defines his social personality." In other words, it classifies a person.[1] Assigning a name to a child classifies the child in various categories. It defines him as Christian (or other group), classifies him as to gender, suggests a social status, and may even imply a time period when he was born.[2]

Most genealogists have encountered, and possibly gained assistance from, the inheritance of given names. Historically, some groups had stringent customs for the assigning of a name to a child. Knowing these customs can assist in determining the correct parentage of the child. Hence,

> **Most genealogists have encountered, and possibly gained assistance from, the inheritance of given names.**

---

[1] Stephen Wilson, *The Means of Naming: A Social and Cultural History of Personal Naming in Western Europe* (Bristol, Penn.: UCL Press Limited, 1998), xii.

[2] Scott Smith-Bannister, *Names and Naming Patterns in England 1538-1700* (Oxford: Clarendon Press, 1997), 19.

knowing the naming patterns used in a given time and culture can be very important to the family historian as she reconstitutes families. This essay addresses how names were assigned to children. Its focus deals with North American and Western European naming customs that have been the subject of scholarly studies.[3]

As parents named their children, the first option they had was tradition. The commentator William Jenkyn stated, "A good name is a thread tyed about the finger, to make us mindful of the errand we came into the world to do for our Master."[4] Names really are cultural documents that can tell us much about our ancestors' culture and environment.

Naming customs have been used for centuries. Of John the Baptist, Luke tells us in the Bible, "... they called him Zacharias, *after the name of his father.* And his mother answered and said, Not so; but he shall be called John [Jehovah has been gracious]. And they said unto her, *There is none of thy kindred that is called by this name.*"[5] It is obvious from this dialogue that naming customs were in effect among the Jews at the time of Christ.

In Saxon England, the child was never named after his father and was rarely named even for a remote ancestor. The latter was increasingly done, however, from the eighth century onwards.[6] Don Steel states:

> Christian names may therefore be of considerable value to the genealogist, but it must always be borne in mind that descent is but one, although the most important, of the ways in which the unusual Christian name may be obtained. The English genealogist is fortunate in that no limitation has ever prevailed on the names which may be given to a child. In France an official list is still issued containing a selection of forenames, and no name of a child will be registered unless it occurs on this list. A similar limitation prevails in several Roman Catholic countries where the choice is limited to names of saints. A whole avenue of research is thus barred to many a continental genealogist.[7]

Two of the questions that arise in the study of children's names are:

1. How prevalent was name sharing among the children of our families and particularly between the children of one generation and the preceding generations?

2. Did children tend to bear unique forenames, implying that the culture saw them as unique individuals, or did they share names with parents and grandparents, uncles and aunts, implying they were construed more as elements of an ongoing family or lineage and less as individuals?[8]

---

[3] D. J. Steel, MA, FSG, "The Descent of Christian Names," *Genealogists Magazine* 14 (June 1962): 34.
[4] John J. Waters, "Naming and Kinship in New England: Guilford patterns and usage, 1693-1759," *New England Historical and Genealogical Register* 138 (July 1984): 161-162.
[5] Luke 1:59-61 (KJV), italics added.
[6] Steel, "The Descent of Christian Names," 35.
[7] Ibid, 43.
[8] Darrett B. Rutman and Anita H. Rutman, *A Place in Time: Explications* (New York: W.W. Norton & Company, 1984), 85.

As stated by Daniel Scott Smith, "Assigning a name to a child is loaded with fundamental social meaning." Bestowing a given name makes the admission of a child into the family group and locates it in familial space with respect to past and future generations. The very act of choosing a name suggests much about the values, traditions, and preoccupations of those involved in making the selection.[9]

> The very act of choosing a name suggests much about the values, traditions, and preoccupations of those involved in making the selection.

Effect of Godparents on Child-Naming

Although kinship is the most common way in which given names are passed on, it is dangerous to assume it is the only way. The most common of the secondary causes concerns godparents or sponsors at baptism. Even here, there are useful clues for the genealogist. Frequently the godparent is a relative.[10]

Godparenthood was an important influence in determining the name given to a child at baptism in many west European countries. Dutch godparents were used to assist in and affirm the baptismal ceremony and to stand for the baptized infant as its spiritual parents. As with names, the choice of godparents could be an instrumental or an expressive act.[11] In sixteenth- and seventeenth-century Scotland, children were normally named for either relations or godparents. Mr. E. Chitty suggests, "In certain periods naming after godparents was the orthodox practice and only the fact that godparents were most often chosen from within the family produces the appearance that 'family names' were deliberately perpetuated."[12]

In the Anglican and Roman Catholic baptismal tradition, parents honored godparents by naming children for them, as recompense for undertaking their spiritual education. Whom did parents usually select as godparents? Parents usually asked grandparents first and then siblings to act in this capacity for each child in turn.[13]

A study of the parish records of Banbury, Oxford, England, from 1558 to 1559 revealed that 86 percent of the children were named for their godparents. Thus, it can be concluded that sixteenth-century English children were named for godparents rather than for the hope of carrying on a family name.[14]

One of the most complete studies of godparentage is that of Jacques Dupaquier, who analyzed families in the Vexin area of France from 1540 to 1900. He concludes that the spiritual

---

[9] Daniel Scott Smith, "Child-Naming Practices as Cultural and Familial Indicators," *Local Population Studies* 32 (Spring 1974): 17-27.

[10] Steel, "The Descent of Christian Names," 39.

[11] Edward H. Tebbenhoff, "Tacit Rules and Hidden Family Structures: Naming Practices and Godparentage in Schenectady, New York: 1680-1800," *Journal of Social History* 18, no. 4 (Summer 1985): 575.

[12] D.J. Steel, MA, FSG and Mrs A.E.F. Steel, *National Index of Parish Registers: Sources of Births, Marriages and Deaths Before 1837* I (London: Society of Genealogists, 1967), 112.

[13] Gloria L. Main, "Naming Children in Early New England," *The Journal of Interdisciplinary History* XXVII, no. I (Summer 1996): 9.

[14] Erik Chitty, "Naming After Godparents," *The Genealogists' Magazine* 16, no. 2 (June 1969): 47-49.

parents were essentially chosen from among the kin. Specifically, "For the first child, [the god-parents were] the paternal grandfather and the maternal grandmother; for the second, the father's eldest brother and mother's eldest sister, then for the rest one went further afield."[15]

Table 1
Naming Patterns in Vexin, France

Child	For Whom Named
1st son	Father's father
2nd son	Father's eldest brother
1st daughter	Mother's mother
2nd daughter	Mother's eldest sister
3rd child	Distant relatives rather than aunts, uncles, or parents

Scott Smith-Bannister studied child-naming in England from 1538 to 1700, using parish registers that named godparents. In the sixteenth-century registers, he found that 80 to 90 percent of children were named for their godparents. However, by 1700, naming for godparents had dropped to 40 percent. In all decades after 1620, there was a steady decline in naming for godparents. This was perhaps influenced by the Puritan beliefs encroaching on the English society. The Puritans in New England did not use godparents, and their naming switched almost exclusively to naming older children for their parents.[16]

Child-Naming in England

The English did not have strong naming customs. The practice of giving a child three godparents in England was made an ecclesiastical rule in 1661. Of these godparents, two were of the child's own sex and was one of the opposite gender. A beneficed clergyman of the Church of England was obliged to perform the ceremony of baptism when required by a parishioner, and he was expected to give the child whatever name the godparents selected. In *The Dictionary of Genealogy*, FitzHugh indicates that godparents were almost certainly the second most powerful influence in the choice of a child's name. He purports that this may be the reason why in the sixteenth century, more than one child of a family often received the same given name, although both children were living.[17]

This author studied English child-naming patterns from 1558 to 1740 and drew these conclusions. From 1621 to 1680, 42.4 percent of oldest sons were named for the father's father and 18.4 percent of first daughters were named for the father's mother. In the later cohort of 1681

---

[15] Girard de Villethierry, "La vie des Gens Maries" (Paris, 1696) in Jacques Dupaquier, "Naming Practices, God-parenthood, and Kinship in the Vexin, 1540-1900," *Journal of Family History* 6, no. 2 (Summer 1980): 154-155.

[16] Smith-Bannister, 29-48.

[17] Terrick V.H. FitzHugh, *The Dictionary of Genealogy* (Sherborne, Dorset: Alphabooks, 1985), 127; E.G. Withy-combe, *Oxford Dictionary of English Christian Names* (Oxford: The Clarendon Press, 1959), xxx.

to 1740, 36.8 percent of first sons were named for the father's father and 36.8 percent of first daughters were named for the mother's mother. This suggests that seventeenth-century English society was patriarchal, especially for firstborn children. In both time periods, about 24 percent of the eldest three children of both genders were named for their parents. The significant find is that first sons were usually named for the paternal grandfather.[18]

Smith-Bannister states, "The most important determinant of the names given to children was the proportion of children named after a godparent. . . . the proportion of children named after godparents was greater than that named after a parent."[19] The naming for parents increased over time. In 1545, 15 percent of boys and five percent of girls were named for parents. This compares to 31 percent of boys and 16 percent of girls by 1700. With boys, there was a clear increase in father-son name sharing in England. There was a deliberate movement toward naming for parents. This change shows a lessening of the use of godparents and the strengthening of the nuclear family over time. This was partly because the responsibility of raising the child spiritually and educationally shifted from godparents to parents by 1700.

Child-Naming in Middlesex County, Virginia

Darrett and Anita Rutman studied the naming of children in Middlesex County, Virginia from 1650 to 1750. The results are shown below. The table shows the percentage of children sharing forenames with parents, grandparents, aunts, uncles, and deceased siblings:

Table 2
Naming Patterns in Middlesex County, Virginia[20]

Birth Order	Parents or Grandparent	Aunt or Uncle	Deceased Sibling
1st son	71.1	17.8	0
2nd son	63.8	26.3	1.3
3rd son	33.7	30.6	8.2
1st daughter	65.5	15.8	0
2nd daughter	58.5	18.6	1.7
3rd daughter	29.9	32.5	5.2

Instances of shared names are highly suggestive of a familial rather than an individual view of children. They are not definitive, however. It is clear that the naming of at least the first two children of each gender was usually for parents and grandparents. Subsequent children were frequently named for aunts and uncles, as well as deceased siblings.[21]

---

[18] Richard Woodruff Price, "Child-Naming Patterns in Three English Villages, 1558-1740: Wickham, Durham; Bottesford, Leiscester; and Hartland, Devon," unpublished master's thesis (Provo, Utah: Brigham Young University, December 1987), 72, 73, 88, 91.
[19] Smith-Bannister, 53, 63, 184-185.
[20] Rutman, 88.
[21] Ibid, 89.

Child-Naming in New England Families

More studies have been done on child-naming in New England than in any other area. Daniel Scott Smith has done major research on child-naming patterns of New England, initially focusing on Hingham, Massachusetts. His results showed that 74 percent of firstborn daughters before 1735 were named for their mothers, and 67 percent of firstborn sons were named for their fathers. David Hackett Fischer proposed that naming children for their parents was a supremely New England folk phenomenon—that the custom originated as a product of covenant theology among Puritan emigrants. This theology eliminated the use of godparents, giving parents the major responsibility to be spiritual guides for their children instead of passing it to someone else.[22]

The settlers of Hingham came from a culture where first children were usually named for grandparents, so why the abrupt change on their arrival in the New World? Three English villages were studied and compared. All three favored naming children for grandparents over parents, especially girls. This same preference for grandparents over parents emerges clearly in Virginia. Fischer identifies "covenant theology" as the source of New England's naming customs, because it enhances the spiritual role of the parents within the family.[23]

Dutch Child-Naming Patterns

One of the cultures with strong traditions for ancestral naming is that of the Dutch. New Netherland (New York) and South Africa both were of Dutch background, and their naming customs mirrored the Dutch in the Netherlands.[24]

In Dutch cultures, the first son was named in most cases (79 percent of the time) for the father's father and the second son was named for the mother's father. The first daughter was usually named for the father's mother (64 percent of the time), and the second daughter was named for the mother's mother. There was also frequent use of the necronym—when a child died, the next child of that gender was usually given the name of the deceased sibling. Also, if a father died while the mother was pregnant, the child would be named for the father. If a mother died in childbirth or shortly thereafter, the child would be named for her. Dutch families alternated between naming for the father's family and the mother's family. The first child was named for the father's family; the second child was named for the mother's family; and names of subsequent children continued to alternate between paternal and maternal relatives.[25]

---

22 Main, 2-3.
23 Ibid, 4-9.
24 Marian S. Henry, "Dutch Naming Practices in Colonial New York," *New England Ancestors* 8, no. 4 (Fall 2007): 31; R.A.P. Hare, "Naming Customs," *The Genealogists' Magazine* 14, no. 4 (December 1962): 121-122.
25 Frans Van Poppel, Gerrit Bloothoft, Doreen Gerritzen, and Jan Verduin, "Naming for Kin and the Development of Modern Family Structures: An Analysis of a Rural Region in the Netherlands in the Nineteenth and Early Twentieth Centuries," *History of the Family* 4, no. 3 (1999): 261-295.

Table 3
Dutch Naming Patterns

Child	For Whom Named
1st son	Father's father
2nd son	Mother's father
Subsequent sons	Uncles or father
1st daughter	Father's mother
2nd daughter	Mother's mother
Subsequent daughters	Aunts or mother

The Dutch in New York and New Jersey almost invariably named children for relatives. There was (1) a strong tendency to name the first child for a paternal grandparent; (2) some tendency to name the first child, if a boy, for the wife's first husband; (3) a tendency to alternate, taking one child's name from the father's side, the next child's name from the mother's side, the following child's name from the father's side, etc.; and (4) the tendency to repeat, giving the name of a child that died to the next child.[26]

Scandinavian Child-Naming Patterns

Scandinavian children were usually named after grandparents. As a general rule, the following table outlines the pattern Scandinavians used in assigning names:

Table 4
Scandinavian Naming Patterns

Child	For Whom Named
1st son	Father's father
2nd son	Mother's father
Subsequent sons	Great-grandfathers
1st daughter	Father's mother
2nd daughter	Mother's mother
Subsequent daughters	Great-grandparents

However, there were exceptions. Sometimes children were named after a father's deceased wife. If a first wife died and the husband remarried, the first daughter was often given the name of the first wife. Also, children named for grandparents might be "out of order" if one of the

---

[26] Rosalie Fellows Bailey, FASG, "Dutch Systems in Family Naming: New York – New Jersey," *Genealogical Publications of the National Genealogical Society* 12 (May 1954): 14.

grandparents had recently died. Likewise, children might also be named out of the usual pattern if an important relative, such as an uncle or aunt, had recently died. If one of the parents died prior to the child being baptized, the child would be named after him or her. If necessary, the name was feminized, such as Oline for Ole. This was especially important for carrying on names of deceased relatives.[27]

Scottish Child-Naming Patterns

Scotland, being a country appreciative of its traditions, had a highly developed system of naming children. The general custom, to which there were some variations, was to name children as follows:

Table 5
Scottish Naming Patterns

Child	For Whom Named
1st son	Father's father
2nd son	Mother's father
3rd son	Father
1st daughter	Mother's mother
2nd daughter	Father's mother
3rd daughter	Mother

A variation exists. The eldest son might be named after the mother's father and the eldest daughter named for the father's mother. Occasionally the second son and daughter would be named for the parents instead of grandparents. Another variation was to call the third daughter after one of the great-grandmothers instead of the mother. In such a case, the fourth daughter would usually be named after the mother.[28]

Naming Patterns of Other Cultures

Other cultures carried child-naming customs. The Jews, Quakers, Germans, and Irish tended to follow certain patterns.

Assigning given names to Jewish children had some strict customs. The Ashkenazi Jews used the following practices. Children were named after their ancestors, but a Jewish child was never given the same name as that of a living forebear. If the grandparents were dead, the first son was named for his paternal grandfather and the second son for the maternal grandfather. If the grandfathers were alive, the names of the great-grandfathers were used. Only a posthumous child was given the same name as his father. Daughters were not always named after their grand-

[27] Richard L. Hooverson, "Understanding Naming Patterns: Will the Real Ole Olson Please Stand Up," *Heritage Quest Magazine* 20, no. 3 (June 2004): 71-72.
[28] Gerald Hamilton-Edwards, *In Search of Scottish Ancestry* (London: Phillimore & Co. Ltd, 1983), 71-72.

mothers, although such was very common. The ban on naming for a living progenitor was just as strict with the women as with the men.[29]

Sephardic Jews had a much simpler custom, which was of far greater help to the genealogist. The eldest son was named for his father's father; the second son was named for his mother's father; the third son was named for his paternal great-grandfather; and thereafter the parents had a free choice. Daughters were similarly named after their female ancestors. There was no hesitation about using the names of living relatives or parents in Sephardic families. The same name was, however, never given to two surviving siblings.[30]

German children were usually given two names. The first was a spiritual biblical name such as Johann or Maria. The second was a secular name and the one they usually went by. It is this second name that was often taken from family traditions. These patterns were not always adhered to, and as German emigrants began new lives in America, many anglicized their names and began to adopt American naming customs.[31]

David Hackett Fischer in *Albion's Seed* discusses four migrating groups, or folkways, who came into North America from the British Isles. They were (1) the Puritans who came from East Anglia to Massachusetts between 1629 and 1641; (2) the cavaliers and their indentured servants who came from the south of England into the Chesapeake Bay between 1642 and 1675; (3) the Quakers who came from the English north midlands to Delaware and Pennsylvania from 1675 to 1725; and (4) the Scots, Irish, and Anglos from the English borderlands who settled in Appalachia between 1717 and 1775. Of these four folkways, the Quakers showed the most distinctive naming pattern. They tended toward a much different pattern from the English, New England, or German customs. They were the only group to show a more equitable honoring of both the father's line and the mother's line when it came to naming children. Though these were not iron-clad, the pattern is clearly discernable:[32]

Table 6
Quaker Naming Patterns

Child	For Whom Named
1st son	Mother's father
2nd son	Father's father
3rd son	Father
1st daughter	Father's mother
2nd daughter	Mother's mother
3rd daughter	Mother

---

[29] Edgar R. Samuel, "Jewish Naming Customs," *The Genealogists' Magazine* 14, no. 2 (June 1962): 44-45.

[30] Ibid, 45-46.

[31] Anne S. Riepe, "German Naming Customs," *Riepe Roots: Surname Genealogy,* http://www.rieperoots.com/pages/Names/customs.htm.

[32] "Quaker Naming Patterns for Children," *The OTHER Chester County Site!,* http://chester-county-genealogy.com/modules/smartsection/item.php?it and David Hackett Fischer, *Albion's Seed: Four British Folkways in America* (New York: Oxford University Press, 1989), 502-507.

According to a study of nineteenth-century child-naming patterns of western Ireland, it was traditional to name the elder children for grandparents, frequently of the paternal side. If the maternal relatives were more influential, then the children might be named more often for the mother's relatives. The first two children of each gender were named for their grandparents. The third child was usually named for other relatives, especially for deceased siblings. If relatives were prominent, such as an uncle who was a Catholic priest, then there was a tendency to name children for them. Children were also often named for unmarried relatives, deceased relatives, and godparents.[33]

Table 7
Irish Naming Patterns

Child	For Whom Named
1st son	Father's father
2nd son	Mother's father
3rd son	Other relatives
1st daughter	Father's mother
2nd daughter	Mother's mother
3rd daughter	Other relatives

Conclusion

A problem often facing the genealogist is which of three John Smiths living in the same village contemporaneously was the ancestor who married Jane Doe. By understanding naming patterns, it may be possible to draw conclusions based on important naming customs.[34] Although naming-patterns can provide powerful clues to identifying family relationships, they can also be frustratingly misleading. When researching any family, it is necessary to analyze all data and, with the preponderance of evidence, use the naming patterns to assist in drawing a final conclusion. Child-naming can be a useful tool when combined with other evidence. But keep in mind that our ancestors didn't necessarily follow a script when they named their children.

> When researching any family, it is necessary to analyze all data and, with the preponderance of evidence, use the naming patterns to assist in drawing a final conclusion.

---

[33] Richard Breen, "Naming Practices in Western Ireland," *Man* 17, no. 4 (December 1982): 703-705.
[34] Penny Bonnar, "Unpuzzling the Past Via Naming Patterns," *GenToday-L Archive* (October 1999), http://www.genealogytoday.com/news/archive/1099news.htm.

Clearly, assigning a name to a child had many different variables. However, understanding the typical patterns used by different cultures and nationalities can be of great help to a family historian. Sometimes the details we discover about an ancestor can be sketchy. At some point, the puzzle we are putting together seems like a brick wall, which needs to come down. Understanding child-naming patterns may be the solution for breaking down the brick wall.

15

Jurisdictions:
Who Created the Record?

Loretta Evans, AG

The John Doe family lives in a small town in the Midwestern United States. Various agencies keep records on the Doe family. Mr. and Mrs. Doe are registered in a voting precinct, which is part of a legislative district. Their children attend schools that are run by a local school district. Their property is protected in a fire district. Mr. Doe runs his own business and keeps all his records locally. Mrs. Doe, however, works for a national chain store, and her employment records are kept locally, regionally, and at the national headquarters. Mr. Doe belongs to the Masonic Lodge, and he has held both local and state offices. The Doe family attends church in a Catholic parish, which is part of a larger diocese. The family medical records are kept at the doctor's office and the hospital, although the hospital has sent its older records to an archiving company out of state. Mr. Doe is a navy veteran, and their son, Jerry Doe, will join the National Guard when he finishes high school. In one hundred years, when the descendants of John Doe become interested in genealogy, they will need to understand jurisdictions in order to locate records of this family.

Many jurisdictions are much like a Russian nested doll. Smaller divisions are found within larger and larger jurisdictions. Some divisions, however, do not fit neatly into local, state, and national categories. A researcher should think about how his ancestors' lives were impacted by various organizations in order to find the records today.

A genealogist needs to know the history of the locality he is searching. Jurisdictional boundaries have changed over the years. The boundaries of church

> **A genealogist needs to know the history of the locality he is searching.**

parishes changed as one congregation grew and another lost members. County boundaries were altered as populations shifted. Different records were kept in different time periods and by different agencies.

Local, regional, and national histories can help a researcher understand the places where his ancestors lived and the changes that may have affected genealogical records. If a town has been in three different counties since its founding, records might be held in three different courthouses.

One of the best sources for learning about jurisdictions and regional jurisdictional changes is the FamilySearch Research Wiki, which can be found on the Internet at https://wiki.familysearch.org. FamilySearch Wiki is a large online library where researchers can find thousands of articles and how-to instructions about doing family history. It contains information about all the states in the United States and the provinces of Canada, as well as many international locations. To learn about jurisdictions and/or jurisdictional changes for a particular locality, click on the link to that locality from the main page of the Web site.

Historical maps can also be helpful in genealogical research. Cities with large populations a hundred years ago could be ghost towns today. One researcher was looking for church records in a small town in Poland. They had been transferred to a larger church in the city across the river. This city is now in Germany.

National Government Records

Most national governments created records concerning the military, citizenship rights, those who crossed their borders, and relationships with foreign countries and with native people. They may also have taken censuses. Most countries hold their records at a national record office or national archive.

Civil Registration

In the United States, birth, marriage, and death records are held on a local or state government level. In many other countries, such records were mandated and are preserved by the national government.

National Census Records

In the United States, a census was taken every ten years, beginning in 1790. These records can be tremendously useful for genealogical research. The population schedules through 1940 have all been indexed, and they are available online. Mortality schedules, agricultural schedules, slave schedules, and other census documents can give additional details. Some of the schedules are online; most have been microfilmed, but many have not been indexed.

Military Records

United States military records include service records, bounty land warrant applications, pension files, records of military hospitals, and numerous other documents. The most useful records for many family historians are the military pension files, although not all soldiers lived long enough to qualify.

Federal Land Records

The United States government held large tracts of land. When an individual obtained land from the federal government by purchase, either by a bounty land warrant or by homesteading, records were created that may be useful for genealogical research. An index to some federal land patent certificates can be found on the Internet. The actual files are held at the National Archives.

In addition to land ownership records, the federal government retained documents relating to the use of federal land. These included the sale or leasing of mineral rights, timber cutting, petroleum exploration, and grazing rights.

Immigration, Emigration, Passport, and Naturalization Records

National governments have traditionally controlled who crossed their borders. The federal government also controlled who received status as a citizen and who could carry a passport.

The United States mandated that each ship create a list of passengers arriving in U.S. ports, especially of those who planned to live in the United States permanently. Many of these passenger lists are indexed and available online. The name of the port, the name of the ship, and the date of arrival are all needed to locate an ancestor in these un-indexed records. The United States also kept records of people who crossed the borders from Canada and Mexico. Some immigration records are indexed and the original images are available online.

The U.S. State Department created records of citizens living abroad. Older passport application records have been microfilmed and digitized.

Early naturalization records are usually found in local courts. However, citizenship records after 27 September 1906 are held by the federal government. To locate those after 1906, contact the U.S. Citizenship and Immigration Services.

Records of Native Peoples

In the United States, most American Indian records are federal. Those with Native American ancestry should become familiar with reservation documents, Indian censuses, and other records held at the National Archives and its regional offices.

Legislative Records

The laws passed by national parliaments are rarely useful to family historians. However, occasionally bills were introduced to benefit private individuals. These can contain genealogical information. United States congressional records from 1789 to 1838 are found in the American State Papers. Records after 1817 are found in the U.S. Serial Set. These are available in print volumes, micropublications, and online.

Federal Court Cases

Records of U.S. federal courts are held by the regional office of the National Archives where the trial took place. If an ancestor was convicted in federal court, it may be useful to locate federal prison records as well.

Federal Employment Records

In the United States, the jobs of postmaster, customs agent, Indian agent, and land office positions were federal jobs. Employment records for federal employees may be found in the National Archives or its branches.

State Records

In the United States, a number of genealogically useful documents were created at the state level of government. Today they might be held by the state agency, a university library, or a state historical society or archive.

Vital Records

In the United States, many vital records are held by the state where the vital events occurred. Because each state sets its own policies, a researcher needs to learn about the laws of each state. Some localities mandated the recording of birth, marriage, and death records in the early 1800s, but some did not do so until the twentieth century. In some places, birth and death records are held by the state health department. However, marriages were held at the county level until well into the twentieth century, when states began recording marriages on the state level. New England began recording vital records in colonial times, but the dates were recorded in the town records rather than by the state or colony.

State Census Records

The United States government took censuses in years ending with 0, beginning in 1790. Some states took additional censuses, often in years ending with 5. Some are only a list of heads of households with the ages of family members. Others ask detailed questions about each person living with the family. A few of these census records have been indexed, but many must be searched page by page.

State Militia Records

Most states did not keep military records. However, some documents do exist on a state level, especially for state militias. It may be useful to check the holdings of a state archive, historical society, or university library to see if such records survived.

Men who served in the Confederacy during the Civil War were not granted federal pensions. Many southern states granted pensions to such veterans and their widows. These pension applications have been microfilmed.

State Court Records

Most court activity takes place in the states' court systems. Most civil and criminal cases are tried under state laws. While they usually begin in the local courts, appeals reach state-level courts. In addition, most states maintained a prison system to incarcerate individuals convicted of serious crimes.

Business Records

The state may have determined qualifications for people who worked as teachers, barbers, doctors, lawyers, and other professions. These licensing records may be useful to add color to a family history. Many states held records of cattle brands, safety inspections of mines, and other business-related documents.

County Records

In the United States, it is at the county level that most people had dealings with government. The county courthouse often holds birth, marriage, and death records; recorded land deeds; divided property when someone died; and dealt with civil and criminal cases, divorces, and some early naturalizations. These county records are used repeatedly by genealogical researchers.

Books such as *Ancestry's Red Book* and *Everton's Handybook for Genealogists* are useful to trace county boundary changes, as well as electronic programs, such as AniMap. Individual county Internet sites on USGenWeb can also give useful information.

Vital Records

In some states, birth, marriage, and death records are held by state agencies. However, county records may pre-date state registration. In many places, these vital records are still held on the county level. Even today, most couples go to the county courthouse to apply for a marriage license. Divorce proceedings were usually recorded in local court documents.

Land Records

Land records are often the earliest documents that survive in any locality. Most land transactions record the name of the buyer [grantee], the name of the seller [grantor], a legal description of the land, and the price and date of the sale. In addition, land records often provide important clues in tracing a person's ancestry. They might name a piece of land that was transferred through several generations of family members, list an individual's heirs if that person's land was divided after he died, or name the wife of a married man when he sold a piece of real estate.

Probate Records

Probate was the process by which a person's property was divided when he or she died. Guardians were appointed for minor children. Most probate documents were recorded at the courthouse in the county where the deceased lived. A deceased individual may or may not have left a will, but the county court determined that his property was divided according to law. If the person who died had no property or he had divided it during his lifetime, there may be no probate records for that person.

Local Court Records

Local court records, including civil cases, criminal cases, adoption records, divorce records, and naturalization records, can be very helpful to genealogists. They are often kept at the county courthouse where the court action took place.

Tax Rolls

Property tax records were usually kept on a county level in the United States. In some places, township and city tax records have survived as well. Property taxes were often levied on farm animals and vehicles as well as real estate. A detailed tax list can sometimes be helpful in determining the ancestor's economic circumstances. Some places had a "bachelor tax," a higher assessment levied on single men. When a man stopped paying this tax, it may be a clue to when he married.

Voter Registration Rolls

Surviving voter registration rolls may be held at the county courthouse or at a local library.

Other Local Government Records
City, Town, and Township Records

Some local governments kept vital records. They may have imposed taxes. In addition, they may have maintained the cemeteries in the locality. Even if good county records exist, other local government documents may have survived. Some of these records contain information not available elsewhere.

Public School Records

Many public school records are restricted because of privacy. An ancestor's report card may be considered private information, but the fact that he attended school during the 1900-1901 school year may not. Yearbooks and student directories may be held at the school or archived at a local library or historical society. If a family member was a teacher, principal, or other school employee, his employment records may be held by the local school district as well.

Records Created by Private Agencies
Church Records

In most parts of the world, church records pre-date vital records kept by governments. Most churches recorded christenings, marriages, and burials, although some recorded only minutes of meetings, financial records, and other records of lesser importance to a genealogist. Dates of christening and burial can substitute for birth and death dates. The records could be held at the local parish, or duplicate transcripts may have been sent to a regional repository. Some denominations have universities that hold religious historical records.

In some European countries, the parish boundaries served political, as well as religious, purposes. As the original parish grew or waned, the government and religious boundaries may not have remained the same.

Mortuaries and Cemeteries

Not all cemeteries are maintained by local governments. The sexton's records are often held onsite at the cemetery office. In other places, the city may have one office that holds records for all city cemeteries. For cemeteries that are maintained by churches, funeral homes, or fraternal organizations, it is best to contact the organization that manages the cemetery today.

Fraternal Organizations

Clubs and fraternal organizations may or may not have records that could be genealogically useful. It is best to contact the surviving local or state organizations to see if such records exist.

Medical Records

Medical records are protected by privacy rules. Most are not available, except to the person named in the record. Some may be released to descendants if the primary individual has died. Medical records may be stored offsite.

Business Records

If business records have survived, they can add details to a biography. The records may confirm that the ancestor worked for the company, but they will be unlikely to provide data such as birth, marriage, and death dates.

Farm and Plantation Records

Occasionally records are kept that deal with very small jurisdictions. Farm records in Norway (*bygd* books) list the people who lived on each farm and include genealogical facts about their lives. In the southern United States, some histories have been written about plantations, including all the people who lived there, both slave and free.

For Further Study

Eichholz, Alice. *Red Book: American State, County, and Town Sources.* 3rd ed. Provo, Utah: Ancestry, 2004.

Greenwood, Val D. *The Researcher's Guide to American Genealogy.* 3rd ed. Baltimore: Genealogical Publishing Company, 2000.

The Handybook for Genealogists. 11th ed. Logan, Utah: Everton Publishers, 2006.

Szucs, Loretto Dennis and Sandra Hargreaves Luebking. *The Source: A Guidebook of American Genealogy.* 3rd ed. Salt Lake City: Myfamily.com, 2006.

16

Getting the Most from Electronic Indexes

Suzanne Russo Adams, MA, AG

For decades, genealogists have created and utilized indexes to records of genealogical value. Indexes are crucial to locating, gathering, and analyzing historical documents. Methods of capturing index information have changed over the last few decades, as have the ways that we might use these finding aids.

When data is electronic, it can change and be manipulated much more rapidly than printed data in a book. Therefore, Web sites that contain a large amount of genealogical data are constantly improving their content. Since millions of records are often added to Web sites, it is important to keep current with any particular site. In the world of digital content, sites might publish and re-publish data weekly, if not daily, allowing for mistakes to be corrected and errors to be resolved in the data.

In order to utilize newly published material, it is important to know a few things about Web sites used for genealogical research. Every good Web site should have a site map, tips on how to use the site, a site tutorial, and, if it contains databases, a search tutorial. These are the first things to look for when using any type of search service but especially when using a Web site that hosts genealogical content. Questions you might ask yourself include:

- "What is the purpose of this Web site?"
- "How can I effectively use this Web site?"
- "Where are the search tips, search tutorial, and site maps?"
- "What are the strengths and limitations of this Web site or search engine?"
- "What are the strengths and limitations of the genealogical records I am using?"

A history of the record sets you might find on the Web, such as county or state vital record indexes and indexes to the census, might require a little genealogical sleuthing about where the records came from and how they were created, in order to better understand and utilize them.

Look for Source Information

Source information is crucial to understanding how a dataset was created and what it contains. The source information about an online-content set can tell you a great deal about what may or may not be included in that particular database. In many cases, the laws governing whether or not record sets are open or closed to the public also help determine which datasets are digitized and placed online. Some sets of information are easier to acquire and digitize than others. Keep in mind that the information in an online database may be determined by what information was available publicly at the time it was digitized. Doing your homework to determine what information is contained in a dataset can save time and headaches in your research.

> Source information is crucial to understanding how a dataset was created and what it contains.

As an example, the Ancestry.com Web site, http://www.ancestry.com, includes a dataset labeled "Nevada Marriage Index, 1956-2005." One might assume the database contains all marriage indexes for the entire state for the dates included in the title. Wrong!

The marriage records indexed from 1966 to 2005 were obtained by the Nevada State Health Division, which should imply a statewide index of marriages, but the data from 1956 to 1966 actually covers Clark County only. This is crucial information, because if you were searching for the index entry of an ancestor who married outside of Clark County before 1966, you would not find him in this database.

Additionally, not all databases may be completely indexed at the time they are posted on the Internet. Ancestry.com and FamilySearch.org release some databases that are "image only" first, with an index to those images following at a later date. Web sites like Fold3.com indicate the level of completion of a collection so that researchers know how complete the record sets and their indexes are at the time they are used.

An Index Is a Finding Aid

Due to continuing technological advances, it is becoming increasingly easier to connect a scan of an original source document to an index. When viewing indexes online, it is important to learn what information is contained on the original document and the "rules" for collecting that information. For example, enumerators of the U.S. federal censuses were instructed to record the state and/or country of birth for an individual. Thus, researchers should not expect to find the city of birth of an individual listed on an original census record or on an electronic federal census index. Moreover, researchers must understand which fields of information were indexed on a specific document in order to effectively use the index.

Names

Anyone who has invested serious time in researching his family history has found that ancestral given names and surnames are often spelled many ways on documents. Names may appear phonetically, abbreviated, or translated. Additionally, an ancestor may have used a middle name or even a nickname on a document. When dealing with electronic records, a name can be mis-transcribed or mis-keyed. Watch for variations of both given names and surnames, particularly for immigrants. For example, an Italian immigrant, Matteo Russo, was listed as Mike Russo on a 1920 census and as Martin Russo on a World War I draft registration card, while his wife, Maria Accetta, was listed as "Mar Chetta Russo" on that same document. Many books on ethnic names and surnames yield information about various spellings of a name. Behindthename, http://www.behindthename.com, is a good Web site for more ideas about alternate name spellings.

Some online publishers of content also use name authority dictionaries[1] and the Soundex[2] to help researchers search for misspelled or variant names. Keep in mind that these sources do not list every possible variation of a name.

Dates and Ages

Dates and ages can be indexed incorrectly for a variety of reasons. First, the date may be listed incorrectly on the original record. Have you ever written the previous year on a document, letter, or check because it is now January and you are used to writing the previous year by force of habit? This is not just a modern phenomenon. Additionally, a census enumerator may have guessed at the ages of persons in a household, and some of our illiterate ancestors might not have known their exact date or even year of birth. Second, what about Julian and Gregorian calendar dates on historical documents? Many areas of the world recorded dates differently than others. It is only in modern times that more uniform time and date systems have been adopted. Third, a date may be correct on the original record but may have been mis-keyed by the indexer of that record. If the person keying the data misinterpreted one number in a four-digit year, a person born in 1825 may be inadvertently indexed as born in 1875.

Places

Historically, place names have changed over time. They can be spelled differently than one might expect, or they can be partial or not very helpful (i.e. the name of a country or a state might be listed on a record, rather than the town, city, or county/province).

---

[1] A name authority dictionary is a compilation of names ranked on relevance to a certain name. For example, when searching for the name "John," a name authority dictionary used by commercial genealogy companies might return the additional following names: Jon, Jonathon, Jno., Johnathan, etc.

[2] Soundex is a phonetic algorithm developed in the early 1900s used to code surnames by similar sounds. Many genealogy Web sites implement Soundex and/or the variation known as Daitch-Mokotoff Soundex, crucial for deciphering Jews with Germanic and Slavic surnames.

Relationships

One cannot always assume that records show complete families. A census taken ten or more years before the last census may not reveal children who were born and subsequently died within that same period. Some recorders, such as enumerators of British censuses, might have been instructed to record only those persons that were at home on the day or night the census was taken, resulting in omissions of persons who may have been traveling in another town when the rest of the family was enumerated. These individuals will not be listed in the original record or the index, although they were part of the family.

State of the Original Documents

Traditionally, indexes have been created for vital records, censuses, obituaries, and the like. Many of these record types have a set format and are easier to index than free-form record sets. With the onslaught of electronic data being placed online daily, there is a noticeable shift in the types of records being indexed. More and more foreign (non-U.S.) vitals and other free-form datasets are now available online. There is great momentum in the genealogical and archival communities to preserve data and make it more accessible to a worldwide community of computer users. This sometimes means that before a record set can be indexed, some preservation preparation has to take place.

> There is great momentum in the genealogical and archival communities to preserve data and make it more accessible to a worldwide community of computer users.

OCR Technology vs. Keyed Data

Optical Character Recognition (OCR) is a tool used to translate handwritten, typeset, or typewritten text into an electronic, searchable format. This technology is used on a variety of content types; mostly for newspapers, city directories, and family and local histories, where it might be otherwise time consuming and costly to transcribe names as fielded data. Because these types of datasets are not fielded (i.e. a person does not manually tell the computer that a word is a name or place), the computer does not distinguish between different usages of the words. For example, an index made with OCR will not indicate whether the word "bell" is used as a surname (Bell), a place name (Bell County, Texas), or another type of reference (Liberty Bell, brass bell, wedding bell, etc.). Some Web sites have partially indexed newspapers, city directories, and family and local histories to simplify finding relevant data. Other tools, such as proximity searching, might also be used.

Additionally, the accuracy of the index using OCR technology is largely dependent upon the quality of the image. If the image is poor, it is more difficult for the OCR tool to read the characters and distinguish the character patterns on a page.

Conclusion

Many online indexes now provide links to images of the actual data. This means there is more accountability for indexes than ever before. Sometimes electronic data can be missing from an index, but because the actual images are associated with the data and one can scroll through the images page by page, it is easier to determine the flaws of an index versus one that is in a printed book format.

Because the Internet is not static, some genealogical Web sites have created ways to annotate indexes, allowing for corrections and comments about data and to facilitate cooperation and collaboration to improve the index quality. These comments and corrections become searchable and allow more users to find the data they seek.

Utilize all available sources. Many commercial and non-profit organizations have duplicated some indexes, such as those for the U.S. federal census. If you don't find what you are looking for in one index, search in another index to see if the name comes up more easily. Consider too that if you do not find the data in an online index, utilize the offline data that is available, such as indexes in book form. Just because an index is no longer online does not make it invalid or less useful. Always bear in mind that an index—and especially an online index—is a finding aid and is not meant to be an exact transcription of the original data.

For Further Study

Gormley, Myra Vanderpool. *The Official Guide to Rootsweb.com.* Provo, Utah: Ancestry.com, 2007.

Lynch, Dan. *Google Your Family Tree: Unlock the Hidden Power of Google.* Provo, Utah: FamilyLink.com, Inc., 2008.

Morgan, George. *The Official Guide to Ancestry.com*, 2nd ed. Provo, Utah: Ancestry.com, 2008.

Powell, Kimberly. *The Everything Guide to Online Genealogy: A Complete Resource to Using the Web to Trace Your Family History.* Avon, Mass.: Adams Media, 2008.

Smith, Juliana. *Evaluating Indexes, parts 1 & 2.* Ancestry.com, 31 January and 14 February 2000. http://learn.ancestry.com/LearnMore/Article.aspx?id=26 and http://learn.ancestry.com/LearnMore/Article.aspx?id=538.

Smith, Juliana. John or Janos: *Tips for Translating Names.* Ancestry.com, 11 June 2009. http://learn.ancestry.com/LearnMore/Article.aspx?id=14406.

Effective Use of Libraries

Chad R. Milliner, MLIS, AG

Libraries are where magic happens, and the librarians are the magicians. But genealogists need to peer behind the curtain and learn how the tricks are done, because it is unrealistic to expect the magicians to always have the time to put on a private pulling-a-rabbit-out-of-a-hat show. Genealogists have to learn how to pull out their own rabbits.

Know Before You Go

Do the obvious before coming to a library. Look at the library's Internet Web site to verify that it will be open on the date of the planned visit. For a large library with different departments, determine not only the overall building hours but also the hours for the relevant departments or reading rooms. For example, at the Library of Congress, some of the reading rooms are closed on Saturdays while others are open. Some of the reading rooms close as early as 4:30 p.m., while other reading rooms on particular days of the week stay open as late as 9:30 p.m.

For libraries with a separate local history or genealogy division, do not assume that this division will be the place where all, or even most, of the ancestral research will be done. Ancestors lived on Earth, not in a formless void, so materials in a library's maps or cartography department might be highly relevant. In addition to being born, marrying, and decomposing, ancestors interacted with earthlings and partook of the earthlings' festivals and historical events. So, really, all departments of a library can have materials that need examination. Therefore, it is important to look at all of the parts of a library's Web site, not just those portions labeled "genealogy."

Learn what materials each library department holds. Then learn all available information about accessing those materials while the trip is still in the planning stages. Some libraries have parts of their holdings on open stacks or shelves, while other less-used parts of their holdings are housed in closed stacks or shelves in high-density storage areas. Sometimes a librarian can retrieve needed items from storage in just a few minutes, but in other instances it can take several days. So unless the library's Web site directs otherwise, notify the library staff by telephone or e-mail several days in advance of the trip if materials need to be retrieved from storage. Also ask whether any member of the general public can make such requests, or whether readers will need an institutional ID card. If the latter, ask about how arrangements for such a card can be made. It is possible that a letter of recommendation will need to be solicited from a scholar, such as a university professor.

The best way to learn whether materials of interest are on open or closed shelving is to examine the records for those items in the institution's online catalog via the Internet. Focus on what the catalog lists for each item's circulation status. Items stored offsite or in an onsite high-density storage facility are usually identified as such in this part of each catalog record. As shown in the following illustration, if your ancestors came from outer space, the Library of Congress has two copies of a book that might be helpful, but neither copy is immediately accessible. The first copy is stored in closed stacks and thus has to be requested from a librarian. The second copy is stored in an offsite facility.

Illustration 1

Library of Congress online catalog.

Make printouts of the full catalog records for those sources that appear relevant to the research objective. Take these printouts along on the trip, just in case the library's internal system is down on the day of the visit or in case a needed source cannot be located on the shelf. If the library has closed stacks, having the printout will save time in filling out call slips. Each of the printouts should note the subject headings that the catalogers assigned. Using the online catalog, find out what other library sources have been cataloged with those subject headings. Make additional printouts of any additional sources. Arrange the printouts in call number order, especially when the volumes are on open shelves, in order to minimize the amount of walking needed.

Intellectual Access to Library Holdings

Even the smallest public library has some method of maintaining intellectual control of its holdings; that is, knowing what materials it has and where those materials are located. While online library catalogs are what most libraries now use for this purpose, most libraries have been in existence far longer than have computers. Thus, libraries used some other method of maintaining intellectual access prior to using the computer; and, for many libraries, vestiges of the earlier system (or systems) still exist. These vestiges (such as a physical card catalog or a printed shelf list) might be the only source of information about the collections they describe.

Because information about some library holdings might not be accessible via the library's Web site prior to making a trip there, it is important to consult with library staff members before or upon arrival at the library to learn about such limitations. Some records might take several days to retrieve if they are stored at an offsite facility. Even if a library staff member provides initial assurance that all materials are now described in the online catalog, ask some probing questions to be sure: What about government documents? What about genealogical materials contributed by community members? What about manuscript materials stored in vertical files?

It is very common for manuscript materials to be cataloged differently than books. This is because these materials *are* different. By their nature, manuscript materials are likely unique, held nowhere else, while books are typically available at multiple libraries. Because of the uniqueness of manuscript materials, the library may require that they be read in a special room and may prohibit photocopying or require a staff member to do it. Thoroughly understand all rules regarding manuscripts.

In addition to having some holdings that might be described only by a system that predates the computer age, a library might have some holdings physically arranged in a system that predates the one used for most library holdings. Large libraries often assign Library of Congress-style call numbers to books and other types of library materials, while small libraries tend to use a variation of the decimal classification system first developed by Melville Dewey. Determining which system is in use is easy—if a call number of something that is not a United States government document begins with one or more capital letters, the library is using the Library of Congress system. If the call number begins with three digits, then it is using the Dewey system. Government documents are usually assigned call numbers from a system known as SuDoc.

Such call numbers may initially appear similar to Library of Congress call numbers, but the systems are totally different.

Call Numbers and Serendipitous Browsing

As noted, large libraries tend to use the Library of Congress system. But large libraries often started out as small libraries. So, a large library that now uses the Library of Congress system may have earlier used the Dewey system when it was a smaller library. Thus, some books about the history of a particular town might be shelved with Library of Congress call numbers beginning with the letter "F" while other books about that same town might be shelved with Dewey books with a call number somewhere in the 970s. It is common for libraries with books in both systems to have such books shelved in completely different areas of the library, or for the Library of Congress books to be in open stacks and the Dewey books (because they are older) to be in closed stacks requiring retrieval.

It is also common for libraries to shelve books that are odd sizes on special shelves that may or may not be located close to the shelves used for the regular-sized books. And of course materials in special formats (such as microform) will be stored apart from regular printed books. So on the first research day at a library, identify how the library arranges its materials. Learn whether the online catalog includes records for *all* of the materials that a library has. Determine whether some books have call numbers with a system different than what is used now and how odd-sized books are stored.

> **On the first research day at a library, find out how the library arranges its materials.**

The Library of Congress and Dewey systems have specific call numbers for books about genealogy. But most books of genealogical value are NOT genealogy books and thus have call numbers that do not begin with CS (Library of Congress) or with 929 (Dewey). One of the best ways to find books of genealogical value is through serendipitous browsing. Serendipitous browsing occurs when you are looking for one book on a shelf and during the process find other books of similar or even greater research value. The Library of Congress and Dewey call number systems both have the same underlying purpose—to arrange books by subject matter so that books about, say, mines, are shelved close to each other. This allows for serendipitous browsing when a library uses an open-stacks system.

Given that both systems have similar purposes, why are there still two different systems for assigning call numbers to books? There is not room in this essay for a detailed explanation, but one reason is that any book is only so wide. There is not an infinite amount of space for writing a call number. Thus, in order for a library to efficiently shelve its holdings, the great majority of the books on the open shelves need call numbers short enough to fit on the book spines. Less room on book spines is usually needed to write a call number in the Library of Congress system than is the case for the Dewey system, for any two identical detailed subjects. Also, the Library of Congress system is easier to use when greater subject separation is needed, which is the case in larger collections.

Family History Library, Salt Lake City, Utah.

Smaller public libraries use the Dewey system because it is easier for the general public to understand a call number that is all digits. Also, a smaller public library usually has only a few books on any particular subject. For example, a smaller public library may have only four total books about mining. By contrast, a large research library may have thousands of books on this subject. Since the large library will still want to facilitate serendipitous browsing, its librarians would want to shelve books about specific aspects of mining, or books about specific mines, near each other while shelving books about lesser-related aspects of mining further away.

In order for serendipitous browsing to work in a large library, call numbers have to be longer. Just like a nine-digit zip code allows for more precision in mail delivery than does a five-digit zip code, a longer call number allows books about any particular aspect of mining (or any other subject) to be shelved closer together. While it is possible for a Dewey call number to be equally as specific as a Library of Congress call number, the Dewey call number is more complex and results in a longer number than a Library of Congress call number. The flexibility of the Dewey system allows libraries with large collections to determine unique numbers for each book, but those numbers can often be quite long on the top line, with three, five, or more digits to the right of the decimal (along with the required three on the left of the decimal). Such long call numbers often do not fit on the spines of most books, which is one reason why libraries with large collections of books on many different topics usually use the Library of Congress system. Libraries with fewer books on most topics usually use the easier-to-understand Dewey system. In addition, the Library of Congress system was designed for larger collections and has more subdivisions. The nature of the numbering system, with multiple lines rather than a single, long subject number, makes it easier to find a specific book of interest, even in a large collection.

If, for example, an ancestor who is the subject of research went to Alaska and became a miner, where would browsing the shelves for a book that might describe the mine at which he worked and the conditions under which he labored be most productive? Does the library shelve this book with books about Alaskan history or with books about mining history?

If research is undertaken at the Family History Library, the answer is that the book will be given a call number that will shelve it with books about Alaskan history. The Family History Library made a decision long ago to shelve all of its books by the geographical areas to which those books relate, except for books about a specific family's history. But at almost any other research library, the book will be shelved with books about mining history. If the library decides to make the call number detailed enough (i.e., long enough), then books about Alaskan mining history will be shelved in closer proximity to each other than books about the history of mining in Wyoming, but in smaller libraries and libraries still using the Dewey system, books about all aspects of mining are more likely to be intermixed, which will result in serendipity being less likely to strike while browsing.

The printouts made before coming to the library contain the call numbers assigned by the library catalogers to the sources. Once the relevancy of these sources has been determined through onsite examination, browse the shelves immediately before and after the books that were most relevant.

Bibliographies

Once the books and other materials identified before coming to the library have been examined and any additional materials found during browsing have been studied, the final step is to examine published and online bibliographies of sources that pertain to the relevant subject. Bibliographies are lists of sources on any given subject. They can be selective, containing only citations to the sources that the compiler found most relevant, or comprehensive, containing everything published on the subject of which the compiler was aware. To determine what a library has that is relevant to the research topic of interest, take the subject headings that the library staff assigned to the sources most useful during the research there. Via the subject browsing feature of the library catalog, search for similar subject headings in the online catalog that list "Bibliography" as the final part of the subject heading. Consult with the library staff if you need help determining how to subject browse in the online catalog.

Once relevant bibliographies have been found, search them carefully and read all of the introductory material. Often, very obscure sources can be identified through this method. Then, use *Worldcat* to locate which libraries have the sources that appear relevant. *Worldcat* is an online union catalog that lists holdings of libraries from all parts of the world. While its coverage is uneven because it lists only holdings that member libraries choose to add to the *Worldcat* database, it is a key tool that should always be utilized, http://www.worldcat.org.

Resources beyond Library Walls

It is impossible to conduct serious genealogical research using just resources available via the Internet. Conversely, it is also impossible to conduct serious genealogical research without using Internet resources. The Genealogical Proof Standard promulgated by the Board for Certification of Genealogists calls for a "reasonably exhaustive" search to always be done. Exactly what constitutes a reasonably exhaustive search depends on the research problem at hand, but if an entire category of materials is excluded from the search, it is impossible to say that the resultant search was anywhere close to being exhaustive.

How can a thorough search be made of Internet resources? Consider that there are many different providers, most of which have unique data not found in other providers' offerings. Consider also that most providers charge fees for access to their resources, and thus it may not be feasible to subscribe to all providers' products. A partial answer in many cases is to use these Internet databases at libraries. But database providers often have multiple versions of their products. One version, for personal subscriptions, might contain functionality or information not available in the version(s) made available to libraries. Say that Company A includes in its consumer version of its database product a source that is licensed to it by Company B. Company B may have previously licensed library rights to that source to Company C. So if you access Company A's database product at a subscribing library, you will not get access to the information that Company B created. Thus, in research notes make sure to note which version of a database is being examined.

Just as libraries have physical holdings with call numbers other than 929 or CS that still have great genealogical value, many libraries have subscriptions to databases that are not explicitly genealogical in nature yet have great genealogical value. Thus, identify all of the databases to which the library subscribes, regardless of the subject matter. Try to focus research time on the library subscription databases that are not available through libraries closer to home.

New Internet databases are being launched all the time, but there are certain categories of databases that are likely to be more useful in performing a reasonably thorough search. Everyone's ancestors lived somewhere on planet Earth, so databases containing images of maps (perhaps overlaying images of the Earth) are likely to have research value in many cases. Use maps that cover a broad area to see the general "lay of the land" in the area in which the ancestor lived. Look for geographic features, such as rivers and canyons, that would have influenced how and where the ancestor would have moved around. Then "zoom in" as tightly as possible. Several companies published maps showing the specific buildings in cities and towns during the nineteenth and early twentieth centuries, such as those published by the Sanborn Fire Insurance Company. Often, large libraries will have subscriptions to Internet databases containing images of these maps, although sometimes a library will limit its subscription to just the maps of the state in which the library is located.

Some online databases provide abstracts (and often images) of theses and dissertations. There are also databases that abstract articles published in historical journals. These types of databases are complementary and thus both useful in conducting the reasonably exhaustive search recommended by the Genealogical Proof Standard. Determine if the library subscribes to databases like *Digital Dissertations, Dissertation Abstracts International, America: History and Life,* and *Historical Abstracts*.

For Further Study

It is impossible to cover all that needs to be known to make library research magic happen in a short essay. There are a number of excellent guides to researching in libraries that go far more in depth and cover many more aspects of the topic. While some of these guides are directed primarily to college students and none of the guides were written by or for genealogists, they all are useful.

Chernow, Barbara A. *Beyond the Internet: Successful Research Strategies.* Lanham, Md: Bernan Press, 2007.

Gates, Jean Key. *Guide to the Use of Libraries and Information Sources.* 7th ed. New York: McGraw-Hill, 1994.

Mann, Thomas. *The Oxford Guide to Library Research.* 3rd ed. New York: Oxford University Press, 2005.

Shaw, Maura. *Mastering Online Research: a Comprehensive Guide to Effective and Efficient Search Strategies.* Cincinnati, Ohio: Writers Digest Books, 2007.

18

Documentation and Source Citation

Amy Harris, Ph.D., AG

Every genealogical researcher has had the experience of reading a report or research completed by previous generations or previous researchers. Excitement grows as we realize the earlier authors found information or made conclusions we did not know about earlier. That spinning euphoria disappears when our eyes stray to the bottom of the page or the end of the research to discover that the citations, when they exist, have limited information. That sinking feeling comes from the realization that we will now have to retrace all of the steps or guess how to retrace the steps of the previous researcher.

For example, in a published genealogy of the Curtis family of Connecticut, there are references to sources used (without specific archival and internal reference information), three cited quotations, and five numbered footnotes—to support over 400 pages of genealogical information.[1] This is not unusual for genealogies written before the last quarter of the twentieth century and is not a criticism of prior generations' work so much as a reminder

> **Professional researchers quickly learn that the mark of excellent research rests on meticulous and complete source citations.**

that the expectations of professional genealogical research have changed and now demand a higher standard of citation. Professional researchers quickly learn that the mark of excellent research rests on meticulous and complete source citations—in research calendars, lineage charts,

---

[1] Harlow Dunham Curtis, comp., *A Genealogy of the Curtiss-Curtis Family of Stratford, Connecticut, A Supplement to the 1903 Edition* (Stratford, Conn.: Curtiss-Curtis Society, 1953).

and written reports and publications. In many ways, it is not whether one receives payment or not that sets apart the amateur from the professional genealogical scholar but rather the standard of documentation that one adheres to in one's work. Professionals understand the important elements of documentation: who produced the source, what it is, where and when it was produced, where it is stored (both location and call number), where and how the researcher accessed it, and specific internal reference information (page, folio number, etc.). As they hone their craft, genealogists also learn to tell a research story with their citations.[2]

Someone with no genealogical training is often surprised to learn the exacting standards of documentation and citation required by professional genealogists. Even beginners, however, quickly realize the importance of source citations for both retracing research steps and certifying that they do not accidentally plagiarize previous work.[3]

Beginners tend to think of footnotes and documentation as references they can come back to when they return to a project—a sort of audience of one. Therefore, as long as the footnote declares the information came from the "1920 Pittsburgh, Pennsylvania census," they feel comfortable having established an original source for their information and the ability to remember where they found the information. If they distribute their work, they think of the report as having a broader audience but often continue to think of citations as primarily information for them, or as signals that original records back up the information. More advanced researchers understand that footnotes, source citation, and documentation have a broader audience. The audience is anyone who reads it, and he or she should be able to retrace the steps and analysis without a struggle. In this context, the "1920 Pittsburgh, Pennsylvania census" not only lacks enough information about who produced the census or where in that census the information was found, but also neglects to specify where the researcher obtained the information. Did it come from a microfilm, a digital copy, a transcription? A complete source citation answers all of those questions.

Advanced researchers also understand that the "use of footnotes enables historians [and genealogists] to make their texts not monologues but conversations."[4] Whether the researcher engages in conversation with paying clients, journal editors, or family members, all professional research has to be scrupulously documented to maintain a professional status.

---

[2] For a lucid history of the footnote and the discussion of the "double story" of footnotes and historical scholarship, see Anthony Grafton, *The Footnote: A Curious History* (Cambridge, Mass.: Harvard, 1997). For a succinct discussion of source citation, see Jacques Barzun and Henry F. Graff, *The Modern Researcher*, 5th ed. (Fort Work: Harcourt Brace Jovanovich, 1992), 296-316.

[3] The development of electronic and digital production and dissemination of written materials has facilitated a booming plagiarism problem. To learn more about plagiarism standards and how to safeguard against it, see http://www.plagiarism.org. The Internet has also allowed for a form of "hyper" citation, as articles and postings can contain hyperlinks to other Web sites, articles, blogs, newspapers, etc. See Jenny Lynn Bader, "Forget Footnotes. Hyperlink," *New York Times*, 16 July 2000. Bader's article addressed Internet sourcing, but also partially addressed the concerns expressed by Gertrude Himmelfarb in 1991. See Gertrube Himmelfarb, "Where Have All the Footnotes Gone?" *New York Times Book Review*, 16 June 1991. I originally found the reference to Himmelfarb's piece in Barzun and Graff, The Modern Researcher, 297. For the text of both Bader and Himmelfarb's essays, <http:/crab.rutgers.edu/~goertzel/hyperlinks.htm>.

[4] Grafton, *The Footnote*, 234.

Style and Standards

Source citation has been part of the western scholarly tradition since at least the Renaissance, but in the nineteenth and twentieth centuries the style and presentation of sources began to develop discipline-specific structures. Though similar to and growing from historical citation formats, genealogy has a particular citation style and standard. Based on *The Chicago Manual of Style,* the most recent and comprehensive explanation of that standard can be found in *Evidence Explained* by Elizabeth Shown Mills.[5] When writing source notes and footnotes, professional genealogists may wish to follow this style as one that promulgates consistency and thoroughness. While *Chicago* has become the foundational text for source citation in many disciplines, *Evidence Explained* is more specifically targeted to genealogical research and writing.[6]

Both texts should be consulted for the details of citation, but a couple of reminders about style are warranted. First, in a written report, the first footnote to mention a source should be completely self-standing (or if a bibliography is used, the full citation should be listed there). In other words, a reader should be able to find the exact source and place within the source from which the information came, without having to consult attached family group records. Second, if the researcher found information in a derivative source that cited an original source, the footnote should include the original source information followed by the derivative source information. This tells the reader not only where the researcher obtained the information but also the location of the original source.

Careful attention to source citation, both during research and writing, will guarantee that the researcher does not inadvertently plagiarize another's work. The combination of the narrative and the footnotes trailing across the bottom of a report or family group record also informs the reader that the researcher has clearly distinguished between original ideas and arguments and those from past scholars. As stated in *The Chicago Manual of Style,* "Ethics, copyright laws, and courtesy to readers require authors to identify the sources of direct quotations and of any facts or opinions not generally known or easily checked."[7] This means genealogical

> **Careful attention to source citation, both during research and when writing, will guarantee that the researcher does not inadvertently plagiarize another's work.**

---

[5] *The Chicago Manual of Style: The Essential Guide for Writers, Editors, and Publishers,* 15th ed. (Chicago: University of Chicago, 2003); Elizabeth Shown Mills, *Evidence Explained: Citing History Sources from Artifacts to Cyberspace* (Baltimore: Genealogical Publishing Company, 2007). For a boiled down, and less expensive, verion of *Chicago,* see Kate Turabian, *A Manual for Writers of Researcher Papers, Theses, and Dissertations: Chicago Style for Students and Researchers,* revised by Wayne C. Booth, Greagory G. Colomb, Joseph M. Williams, and the University of Chicago Press Editorial Staff, 7th ed. (Chicago: University of Chicago Press, 2007).

[6] There are numerous online and print descriptions of citation style that are more portable and less expensive than these manuals, but no matter what resource a genealogist/family historian uses as a style guide, it should conform to *Chicago* or the genealogically applied *Chicago* found in *Evidence Explained.*

[7] *Chicago Manual of Style,* 594.

researchers must be very careful to cite any work not their own, whether that be a direct quotation (set apart with quotation marks or a block quote) or a summary of another's work.

Documentation While Researching

Excellent source citation and documentation begins with the research, not the writing. Whether entered into family tree software, a spreadsheet, or a word processor, research logs and calendars should contain full citation information. This streamlines the process of sourcing information in a written report or compiled lineage and confirms that research shared in its preliminary stages takes with it all the relevant source information. It also simplifies returning to research after a gap of days or even longer. Strict adherence to citation standards also guarantees that the researcher

> **Excellent source citation and documentation begins with the research, not the writing.**

always clarifies his own work and analysis from that done by others—thus preventing the legal and ethical questions about intentional or unintentional plagiarism.

Documenting sources while researching can also be a way of analyzing and interrogating sources. Including complete source information can provide the researcher with the opportunity to think about the source, its content, its producer, its archival status, and how it connects with other records. It can also stimulate further research questions. For example, citing an oral history would require that the researcher make note of who conducted the interview, who was interviewed, when and where the interview was conducted, where the recording and/or transcription is stored, and in what medium it is stored. A citation for an oral interview with a woman in her sixties, made in the 1980s, in which the woman recounted events of the Depression or World War II, should have the researcher asking questions about the distance between the events and the report. The content and scope of the interview will be different if the interview was conducted by a local archive collecting stories for a documentary rather than a granddaughter writing a family history for a family reunion, and these differences should be carefully analyzed by the researcher. Careful attention to the source citation in these early stages can help the researcher raise questions that will benefit later research steps.

Narrative of the Research (Research Reports, Proof Summaries, Journal Publications)

Since genealogy, like history, "is an investigative discipline as well as a form of story-telling,"[8] the source citation should support any narrative report of the research process. Once a researcher has decided to share her research in written form, the challenge becomes how to make the narrative of the research and the footnotes tell two mutually reinforcing stories. A research report, proof summary, or journal article is typically written to show the depth, breadth, and thoroughness of the research or to prove a particular point. Family histories, biographies, and compiled lineages are written to tell a life story.

---

[8] Grafton, *The Footnote,* 232.

In either case, the footnotes should demonstrate the research steps and show that the information came from reliable sources. For though "no accumulation of footnotes can prove that every statement in the text rests on an unassailable mountain of attested facts," footnotes can and should persuade a reader to accept the researcher's conclusions and indicate which records the researcher has consulted.[9] In other words, the footnotes should be the undergirding of the story. The Curtis genealogy mentioned above is no longer standard for this very reason—we no longer expect hundreds of pages of research to rest on just a few specifically documented sources.

> **Footnotes should demonstrate the research steps and show that the information came from reliable sources.**

Biographical Writings (Compiled Lineages, Family Histories, Biographies)

In a report detailing research steps, footnotes often have the simple purpose of providing full archival information for the sources discussed and analyzed in the narrative above. In biographical writings, however, the footnotes must tell a separate but complimentary story to the narrative. For example, when describing the rate of infant mortality among a particular family in eighteenth-century England, a supportive footnote can explain if the rate was unusual or typical and provide the reader with further resources on the topic.[10] How much of this information goes into the main narrative and how much goes into the footnotes remains the prerogative of the author.

Additionally, researchers can use footnotes to fill gaps, explain reasoning, and provide supplemental resources that do not fit with the biographical structure of the writing. For example, unlike their American counterparts, many women in early modern England did not marry (upwards of 25 percent in certain locales at certain times). When writing a biography of a seventeenth-century English family, a discussion of the family's unmarried daughters could benefit from a footnote supplying the historical and demographic research that explains the context of marriage and singleness—even if the information is not incorporated into the main text.[11] Though this can lead to long footnotes, it leaves the main biographical text easier to read and navigate.

---

[9] Grafton, *The Footnote*, 22.

[10] Peter Laslett, *The World We Have Lost Further Explored* (New York: Scribner, 1984), 112. Laslett, using the work of the Cambridge Group for the History of Population and Social Structure, demonstrates that an average 70 percent of children survived to their tenth birthday. Only 54 percent of the children in this family survived to ten, but the average figure used by Laslett still allows for many families with higher and lower mortality rates.

[11] Judith M. Bennett and Amy M. Froide, eds., *Singlewomen in the European Past, 1250-1800* (Philadelphia: University of Pennsylvania Press, 1999); Bridget Hill, *Women Alone: Spinsters in England 1660-1850* (New Haven and London: Yale University Press, 2001); Amy Froide, *Never Married: Singlewomen in Early Modern England* (New York: Oxford University Press, 2005); E.A. Wrigley and R.S. Schofield, *The Population History of England, 1541-1871, A Reconstruction* (Cambridge: Cambridge University Press, 1989); Peter Laslett, *The World We Have Lost: England Before the Industrial Age*, 3rd ed. (New York: Scribner, 1984).

In conclusion, citation smoothes the research and writing process, ensures that the researcher does not claim another's writing as his own, and supports the claims of reports and biographies. The narrative report contains the analysis, but the footnotes are the framework upon which that analysis hangs. Careful attention to the style and content of citations both in research calendars and in final written products is the badge of an advanced genealogical researcher.

For Further Study

Bader, Jenny Lynn. "Forget Footnotes. Hyperlink." *New York Times,* 16 July 2000.

Barzun, Jacques and Henry F. Graff. *The Modern Researcher.* 5th ed. Fort Work: Harcourt Brace Jovanovich, 1992.

The Chicago Manual of Style: the Essential Guide for Writers, Editors, and Publishers. 15th ed. Chicago: University of Chicago, 2003.

Curtis, Harlow Dunham, comp. *A Genealogy of the Curtiss-Curtis Family of Stratford, Connecticut, A Supplement to the 1903 Edition.* Stratford, Conn.: Curtiss-Curtis Society, 1953.

Grafton, Anthony. *The Footnote: A Curious History.* Cambridge: Harvard, 1997.

Himmelfarb, Gertrude. "Where Have All the Footnotes Gone?" *New York Times Book Review,* 16 June 1991.

Laslett, Peter. *The World We Have Lost Further Explored.* New York: Scribner, 1984.

Mills, Elizabeth Shown. *Evidence Explained: Citing History Sources from Artifacts to Cyberspace.* Baltimore: Genealogical Publishing Company, 2007.

Turabian, Kate. *A Manual for Writers of Researcher Papers, Theses, and Dissertations: Chicago Style for Students and Researchers,* revised by Wayne C. Booth, Gregory G. Colomb, Joseph M. Williams, and the University of Chicago Press Editorial Staff. 7th ed. Chicago: University of Chicago Press, 2007.

19

Writing a Quality Research Report

Linda K. Gulbrandsen, AG

Ask any researcher to envision a perfect day in the world of genealogy, and you may hear about a visit to a particular library, courthouse, or archive, immersed in wonderfully old, musty records. Or that researcher may wax eloquent about an expedition to a cemetery or ancestral home town, or a connection with a new-found relative. For others, this ideal day might include the discovery of an elusive record or a DNA report that answers a decades-old ancestral quest. Very rarely will be found the researcher who envisions a perfect day ensconced in front of a computer, compiling research results into a fully documented and cited report!

The reality for an excellent genealogist is that a portion of his research time is committed to the necessary, sometimes tedious, task of committing his research work to some permanent format. Few, if any, researchers can or will delegate to others the preparation of source-cited reports, research logs or calendars, lineage charts, tables, and timelines that are the natural byproducts of their research.

What happens if you as a genealogist don't take the time to commit the results of your research to some type of permanent memory? Your important research work is likely to be lost forever. Even if

> The time you expend in synthesizing thousands of facts and minutiae into comprehensive, meaningful reports or articles will constitute some of the most valuable time you can spend as a genealogist.

your files (or hard drives!) are stuffed with documents and facts representing months or years of diligent work, that evidence will be of less value to others without any corresponding written analyses and summaries of evidence. Whether your research is undertaken for personal research or as a professional researcher for clientele, the time you expend in synthesizing thousands of facts and minutiae into comprehensive, meaningful reports or articles will constitute some of the most valuable time you can spend as a genealogist.

The written report or article summarizing your research on a particular ancestor, family, or community of people is one of the most effective means of committing your work to permanent memory. It represents the "showcase" of your labors and is the most tangible evidence of what you have accomplished as a researcher. Through a report, you can share new discoveries about individuals and family relationships and communicate the progress or resolution of a specific research problem. You can describe challenges still ahead and outline plans to tackle them, setting the course for future research. And if you set that project aside for any period of time, a written report allows you or anyone else to easily resume research years later where you left off.

A professional, well-written report communicates and educates its readers about a particular research problem, while apprising them of evidence, or the lack thereof, that supports certain facts and conclusions. A well-written report embraces sound research methodology, solid analysis of evidence, and reasonable conclusions. A poorly written or presented report that is missing these elements detracts from the focus of the research. Reports with deficient analyses and explanations may even confuse or mislead the reader, who may then question your conclusions and recommendations for future research.

Writing a summary report as a standard practice in all your research endeavors will provide additional bonuses for your own research. Through the writing process of analyzing evidence and synthesizing data with reason and logic, certain "holes" or gaps in research are often illuminated that might otherwise never be noticed. These "holes" may include an overlooked record source, a possible avenue for future research not considered earlier, or a connection between neighbors and associates of the ancestor not previously recognized. It might be the sudden realization of the significance of certain details within a particular record already in your possession. A willingness to address these "holes" and exhaust every reasonable resource in seeking resolution to problems is part of what defines an excellent genealogist.

Components of a Research Report

Research reports vary in content and purpose, and no single style or format dictates the actual structure. Many different options and templates are acceptable in report writing. A major key to an excellent written report lies in a clear writing style and well-organized pres-

> **A major key to an excellent written report lies in a clear writing style and well-organized presentation of the research problem.**

entation of the research problem, using evidence that incorporates sound research methodology and reinforces solid conclusions.

A well-written report also includes certain components that support a clear and easily understood process of logic and flow. The inclusion or absence of these components often distinguishes the well-written report from a mediocre one. A professional research report will include these components, albeit not always in this order:

- a clear research objective;
- a brief synopsis of the background information upon which the research is based;
- a full analysis and explanation of all evidence examined during the research process, with any resulting conclusions;
- a summary of the evidence, with future research recommendations.

Research Objective

A well-defined statement of the research objective(s) in the introductory paragraph of the report establishes the purpose for what will follow. The stated research objective is usually simple and conveyed with one or two sentences, although it may expand to an entire paragraph. Sample research objectives: locating the marriage of an ancestral couple in Kentucky, identifying the maiden name and parents of a female ancestor, or determining the town of origin in New York of a family that settled in Ohio. The research objective should include specific names, dates, and events that clearly identify these individuals. Whatever the research objective, it should be reflected in the research work that follows.

When working as a professional researcher with a client, clearly understand the stated research objective of the client prior to your work on the project. A research report that is excellent in content and analyses may go largely unappreciated by the client if his *intended objective* was ignored, resulting in wasted valuable work time on your part. Also keep all subsequent research focused on the agreed objectives unless an alternative direction has been discussed and agreed upon in advance with the client.

A brief recapitulation of your research objective in the summary section of a research report is an effective way to bring it full circle. This restatement of the research objective, along with a summary of the research process, reinforces within the reader's mind the original purpose of the research and how it was resolved.

Background Information

A background summary of the ancestors or families of interest comprises another important component of the research report. Background information offers context and foundation for the research problem by establishing the facts and premises upon which the research was based. This summary usually includes a brief synopsis of previous research undertaken by you or others that is pertinent to this problem. It may also include unresolved issues that could be impacted by the anticipated research. The amount of detail given as background will vary, depending on

JANE DOE SMITH, AG®
ACCREDITED GENEALOGIST

P.O. Box 12345
Small Town, CA 99999
Phone 000-123-4567
JaneSmith@anywhere.com

HILL RESEARCH REPORT

1 January 2012

Rachel "J." (Hill) Keller was born 29 February 1839 in Pennsylvania.[1] Family records indicate that she was born in Monongahela City in Washington County. Rachel's death certificate states that her father's name was William Hill, and her mother's name was unknown.[2] Rachel Hill Keller died 29 May 1914 in Siskiyou County, California, and was interred in McLouth, Kansas, near her husband's grave.

Little is known about Rachel Hill prior to her marriage with Garret V. Keller of Leavenworth County, Kansas, in 1871. After their marriage, Rachel and Garret Keller resided in Alexandria Township, Leavenworth County, Kansas;[3] and by 1900 they resided in Union Township in neighboring Jefferson County.[4] Rachel moved to California sometime after the death of her husband in1901 to live near her daughters, where she died in 1914. Garret and Rachel's three children included Mary [May], born about 1873; Nancy, born about 1875; and Bertha (Birdie), born August 1879.

This research session focused on the identity of the parents of Rachel Hill, who were tentatively identified in this session as Samuel and Elizabeth Hill of Washington County, Pennsylvania. This theory disagrees with the father's name given on her death certificate as William Hill, which may be incorrect. Rachel's marriage to Garret V. Keller was also located during this research session in Dickinson County, Kansas. The following report details the research completed this session and provides suggestions for continued research to determine if Rachel was indeed the daughter of Samuel and Elizabeth Hill.

IDENTIFYING THE PARENTS OF RACHEL HILL

Obituaries obtained for both Garret and Rachel Keller provided valuable genealogical information and insights about their lives.[5] Rachel's obituary did not indicate the names of her

[1] Death record of Rachel Hill, County recorder's office, 1914, Siskiyou County, California, obtained through correspondence with county recorder's office. - See Document 20 in Research Report dated 30 June 2011.
[2] *Ibid.*
[3] 1880 U.S. Federal Census (Population schedule), Alexandria Township, Leavenworth County, Kansas, ED145 Sheet 10, Dwelling 80, Family 80, G.V. Keller household. National Archives T9_385. Ancestry.com 1900 United States Federal Census [database on-line]. (Provo, Ut. Ancestry.com Operations Inc., 2002). --See Document 21 in Research Report dated 30 June 2011.
[4] 1900 U.S. Federal Census, Union, Jefferson County, Kansas, Enumeration District 81 Sheet 49, Dwelling 202 Family 203, Garret V. Keller household. National Archives T623_483. Ancestry.com 1900 United States Federal Census [database on-line]. (Provo, Ut. Ancestry.com Operations Inc., 2002). --See Document 22 in Research Report dated 30 June 2011.
[5] Obituary of Garret V. Keller, *McLouth Times*, 4 July 1901, Page 1, obtained through correspondence with Kansas State Historical Society, November 2011; Obituary of Garret V. Keller, *Oskaloosa Independent*, Oskaloosa,

Sample Research Report.

the problem. At the very least, it should include the names of the primary ancestors of interest; relevant event dates that are known, e.g., birth and death dates; and the localities in which these events occurred. Relationships to other family members may also be mentioned, especially as they apply to the stated research problem.

As an example, the research objective in a particular case study was to identify the parents of Mary Wheeler who was born in 1875 in Hamilton County, Ohio. Background information included Mary's maiden name as Mary Jackson, her birth year and death date, and her birthplace in Indiana as provided by her death certificate. This certificate did not identify her parents' names, nor did her obituary. Previous research also located Mary in several federal census records as a married adult but not before her marriage. This background information can be summarized with details in a few brief sentences.

Unresolved issues also related to this research problem included an unpublished family history compiled by a great-granddaughter. The history reprised a family tradition in which Mary Jackson's parents died young, and she was farmed out to relatives as a child. A will was discovered in previous research for a Henry Jackson who resided in the same county where Mary may have resided as a child. Henry Jackson left a small personal bequest to his "beloved granddaughter, Mary Jackson," and Henry's calculated age allowed the possibility that he was Mary's grandfather.

A third background item included a federal census search that resulted in three different Mary Jacksons of similar age to the ancestor who were identified as children in different households of that same county.

Was the ancestor Mary Jackson one of these three girls in the census records of that particular county? Did Mary's parents die young, and was her father the son of this Henry Jackson? These types of unresolved issues, pertinent to the research problem, also merit inclusion as background information. With this information provided as a foundation to the research problem, the reader is now apprised of the pertinent facts that might impact subsequent research on this problem.

Providing adequate background information in a report not only clarifies the research problem for the reader (or client) but also protects you as a professional researcher. If your research ever comes into question, you have ensured that any records given to you by the client at the beginning of the project are documented and evaluated within the report and that your research was built upon this foundation of knowledge.

If you resume work on a project left untouched for some time, you can save significant time refreshing your memory with case details if you included background information in your previous reports. Even if you anticipate that the client is familiar with the facts surrounding the research problem, include a brief summary in the introductory section of the report that reviews the established evidence in the case upon which all subsequent research was based.

Research Process

The body of the research report should focus primarily on research results and the conclusions drawn from evidence gathered through that work. All records examined and the subsequent results of these searches, both positive and negative, should be included in this written report. Some evidence presented may provide direct proof of certain facts and relationships and require less explanation, e.g., a death certificate that documents an ancestor's date of death. That same certificate may also include other less direct, but equally pertinent, information relating to the research problem that requires additional explanations, e.g., the name of the informant who was a possible relative; the number of years the decedent was a resident of that city or state before death; or the place of birth, which could point to the ancestor's place of origin.

> **The body of the research report should focus primarily on research results and the conclusions drawn from evidence gathered through that work.**

Multiples pieces of evidence (or lack thereof) may be necessary to build a case of probable circumstance, in which no clear direct evidence can be found to prove a hypothesis or theory. Rather, many disparate pieces of evidence, when placed together, combine to support that hypothesis or to show its plausibility. In these instances, each piece of evidence must be analyzed by the researcher in a way that will be meaningful and clear to the reader, to show how that indirect evidence (piece of the puzzle) supports—or disproves—the hypothesis or theory of the research problem and any eventual conclusions. The report must help the reader understand the significance of the evidence, as well as any possible limitations, in providing definitive proof of a theory.

Keep in mind the potential reading audience as you present evidence in a research report, especially in cases involving circumstantial evidence. The points of evidence that support a particular conclusion may be crystal clear within your experienced researcher mind. But unless you present this information in a way in which the reader understands your flow of logic and the reasons for your conclusions, your research may not be valued in the way that is deserved by those who read it. Unless you know that your audience has extensive experience and knowledge of the records and research methodology of that ancestor's region, you may wish to gear your report to the reader as a novice researcher with little or no exposure to these records. Don't assume that the reader will understand such terms as "ecclesiastical jurisdictions" or "chattel deeds" or the potential significance of a witness's name on a land deed.

Include the results of pertinent negative searches, as well as positive ones, in a report. Documenting negative searches is a time saver in future research for you or another researcher who tackles this research problem again. Professional researchers are sometimes reticent to include the results of negative searches in their reports because they fear that a client will think these searches represent wasted time and money. If you as a researcher can justify the reason for the record search, your search is justified. You showed where the records don't include evidence of that particular ancestor, which leaves other options open to pursue in future research where the sought-for evidence may exist.

Summary of Evidence

Every research report should include a written summary of evidence located (or not located) during the research process and show how those results address the research objective. New evidence found should be reviewed to show how it supports or proves a theory, followed by any resulting conclusions. If new evidence does not resolve the research problem, clear explanations should show how the evidence has impacted or eliminated one or more theories and created new ones. Provide clear direction for future work through specific recommendations of research through available resources. Resources may include records found onsite in the immediate area or locale and those that require travel or correspondence to examine them.

Some researchers include a summary of their research results in the introductory paragraph of the report (after the statement of the research objective) that provides a preview for what will follow in the report. Again, report styles will vary, depending on personal preferences, and are not nearly as important as the content of the report itself.

Too many professional researchers gloss through or omit the final step of including recommendations for future work in the written report, especially when the research problem is still unresolved. They may feel pressure to finish the report quickly or fear that they are giving away "trade secrets" or research ideas that the client will then follow up on his own and discontinue the future services of the professional researcher. Rarely does this scenario actually occur. In fact, the opposite is more likely to occur. Most clients hire a professional researcher because they want someone else to do the research, either because of lack of time or interest or because they just don't know how. Surprisingly, it is more often through providing many suggestions and possible future scenarios that a client's interest and curiosity is piqued, with a greater desire to continue research to see "what lies ahead" in the ancestral search.

An important hallmark of an excellent genealogist is that he sees possibilities where others have given up and that he is willing to think "outside the box" in exploring records and ideas that others might not consider. It is more frequently the researcher who continually stretches his mind to consider these other possibilities who will find answers and resolve problems when others have long given up.

Writing to the Reader Audience

As you write any research report, consider first and foremost how it will be read and understood by the reader audience who will read it. This technique may facilitate how you organize and present your evidence in a sequence that flows smoothly from one section to the next and makes logical sense to the reader. A report often fills a dual role of "educating" the reader to sound research methodology as it presents research results. Hence, any research report should be geared to the reader's basic level of knowledge and experience with the research process but in a way that is not patronizing or condescending.

Brief explanations of research methodology utilized in the research process may also help the reader understand your course of action as a researcher. Explaining the significance of certain records or the purpose behind a certain research path may engage the client more fully with the project and spark his desire to learn more.

Include documentation that supports the facts and conclusions of the report. Documents are usually cited in the report through footnotes or endnotes. Always include complete source citations within the research calendar and the research report. Citation styles differ, but the source citations should be clear and consistent within the report and supporting documents.

Research calendars, photocopies of evidentiary documents, maps, lineage charts, and other records constitute important ancillary parts of a research report. Provide photocopies or digitized images of the original documents with the report, where possible, with the exception of certain records that can be easily abstracted, such as certain deed records. Inclusion of actual documents related to the report allows the reader to review the original records and follow the analysis of evidence. It also provides a visual support of conclusions and a reference point for future work.

Creating a Professional Research Report

Always take time to prepare research reports in a professional, well-written manner. Check for typographical errors and good use of grammar. (See the following essay in this book by Tristan Tolman on "Good Writing: Essential to Becoming an Excellent Genealogist.") Review the content of a report for consistency in logic and thought. Focus on brevity and clarity in expression. Avoid unnecessary verbiage and trite phrases.

Keep reports consistent to the particular "person" or "voice" in which it is written. A narrative format written in *third person* generally sounds more formal and may be preferable when the report will be shared with many. Example: "Robert Barker resided in Williamson County, Tennessee, during the Civil War, where he enlisted in the 49ᵗʰ Volunteer Infantry. . . ."

A report written in *second person* is a more informal report style with a personalized flavor that some researchers may prefer. Example: "Your ancestor lived in the parish of. . . ." Or, "Your ancestral line extends to. . . ." This style works well in a letter-report format.

Writing a report in *first person* is appropriate with a less formal letter-type report to a client or family member or in a cover letter that accompanies a formal research report. The cover letter may include a brief summary of research results with special explanations for unusual aspects of the session. Example: "I located the original document in the state archives rather than the county courthouse, as expected. . . ."

An alternate report-writing style, less preferred but occasionally used, reflects the researcher's "flow of consciousness" as he works through successive records during a research session and explains how evidence was located and analyzed. This report-writing style tends to focus more on the movements of the researcher than on the facts of the research, which may be distracting to the reader and make it more appropriate as a brief cover letter to the client.

For similar reasons, you may wish to avoid "travelogues" in research reports that recount a researcher's expeditions at various archives. A possible exception to this rule might be the mention of a significant document located in a unique location. In general, the more detailed descriptions of archival visits are better kept within a cover letter that accompanies the research report.

When possible, set aside a research report for a few days after writing it and then read it again for clarity and accuracy. Imagine that you are the client who is reading this report for the first time. Are your thoughts and rationale presented clearly and concisely? Does the report flow evenly from section to section? Was the research objective clearly addressed throughout the report in a way that the client will understand and follow easily? Was the research presented in the report consistent with the research objective, along with any conclusions? Were numerous recommendations provided to the client for continued research on this problem?

A cover letter that accompanies a formal research report provides a more personal forum through which to elaborate on informal aspects of the research project. Example items of discussion in a cover letter might include describing in greater detail how a particular record will be obtained, responding to client requests about data sharing and Web sites, establishing a timetable for completing future work, or dealing with the logistics of data entry with new records.

An important but sometimes less recognized aspect of excellent report writing is cultivating a positive tone in research report writing. A research report can be replete with negative searches and yet still reflect great possibilities with future work. Highlight the many places in which that ancestor did *not* show up, and point to other sources still available in which the needed evidence may appear. Avoid promises with unrealistic expectations or impossible solutions, and keep an open mind to unusual, valid possibilities when providing suggestions for future research. Many good researchers abandon a research problem long before all possible record sources and strategies have been exhausted.

Report Writing Time

The ratio of time spent in actual research versus time spent in report writing is a frequent question asked by novice professional researchers. This ratio varies among professional researchers, with some estimating that they spend one hour of report writing for every two to four hours of research, while others use one hour of report time for every hour of research. This wide variance in research versus report-writing time depends on a lot of factors, including the complexity of the research problem. A complex-evidence case will often require substantially more time to report and summarize effectively than a case that involves all direct evidence from primary sources.

Some researchers will conduct all of their research within a particular framework of time and write their summary report afterwards, while other researchers will write the research report as they move through the research process. This latter style can be very effective if a researcher isn't distracted by alternating back and forth between records and report. The researcher who "writes as he works" will often include more details that come to mind spontaneously during the research process, rather than trying to recall those same details several hours, days, or weeks after memories have faded.

Final Considerations

Write research reports on personal ancestral research, not just for clients, even if you don't anticipate that someone will read them. You will be taking important steps to preserve the valuable research work you have accomplished over many years. You may also be amazed with the frequency that a previously unconsidered record source comes to mind during the writing process that opens a blocked research path.

Write research reports on personal ancestral research, not just for clients, even if you don't anticipate that someone will read them.

Writing a research report may seem like wasted time to an inexperienced researcher who hasn't yet discovered its intrinsic value in the research process. Writing sometimes represents a monumental challenge to those less comfortable with synthesizing thoughts into a condensed, logical format. Ongoing practice in writing brief, informal reports with smaller, less-complicated research projects will provide a natural way for any researcher to develop his own style of report writing. The writing process will begin to flow and feel more comfortable.

People envision a time when pressing a magic button will automatically display a complete family pedigree that connects with every other human being who ever lived on this planet (all perfectly sourced and absent of any errors, of course!). Whether or not such an event might be realized in our lifetime, would it eliminate the need for a written genealogy of that family? Capturing your research work through a written record will enhance your research abilities and also provide an important means of preserving your work for generations to come.

For Further Study

Clifford, Karen. *Becoming an Accredited Genealogist: Plus 100 Tips to Ensure your Success!* Salt Lake City: Ancestry, 1998.

Mills, Elizabeth Shown. "Research Reports." In *Professional Genealogy: A Manual for Researchers, Writers, Editors, Lecturers, and Librarians,* ed. Elizabeth Shown Mills. Baltimore: Genealogical Publishing, 2001.

Remington, Gordon L. *Preparing the Client Report.* Audiotape of lecture presented at Federation of Genealogical Societies, August 1990. Online: Audiotapes.com, 1990.

Storey, William Kelleher. *Writing History: A Guide for Students.* New York: Oxford University Press, 1999.

20

Good Writing: Essential to Becoming an Excellent Genealogist

Tristan L. Tolman, AG

Good writing isn't just for English teachers and their students. Writing is a skill that many professionals, including genealogists, must develop in order to become excellent at what they do. Genealogists write reports to communicate with their clients, lesson plans to guide communication with their students, and books and articles to communicate with their colleagues. Good writing is an indicator that a genealogist is educated, articulate, and professional. It is critical that it is done well.

How do you become a good writer? First of all, learn and follow the rules of good writing. Too often, genealogists don't learn these rules, so they simply do whatever they think looks good at the time. Good writing isn't arbitrary—like any other discipline, there are rules for doing it correctly. Every excellent genealogist should have a style guide and a dictionary within easy reach of his desk and should refer to both of them often.

Second, in order to become a good writer, read! Good writers learn by reading the works of other good writers. The more you read, the more you learn how to write. Specifically, genealogists striving for excellence should take time to read genealogical literature written by excellent genealogists and learn not only about new methodologies and record sources but also about how to write concepts in a clear, correct way.

Following is an overview of some of the fundamental rules that excellent writers follow.

Write Clearly

In *Writing with Precision: How to Write So That You Cannot Possibly Be Misunderstood,* Jefferson Bates gives ten principles for improving clarity and precision of written documents:[1]

1. Prefer the active voice.
2. Don't make nouns out of good, strong "working verbs."
3. Be concise. Cut out all excess baggage. Keep your average sentence length under twenty words.
4. Be specific. Use concrete terms instead of generalizations.
5. Keep related sentence elements together; keep unrelated elements apart. Place modifiers as close as possible to the words they are intended to modify.
6. Avoid unnecessary shifts of number, tense, subject, voice, or point of view.
7. Prefer the simple word to the far-fetched and the right word to the almost right.
8. Don't repeat words, phrases, or ideas needlessly. But don't hesitate to repeat when the repetition will increase clarity.
9. Use parallelism whenever it is appropriate—that is, when you are expressing similar thoughts, make sure you write your sentences so that the elements are in similar or parallel form. But do not use parallel structure when expressing thoughts that are not truly similar.
10. Arrange your material logically. Always begin with ideas the reader can readily understand. If you must present difficult material, go one step at a time. Do not skip any steps. Arrange your format to give the reader every possible "handle" on the material.

Format Your Report or Article

Whether you are writing a research report, an article, or a lesson plan, your writing will usually be aided by the use of headings, subheadings, and captions and in some cases by appropriate charts and graphs. When writing or reviewing your own writing, ask yourself if the information you are providing relates to the given heading, or if it might better be presented under a different one. Perhaps the heading ought to be changed to be more expansive in its coverage, or with sub-captions to identify the component parts.

The format of a research report or article could be organized in any of the following methods:

- Flow of Research Analysis
- Chronological (either as work was done or by event dates)
- Geographical
- By Individual
- By Family Group
- By Specific Research Issue
- By Record Type

---

[1] Jefferson D. Bates, *Writing with Precision: How to Write So That You Cannot Possibly Be Misunderstood,* rev. ed. (New York: The Penguin Group, 2000), 21-22. This book gives a detailed description and many examples of these ten principles. It should be read by all serious writers.

Use Proper Grammar and Punctuation

Excellent writers know and adhere to the rules for proper grammar and punctuation. Poor use of grammar and punctuation flags your writing as sub-standard and may imply (however incorrectly) that your research is sub-standard, as well. Master basic grammatical rules, and refer to a style guide whenever you are in doubt. Following are several basic rules that every excellent genealogist should follow:

> **Excellent writers know and adhere to the rules for proper grammar and punctuation.**

Capitalization[2]

In addition to the words that begin a sentence, the general rule for capitalization is that proper nouns are capitalized. That is, the formal or official names, including titles, of persons, places, or things (i.e.: nouns). Titles are usually lowercased unless they come immediately before a person's name. Thus, *President George Washington* led our country, but *George Washington was the president of the United States.* This rule applies to military titles, academic titles, business titles, etc.

General Gates; the general
Professor Brown; the professor

Watch out for titles that are used in apposition before a name; these are not capitalized. In *Uncle Joe Brown,* uncle is capitalized because it is part of the name. However, in *my uncle Joe Brown,* uncle is a descriptive modifier (an appositive), not part of the name, so it is not capitalized.

General titles of genealogical sources, such as census records, probate records, and birth certificates, do not require capitalization. However, a specific title, such as the U.S. Census Bureau, is capitalized. Internet and the Web are both capitalized.

I learned about census records and the U.S. Census Bureau on the Web.

Names of ethnic and national groups, such as African Americans and Jews, are capitalized. However, designations based solely on color are usually lowercased.

Lowercase north, south, east, and west unless they represent regions, such as the South or the East Coast. Places that appear on maps are always capitalized, and so are adjectives derived from them. Names of mountains, rivers, and oceans are capitalized, as are the generic nouns that accompany these names.

Ireland; Irish
Mississippi River; the river

---

[2] For a much more detailed discussion of the rules of capitalization, see *The Chicago Manual of Style: The Essential Guide for Writers, Editors, and Publishers,* 15th ed. (Chicago: University of Chicago, 2003), chapter 8.

Names of many major historical events are capitalized, but common and more recent events are often lowercased. Names of religions are capitalized. Names of most major wars are capitalized, but the general term war is lowercased when it is used alone. Numerical designations of a time period are lowercased unless used as part of a proper name. Check a style guide for the rules on capitalizing specific time periods.

> *Boston Tea Party; the baby boom*
> *Civil War; the war*
> *The twenty-first century*
> *Baptist*
> *The Middle Ages; the medieval era*

Abbreviations[3]

Do not abbreviate United States as U.S. unless you're using it as an adjective. When you are abbreviating the name of a state, use its two-letter, no-period postal code only in the context of a full mailing address. Otherwise, either write out the full state name or use its accepted abbreviation.

> *U.S. regions; the United States*
> *Arizona* (for running text), *AZ* (for a postal address), *Ariz.* (when an abbreviation is needed, such as in a table or bibliography)

Commas[4]

Items in a series are normally separated by commas. There has been widespread debate about whether a serial comma is needed before the conjunction that joins the last two elements of a series. *The Chicago Manual of Style* strongly recommends adding the serial comma. If any elements of a series already contain internal punctuation, use semicolons rather than commas to separate the elements of the series.

> *Probate records, census records, and land records were searched.*
> *We examined birth, marriage, and death records; church records; and the census.*

Although it is not imperative to add commas around Jr., Sr., and Inc., if commas are used they must appear both before and after the term.

> *Both John Yeamans and John Yeamans Jr. were included on the tax list.*
> *Both John Yeamans and John Yeamans, Jr., were included on the tax list.*

---

[3] See *Chicago*, 15.29 and 15.34. A list of standard abbreviations can be found in *Chicago*, 15.29.
[4] For a much more detailed discussion of the proper use of punctuation in writing, see the following sections of *Chicago:* for commas, 6.18-56; for hyphens, 5.92-93, 6.80-96, 7.82-90; for apostrophes, 7.16-31, 9.34, 9.37; for quotation marks, 6.8-9.

Hyphens

It is generally correct to hyphenate compound modifiers that come before a noun. However, some stylebooks argue that familiar terms such as real estate, high school, and law enforcement are read as single units and therefore require no additional linkage. Do not hyphenate adverbs to the words they modify, even when the two words make up a compound modifier. Names of ethnic and national groups can be hyphenated if they act as a compound modifier before a noun.

> *The poverty-stricken family*
> *British-American trade*
> *African-American culture*
> *A widely known publication*

Apostrophes

Apostrophes are not generally used to make words plural. They are used to create contractions and make nouns possessive. However, there can be exceptions to this rule. To indicate two or more of the letter "a," it is permissible to write *a's* rather than *as,* to avoid confusion. The possessive form of *it* is written without an apostrophe, *its,* while the contraction of *it is* is written *it's.*

Apostrophes are not used to write out decades. Write 1850s, not 1850's. If an abbreviated form of a decade is needed, the apostrophe should be placed where part of the number was removed. The 1850s are the *'50s,* not the 50's.

> *Its settlers arrived in large numbers during the 1850s and 1860s.*
> *It's time for our annual conference.*

Quotation Marks

Commas and periods always go inside quotation marks, but colons and semicolons never do. Question marks and exclamation points go inside quotation marks if the quote is the question or exclamation.

> *The article, which is entitled "Research in Maryland," is excellent.*
> *The following individuals were "indent men":*
> *How does one define "reasonably exhaustive research"?*

Numerals[5]

Some stylebooks recommend writing out numbers one through nine and using numerals for 10 and above. Others suggest writing out numbers one through one hundred and using numerals for 101 and above. *Chicago* generally recommends writing out numbers one through

---

[5] For a much more detailed discussion of writing numbers correctly, see *Chicago,* chapter 9. For writing dates, see also *Chicago,* 6.46.

one hundred, round numbers, and any number beginning a sentence. However, in a list of several numbers or in a comparison of two or more quantities, consistency should be maintained so that if one must be written as a numeral, all of the numbers in the list should be numerals.

> *The building is three hundred years old.*
> *Howard Cash owned three parcels of land: 300 acres, 170 acres, and 80 acres.*
> *One hundred and ten acres were purchased*

Percentages are always given in numerals. It is generally preferred to use the word *percent* rather than the symbol % in running text, unless numerous percentage figures are being discussed.

> *The American population increased by 35 percent between 1790 and 1800.*

Although the most common way to write dates in the United States is the month-day-year style, genealogical writing usually uses the European day-month-year system. The month-day-year style requires a comma both before and after the year, while the day-month-year system needs no commas. In either case, always write out the month; do not use a number (such as 5 for May) to abbreviate the month. When a month and year are given with no day, do not use commas.

> *On February 22, 1732, George Washington was born.*
> *George Washington was born on 22 February 1732.*
> *The Constitution was ratified in June 1788.*

Correctly Use Diacritics and Symbols

Diacritics are marks near or through one or more letters that indicate a phonetic value that is different from the unmarked letter. Genealogists, especially those who research in countries other than the United States, should become familiar with the diacritical marks of the languages they deal with and learn how to re-create those marks in their writing when necessary. It is possible to create most international language accent marks on American computer keyboards using ALT key codes and charts, which can be found online and in the word processor's program (look for the character map).

Beware of marks and symbols that may confuse the reader, such as the English pound sign: £. Many people do not know what various symbols mean, so always explain an uncommon symbol before using it in running text, or in an appropriate footnote.

Use Parallel Construction[6]

When writing a series of elements, each item in the series should be parallel with the others. For example, if one element contains a verb, then the other elements in the series should also contain a verb.

Emigrants left England, sailed to America, and settled in Massachusetts.

Bulleted lists need parallel construction. If the first item in a bulleted list contains a subject and a present-tense verb, then the rest of the items in the list should also contain those same elements. Each item in the list should be a continuation of the introductory sentence and should contain the same key components as all the other items in the list.

Our objectives were to do the following:
- *Locate John Vail in the 1850 census.*
- *Determine whether John Vail left a will.*
- *Identify all of John Vail's children.*

Time spans can be expressed conversationally (with *from* and *to* or *between* and *and*) or as units (with a hyphen between the years). However, the styles should not be mixed. For example, do not write *from 1882-1900.*

Italian immigrants settled in the area from 1880 to 1900.
Italian immigration was heavy between 1880 and 1900.
Italian immigration peaked in 1890-1891.

Develop Your Writing Style

Every writer develops a writing style, and your style will help reflect who you are and give your writing personality. "Style" refers to a choice of one correct alternative over another for the sake of consistency and an appropriate level of formality.[7] Although there are many rules for good writing that must be mastered, not every situation has a definitive rule. On matters of style, select a style and stick with it—be consistent.

Whether you have been hired to perform research for a genealogical company or you are writing an article for a genealogical magazine or journal, find out that company's or publication's style before writing the report or article. Do they prefer active or passive voice? Bulleted lists or narrated paragraphs? Footnotes, endnotes, or citations in parentheses within the text of the report? On matters where *The Chicago Manual of Style* and *The Associated Press Stylebook* differ,

---

[6] For an excellent discussion about parallel construction, see Bill Walsh, *Lapsing Into a Comma: A Curmudgeon's Guide to the Many Things That Can Go Wrong in Print—and How to Avoid Them* (Chicago: Contemporary Books, 2000), 74, 110-111, 140-141, 175-176, 182-183.

[7] Bill Walsh, *The Elephants of Style: A Trunkload of Tips on the Big Issues and Gray Areas of Contemporary American English* (Chicago: McGraw Hill, 2004), xi.

Becoming an excellent genealogist requires that you not only know how to research but that you also know how to present your findings in a clear, correct, and understandable way.

which stylebook do they prefer? Does the company or publication provide a style guide that indicates its preferences on these and other matters? If so, get one and follow it.

Genealogists will face many more situations in their writing than is possible to cover in a single chapter or essay. When you are writing and you have a question about how to do it properly, find out the answer! Look it up in your style guide or dictionary, and then follow the rules. Becoming an excellent genealogist requires that you not only know how to research but that you also know how to present your findings in a clear, correct, and understandable way. Learn to write well!

For Further Study

Bates, Jefferson D. *Writing with Precision: How to Write So That You Cannot Possibly Be Misunderstood,* rev. ed. New York: The Penguin Group, 2000.

The Chicago Manual of Style: The Essential Guide for Writers, Editors, and Publishers. 15th ed. Chicago: University of Chicago, 2003.

Hoff, Henry B. *Genealogical Writing in the 21st Century,* rev. ed. Boston: New England Historic Genealogical Society, 2006.

Walsh, Bill. *The Elephants of Style: A Trunkload of Tips on the Big Issues and Gray Areas of Contemporary American English.* Chicago: McGraw Hill, 2004.

Walsh, Bill. *Lapsing Into a Comma: A Curmudgeon's Guide to the Many Things That Can Go Wrong in Print—and How to Avoid Them.* Chicago: Contemporary Books, 2000.

21

Making Sure Your Work Survives You

Anne Leptich, AG

The obituary of the family genealogist appeared in the newspaper. The dates and places were properly noted. The life story was detailed; the personality and accomplishments of the recently departed were praised and elevated to an abnormal height; and the survivors were listed with their families and geographic locations. But wait! She was also survived by an enormous collection of genealogical research material and many shelves of family history books. Piles and piles of loose papers reside on the desk and dining room table of the dearly departed. Then there is the matter of all of the computer equipment and family heirlooms. And what will happen to all of the yet-to-be-identified family photographs?

How many stories have been whispered throughout the genealogical community concerning the disposal of the assortment of collected family history materials and boxes of papers upon the passing of the researcher? There are tales of family gathering at backyard burnings, flea market sales of old photos and family Bibles, and storage in the attic. As each of these stories has been related to us in social settings, we have all gasped in amazement at the waste of thousands of hours of good genealogical research. Although these stories horrify us at the time we hear them, they usually do not move us to action with our own holdings. Perhaps we seriously consider steps toward organization, but the business of everyday life soon overtakes our thoughts and actions.

I personally have cleared out four homes of loved ones after their demise. The most difficult part, aside from the emotional trauma and sadness, was trying to understand their intent for the distribution of each item. And none of these relatives was into genealogy. As children, we used to laugh at the pieces of masking tape on the bottom of family treasures, naming the person earmarked for inheritance. During each time of cleaning, I wished for pieces of masking tape with a name clearly written by the deceased. I wished for any clue that could make me feel compliant with their wishes.

Think of your own collection. Is it safe in a room dedicated to the pursuit of dead ancestors? Or is it co-mingled with the dining room decor? Perhaps it is under, around, and on top of the extra bed. Is it even collected, or is it mixed with other papers and publications throughout your home? Does anyone else know where it is or how to find it, let alone how to disperse it?

Now that you have a picture in your mind of the fruits of your endeavors strewn about in various places, try to imagine organization brought to the chaos. Think of your living next of kin. Does anyone in your family value your collection as you value it? If they value each piece of information as having been part of you, do they understand the significance and intended placement of each? Would they know the difference between a pedigree chart and a family group record, or a research log?

What about your computer? Do you have your database program current, properly documented, and copied? Have you shared a copy of it with someone outside the family?

Remember the family stories and traditions. Are they still simply in your head? Have you tried to interest someone in your family with listening to the stories? Have you passed them on to your children? Do you think it might be time for you to put them in writing?

Have you labeled old photographs and scanned them into your computer program or saved them onto a CD? This would be a fun project to do with your grandchildren. You could share stories and your love of family history with them while saving an important piece of their heritage.

It is later than you think! Now is the time to prepare your collection to outlive you. An overall plan with goals and checkpoints would be the ideal beginning for your organization. There are several parts to your collection, and they all need to be handled differently. But basically you will label it, donate it, compile it, store it electronically, or toss it.

> **Now is the time to prepare your collection to outlive you.**

Try to organize your collection into categories. You can make lists, use the tried-and-true masking tape program, or place the items together in stacks.

Label It

The concept of the label is simple. Create some type of labeling system for self-contained items that will remain in your possession. For example, you might have photocopied an out-of-print book, or part of a book, that was necessary for your family research. It is housed in a binder on a shelf. Because this book is a clear violation of copyright laws, it will need to be destroyed rather than donated to a repository, unless it is in the public domain. You will need to give a clear directive to that effect. Place a label in the front cover of the binder, directing a toss into the recycle bin.

Books are part of this category. Books still in use can be labeled now and placed back on the shelf, while books you have finished using can be donated for the benefit of others. The label on each shelved book should give clear instructions to the "cleaner and sorter." Name the intended recipient specifically with contact information. I use fluorescent colored mailing labels and print them in quantity from the label-making program on my computer. Here are examples of several I use.

"This book is to be donated to _____" (list address and contact information)

"This binder was used for research only and needs to be recycled"

"This compilation is of my _____ family and can be given to anyone who would like to have it. There are electronic copies in several places."

"This is the supporting information for _____computer"

"This _____ came across the plains and belonged to _____. Please donate to the DUP museum."

At this point, you can label everything in your office and collection that you decide to keep, including furniture, furnishings, and computer equipment. Remember the value of the torn pieces of masking tape on the bottom of fancy dishes.

Donate It

You will have to do the work to choose a suitable place for your donation. Contact repositories for their guidelines concerning donations. Remember that anything donated becomes the property of the recipient, and you then lose all control over what happens to the item. Here is a sample of some repositories and their rules.

The Family History Library in Salt Lake City has a donation guideline sheet that can be requested. Basically they outline the same thing other organizations tell you—when you donate something, it becomes the property of the repository. If you donate a family history book or CD that you have created, the Library will ask you to sign a document giving them permission to film or digitize the material. The material then becomes usable on the FamilySearch Web site for the benefit of a greater number of people.

Allen County Public Library no longer has a guideline sheet. Unless the money to organize the collection is donated with the collection, it cannot be organized and will not be accepted. They prefer books or compilations or money to buy books of their choosing.

The Genealogical Forum of Oregon accepts all donations. They sort them and make the following decisions: place on the shelves or in the vertical file; sell duplicate items at white elephant sales; store in boxes in the back room; or simply toss. As with most institutions, they are limited by the lack of willing volunteers and workers.

Multnomah County, Oregon, Library accepts only books or carefully prepared manuscripts. The items may be kept at the main library, sent to a branch, or tossed. They like money or promises of money in the future.

Universities usually accept only the collections of famous characters, historians, or researchers. Others need not apply. The exception to this rule is a collection that is truly valuable for research. Examples would be something like the Draper Manuscripts or the Zabriskie Collection.

Museums, in the cases of artifacts and heirlooms, are a little more lax in their guidelines. They usually keep and store most items but do not necessarily place them in displays. The exception is in the case of famous or infamous ancestors.

If your donation is made to a non-profit organization, a tax deduction can be taken. The value of the collection is the true value, not the sentimental value or your hourly wage over a forty-year period. Since these rules change from time to time, it is always best to consult the society or your personal accountant about the amounts and the rules of donation.

Compile It

This is all about the large family history book you intend to publish. Break it down into pieces and finish a chapter or a section. Write stories about each ancestor or family and share the stories with living family members now. Enjoy the ancestral epic together. Talk about your family; get to know them—that means the ancestors and the descendants. Create a timeline and outline to finish each part of the whole. Stay on task.

Create a book of ancestral stories for your grandchildren, nieces, and nephews. Some adults might also prefer the illustrated method of learning about their heritage.

After you have completed each part of the huge book, throw away the leavings. They are no longer needed and only serve to keep your surroundings cluttered. If it is too hard to throw away the leftover sheets of paper, place them in a box with a toss directive on the label. When the project is complete, then toss the clutter.

If you do not wish to publish the book you have created, barter the job to a cousin who does no research but wants to have the information. The cousin can publish and market the book, if you research and compile it.

Keep in mind that it is less expensive to create a CD than a printed version of the book, and it is easier still to share the information on a family Web site. Think digitally when sharing your family heritage. I can remember trying to make a decision concerning the use of microfilm or microfiche as the best medium to preserve my collection of records. I have used both over the years, but now all we have to do is think digitally. However, you still need to make sure your Web site will survive you; insure that it is on a permanent Web site. Or, better still, burn it to a CD-ROM and distribute it to several libraries.

This is also about your computer database. Choose a computer genealogy program you can use. Choose one that will allow you to include photos, maps, and documentation of all information in the database. Hire someone to do the data entry for you, if necessary. Be sure to choose a program that has GEDCOM capabilities so that you will be able to share your information, including the photos and documents, with others. Your family history work is a work in progress—it will never be finished. Develop a system to back up data after each and every research and data entry session, to avoid loss of information and valuable work time.

Make a copy of your material every three or four weeks, and share as you go. Choose a relative or friend who does not live in the same house as you do, and give this person a copy of your records. Make sure there is always a copy of your material in another location. One way to share is to place the information on a personal or family Web site and remember to keep it current.

Preserve It Electronically

Due to the ever-changing and improving technical landscape, it is difficult to give a detailed step-by-step outline about how to save your material. The best advice would be to check out the options and make a choice based on the stability and longevity of the medium you choose. About twenty years ago, I thought the best medium would be microfiche. Well, today there are few fiche readers available, and although the medium is relatively stable and the material could be harvested from the fiche, it is rarely used as the "go-to" medium.

We are now in the computer and Internet phase of electronic storage. Basically, we think we have reached the pinnacle of information storage; however, the same principles of stability, accessibility, and longevity should guide your decisions today.

Toss It

After the decisions have been made to label, donate, compile, and preserve your information, what is left? You might still have things laying around, such as: marriage information about a couple with one of your surnames, who was married in the 1600s; family group records that do not fit into your tree anywhere; a pedigree chart you do not recognize; an address and telephone number of someone you do not remember; and a paper with just a name and date on it. If any of the information on these sheets of paper can be interpreted and documented and placed in your database, do it. Otherwise, if it is of no good to you, no one else will want it either.

Then you have the pens and pencils. Try them, many of them no longer write. There is a stack of old ring binders on the shelf. They will not be used because your database is in electronic format. In one desk drawer there are old floppy disks. These floppy disks no longer fit any slots in your current computer. Hopefully you harvested all of the valuable information from these disks long ago.

There is also the old computer and printer on the floor in the corner. Take these relics to the recycle location for old electronics. It will make you feel better to have an empty spot on the floor.

A large box—or several large boxes—contain the leftover photographs. These are not the treasured family pictures, because you have already scanned and saved and shared all of those. These are photos that can be expendable. Have you ever taken a photograph of your foot by mistake—and then kept it?

Toss it all.

Finally

Now that you have organized your collection to outlive you, consider the convenience of no-clutter research. As each research item is completed, it can be handled with the label, donate, compile, store electronically, or toss method of storage. It is easier to "live" with less clutter. Do not think of this process as morbid. Think of it as making life simpler for those who will be left to decide the ultimate outcome of something they do not understand or value properly. Think of the "cleaner and sorter" job and offer a little help with your own version of the masking tape process. How happy would you have been at any time in your life as a researcher to have received an organized, documented package of genealogical material?

22

Paleography: Abstracting, Transcribing, Translating

Ruth Ellen Maness, AG, and Heidi G. Sugden, AG

There's simply no getting around it. Records are written in the handwriting style of the recorder. That style reflects the time period, the training, the personality, and perhaps even the physical condition of the recorder. To become an excellent genealogist, you will have to learn to read the handwriting style for all the time periods and records you are dealing with. That may be Germanic or Scandinavian Gothic, English, Early American, French, Flemish, Dutch, or Polish. However, no matter the country or time period, no matter if it's a land record, church record, census, will, probate inventory, or civil registration record, there are paleographic principles and procedures that, if followed, will lead to success. Those

> To become an excellent genealogist, you will have to learn to read the handwriting style for all the time periods and records you are dealing with.

principles are: (1) you learn to read the script by reading it, and (2) you learn to read the script by writing it. The first procedure is: practice, practice, practice, practice, and the second procedure is more practice, of both principles!

Record keepers all over the world use the writing style that they were taught for their time, but changes in the simple system can and do occur. Age, illness, stress levels, personalities, and maybe even an accident with the milk cart, or falling down after celebrating too many marriages, all take their toll on handwriting styles. Consequently, the handwriting of each record keeper eventually started to look somewhat different from that of his classmates. The one thing that remained a constant is that they all learned to form their letters the same way.

Practice Writing the Script

The letters they wrote began on the writing line and then went along the line and sometimes also above or below the line, depending on the letter. As you learn to recognize the ascenders, descenders, and letters written along the writing lines, you'll be able to read the record. That

means if you will take a few minutes each day and practice writing the basics of the letters the record-keepers used, you will also be able to read the handwriting style used in that country and time period.

> ## As you learn to recognize the ascenders, descenders, and letters written along the writing lines, you'll be able to read the record.

As you form the letters with your pen and follow the movements of how the letters were written, a connection is made between your hand and your brain. Then, as you trace the letters in an actual record, you will be able to decipher the letters that are there. Even if the words and place names are foreign, once you have the letters down, you can always check a dictionary or gazetteer to identify that word or place name.

Compare What You See with What You Already Know

The second procedure to use when deciphering the letters in a name, place name, or word is comparison. Find what looks like that same name, place name, or word in the same record and time period. Write or transcribe the letters you can recognize, leaving blank spaces for those you don't. When you then look at the parts, your mind may automatically fill in the rest. If you are dealing with foreign languages, remember that the English language already contains two of the major language bases of the world: the Germanic language base and the Romance (Latin) language base. Sometimes if you "get out of the way" and let your mind work, it will recognize things you did not even know you knew when reading the records.

Isolate the Letter

Isolate the letter(s) you are trying to read and compare it with others. Put your thumbs, fingers, pieces of paper, or cards on either side of what you think is the single letter. As you note the writing motions that were used to create the letter, you may discover what the letter is, because you've practiced writing it!

Try another Letter

Try another letter in place of the one you think it is. Does the word, place, or name make phonetic sense with that letter there? In other words, does it sound right? For example, in German Gothic script, the Gothic script small *e* looks like an English *n*. By inserting an *e* for what looks like an *n* in the record, the word, name, or place name may make sense.

Locate Vowels

If the same-shaped letter appears over and over in many words, it is probably a vowel. The Germanic- and Romance-based languages of the world use the same vowels you already know: a, e, i, o, u and sometimes y and w.

Think Phonetically

Remember, the record keeper recorded what his ears heard, and he wrote it down the way he thought it should be spelled, both for names of people and also for names of places. Think phonetically when doing any kind of research, but particularly European.

Remember That Letter Usage Changed

Letter usage may have changed over time. For example, in older Scandinavian records, instead of Å or å , two a's could have been used. That person or place name would then come at the beginning of the alphabet in older indexes or gazetteers. For example, Håkongard is the same place as Haakongaard. In older Scandinavian records, an E could replace the Ä at the beginning of a place name. Älvsborg County, Sweden is the modern spelling of the older "Elfsborg" County, Sweden. In Germanic records, Ä, ä, Ö, ö, Ü, and ü could be written as Ae, ae, Oe, oe, Ue, and ue.

Also, keep letters and letter combinations in mind that could be used in place of others such as the small sampling here:

a used for *e*	*g* used for *k*	*tj* used for *ki*
b used for *p*	*i* used for *j*	*u* used for *i*
c used for *k*	*ig* used for *ich, isch*	*ch* used for *k*
ch used for *k*	*k* used for *ck, ch, g*	*v* used for *w*
d used for *t*	*q* used for *k*	*w* used for *v*
e used for *ae, oe*	*s* used for *c, z*	
f used for *v*	*t* used for *th*	

Find the Same Person in a Different Record

The vital events in a person's life recorded in church records could include christening (infant baptism), birth, confirmation (age 11-20), engagement, marriage, death, burial, vaccination, moving in or out, public absolution (illegitimate child), communion (taking the sacrament), pew tax, and so forth. Civil records, such as censuses, tax lists, probate records, land records, and state recording of births, marriages, and deaths (when required), could also list your ancestor. Any or all of the above types of records might be written in a clearer hand than the one giving you trouble. Search all the records that cover the time period in which a life event could have been recorded for your ancestor. One may be more clearly written and/or include more information than the other.

Construct an Alphabet

Construct an alphabet using the letters the writer used. The minister and/or official generally served for a long time in the same place. Even though his general writing pattern remained the same over time, some entries will likely be easier to read than others. By constructing an alphabet using the writer's own letters, comparison will be easier.

> **Construct an alphabet using the letters the writer used.**

Take a piece of paper and fold it lengthwise. List all the letters of the alphabet in print form for the country in which you're working, both capital and small letters. Then, go through the records. Eventually, you will find a capital A that you know for sure is a capital A. Write that letter on your sheet *exactly* as the record keeper has written it, next to your printed version. Find a small "a" and do the same thing, all the way through the alphabet. Then, as you come across difficult-to-read letters, you can refer to your own homemade guide to identify it. In this way, if you leave the record for awhile, you can minimize the time needed to familiarize yourself with the handwriting style again.

Look for Patterns

Analyze several pages before and after the page you need to decipher, and become familiar with the way the record keeper organized the information on each page. Ask yourself the following questions:

- Is the name of the child, the mortgagor, the person writing the will, or the taxpayer, etc. being underlined or written in a larger or different script?
- Are the names of the groom and bride underlined or written in a larger or different script?
- Is the name of the child, bride, groom, grantor, or grantee, etc. written alongside the entry or in the margin?
- Is the principal event date always given first in the entry?
- Does the "legalese" follow the same pattern?
- Is the occupation and/or residence given before or after the name of the father or the principal person in the entry?
- Are the places of residence always listed after the witnesses' names in the birth, christening, or marriage entries?
- Does each entry begin its own line, or does each entry begin where the last one left off?
- Are there other pieces of information centered in the middle of the page or in a column down one side or the other?
- Are there columns labeled *birth, marriage,* and *death,* with check marks in the appropriate columns?
- Is the entry indented or out-dented?

Many other items besides those listed above could constitute a pattern in the record. Take time to study the record you are working with, and the pattern will eventually appear and make sense to you.

When reading foreign language records, keep in mind that the record keeper often wrote the name of the principal(s) in the Latin or Roman style of handwriting you learned in school. The additional details, such as place name, occupation of father, witnesses, and so forth may have been written using letters of that country's script style. By taking a few steps upfront to familiarize yourself with the record keeper's patterns, you will save time. Your eyes and mind will tell you if something is out of sync, out of place, or somehow different than the pattern, as you go through the records. Learn to listen to those hunches with writing- and record-keeping patterns.

For example, because most country parish church buildings and civil record-keeping offices were small, the number of witnesses at a child's birth registration, christening, or marriage was often limited. A study of the patterns within a record will alert you to information you may otherwise miss. For instance, if you notice that each entry in a record is given a standard three- or four-line space before the next entry, but you see one entry taking more than those standard lines of space, it will signal your subconscious mind to stop and identify what is happening in that entry.

If you're reading a church record, an extended entry might indicate unusual circumstances surrounding the birth, which the recorder has noted. The mother may have been traveling through the village and her time to deliver a baby came right then. Or the child may have been illegitimate, or the mother may have been pregnant by force. Such notations, if they happen to be recorded for your ancestor or his family, are the substance that adds meat to the bones of your family history.

The pattern and content of the records themselves can help you read them. Keep in mind the following items of information that might be included—any or all of them—as you work with vital records of any country:

Birth or christening record: child's given name, birth date, christening date, whether the child was legitimate, parents' names, father's residence, godparents and their residences, witnesses to the christening and their residences, mother's age, infant's death date, vaccination date, and date of the mother's introduction back to the church. Generally, the further back in time, the fewer pieces of information will be recorded.

Engagement or marriage record: groom's name, bride's name, respective residences prior to marriage, occupation or position in the family, ages or birth or christening dates, birthplaces, dates and places of confirmation, parents' names, parents' residences, marriage date, date of banns or engagement, morning gift, whether it is a previous marriage for bride or groom, probate information, names of the bondsmen or marriage witnesses, and place of marriage if not in this parish church or this civil jurisdiction.

Death or burial record: name of the deceased or reference to the principal male figure in his life ("Johan Schmidt's wife / child"), occupation or position in family, date of death and/or burial, father's name, mother's name, spouse's name and occupation, martial status, residence, cause of death, age or birth or christening date, obituary or biographical information, place of burial, cost of burial and/or bells, and date of death memorial.

In other types of records, look for the pattern of the "legalese." Familiarize yourself with the words and the positions where the names of the parties involved would be written. Then, as you look through the records, your mind will again let you know if something is "out of sync."

Use Indexes

As a general rule, entries in parish and civil records are entered in chronological, not alphabetic, order. However *always* look in the front, back, and middle of the record book for an index, and check the library catalog reference for those records to see if an index is available. Sometimes you might be pleasantly surprised. Look for typed or transcribed indexes that may cover other types of records found in the geographic area you're researching. They may help you read the names you're struggling with. Even if the index doesn't begin until much later than the actual record, searching it will give some idea of the surnames used in the area.

Use Logic

Do the letters you are stringing together phonetically make sense within the context of the language you are reading? If it looks like gobbledygook, it possibly is.

Months of the Year

The first three letters of the months in Germanic-based languages (used in Germany, "Germans from Russia" colonies, Denmark, Iceland, Norway, Sweden, Finland, Austria, Switzerland, and the Netherlands) are the same first three letters as in English. However, the spelling of the months in the Romance languages (Spanish, French, Italian, and so forth), the Slavic languages (Polish, Russian, Hungarian, and so forth), and anything recorded in the "Cyrillic" writing style will probably be different.

Numerals

Numbers written in numerical form are still numbers, even in records of a different language. For example, although a record keeper may have written words in Gothic script, his numbers will appear basically the same as those with which you are familiar. Remember, however, that Roman numerals were also a part of the Latin language system (Latin being the language of the learned), so those may also be used in records all over the world. In some of the older western European records, including Scandinavia and Germany, the Roman numerals listed below may be used to designate the indicated month of the year.

VIIbr or 7br = September	IXbr or 9br = November
VIIIbr or 8br = October	Xbr or 10br = December

Generally, when a date is written as "12/8 1750" in foreign records, the day of the month is the first number listed (the one on top) if the entry is recorded in that manner. This example is 12 August 1750, not 8 December 1750. Scan several entries to be sure you understand the date pattern of the particular records you're reading. Occasionally, record keepers reversed the dates with the month on top, or listed first. Cross check the date against other records for that person and other dates in the record you are reading.

As a final note: The religion of many Eastern European countries was Catholic. Their records were very often kept in the Latin language until the mid to late 1800s, and the records were written in the Latin script which we use—so don't be afraid to at least try and read records of your ancestors who may have come from those countries.

To become an excellent genealogist, use the principles and procedures mentioned herein, and use common sense. Look for the patterns and common elements in each record. Practice the handwriting style of that which you're trying to read. "Get out of the way" and let your mind work, and you'll be pleasantly surprised at how much you really can read, no matter which country, which language, or which record type you have to deal with. You can do it!

For Further Study

Aiplatov, G.N. & A.G. Ivanov. *Russkaia Paleografia.* Moscow: LOGOS, 2003.

Beránek, Karel. *Pismo Našich Llistin a Listůod 12. Do 20. Století* (The development of Czech alphabets used in manuscripts from the 12th to 19th centuries), Praha, 1976.

Brouwer, Hans. *Beknopte handleiding tot de kennis van het Nederlandsche oude schrift:* (*Reading old Dutch script*) Naarden (Nederland): N.V.Uitgevers-Mij A. Rutgers, 1941.

The Church of Jesus Christ of Latter-day Saints. *French Records Extraction: An Instructional Guide.* Salt Lake City: Family History Department, 198-?.

The Church of Jesus Christ of Latter-day Saints. *Scandinavian Records Extraction: An Instructional Guide.* Salt Lake City: Family History Department, n.d.

The Church of Jesus Christ of Latter-day Saints. *Spanish Records Extraction: An Instructional Guide.* Salt Lake City: Family History Department, 1981.

Grun, Paul Arnold. *Leseschlussel zu Unserer Alten Schrift.* Limburg an der Lahn: C.A. Starke Verlag, 1984.

Haarstad, Kjell and Aud Mikkelsen Tretvik. *Gotisk Skrift: En Tekstsamling.* Trondheim: Tapir, 1981.

Jensen, Larry O., *A Genealogical Handbook of German Research.* Rev. ed. USA, 1978.

Johansson, Carl-Erik. *Thus They Wrote: A Guide to the Gothic Script of Scandinavia.* Provo: Brigham Young University Press, 1970.

Kirkham, E. Kay. *The Handwriting of American Records for a Period of 300 Years.* Logan, Utah: Everett Publishers, 1973.

Minert, Roger P. *Deciphering Handwriting in German Documents.* Woods Cross, Utah: GRT Publications, 2001.

Ribbe, Wolfgang and Eckart Henning. *Taschenbuch fuer Familiengeschichtsforschung.* Neustadt an der Aisch: Verlag Degener & Co., 1975.

Sperry, Kip. *Reading Early American Handwriting.* Baltimore: Genealogical Publishing Company, 1998.

Thompson, Edward Maunde. *A Handbook of Greek and Latin Paleography.* Chicago: Argonaut, 1966.

Free Online Tutorials and Resources for Learning to Read Early American and Foreign Handwriting (Script)

BYU free online tutorials. http://cebyu.edu/is/site/courses.

Czech Republic Script.
     https://www.familysearch.org/learn/wiki/en/Czech_Republic_Handwriting.

Dutch Script. https://familysearch.org/learningcenter/lesson/reading-dutch-handwritten-records-lesson-2-dutch-words-and-dates/29.

Early American Script.
     https://www.familysearch.org/learn/wiki/en/United_States_Handwriting.

English Script. https://familysearch.org/learningcenter/lesson/english-script-tutorial/90.

French Script. https://familysearch.org/learningcenter/results.html?q=French%20handwriting.

German Gothic Script.
   https://familysearch.org/learningcenter/results.html?q=German%20gothic.

Italian Script. https://familysearch.org/learningcenter/lesson/reading-italian-handwritten-
   records-lesson-3-reading-italian-records/20.

Polish Script. https://familysearch.org/learningcenter/lesson/reading-polish-handwritten-
   records-lesson-1-polish-letters/210.

Portugese Script. https://familysearch.org/learningcenter/lesson/reading-portuguese-hand
   written-records-lesson-1-portuguese-letters/213.

Russian (Cyrillic) Script. https://familysearch.org/learningcenter/lesson/reading-russian-hand
   written-records-lesson-1-the-russian-alphabet/31.

Scandinavian Gothic Script. https://familysearch.org/learningcenter/results.html?q=*&fq=
   place%3A%22Scandinavia%22.

Slovakian Script.
   https://www.familysearch.org/learn/wiki/en/Slovakia_Language_and_Languages.

Spanish Script. https://familysearch.org/learningcenter/lesson/spanish-script-tutorial/92.

23

A Brief History of the Accreditation Process

Jill N. Crandell, MA, AG

The study of history frequently reveals events that have transformed our world, events which may not have seemed momentous at the time they occurred. Looking back, historians are able to analyze these historic changes with the knowledge of what followed, thereby recognizing their relative importance. The early 1960s brought forth several such events in the field of genealogy, culminating in the birth of credentials for professional genealogists. By 1964, two credentialing programs had been developed by two separate sponsoring organizations, forever changing the world of professional genealogy.

The concept of credentialing genealogists was not a new idea in the 1960s. Donald Lines Jacobus had expressed his concerns about the profession and its lack of credentials as early as 1930:

> Conditions in the genealogical profession are unsatisfactory. Any person, regardless of education, experience or natural ability, can set up to be a professional genealogist. No course of training is required, no examinations as to fitness have to be passed. For this very reason, the profession appeals to many who lack the mentality for this kind of work, and who might be unsuccessful in other professions.[1]

On 30 December 1942, Milton Rubincam presented a paper at the second annual meeting of the American Society of Genealogists (ASG) and stated that "too many inexperienced per-

---

[1] Donald Lines Jacobus, *Genealogy as Pastime and Profession* (Baltimore: Genealogical Publishing Company, 1971), 40.

sons are calling themselves professional genealogists when they lack proper training in this specialized type of work." He concluded, "The Society should investigate the capabilities of professional genealogists, and, if satisfied with their qualifications, should permit them to state on their letterheads and in their advertisements, 'Approved by the American Society of Genealogists.'"[2] In spite of these concerns, it would be another twenty years before a credentialing program was begun. After so many years, what were the needs of the genealogical community that finally provided the impetus to begin professional credentialing?

The Beginnings of Accreditation

The Church of Jesus Christ of Latter-day Saints founded the Genealogical Society of Utah (GSU) in 1894 for the purpose of assisting Church members in identifying their ancestors.[3] By 1924, the GSU board established a Research Bureau assigned to oversee the instruction of members, to coordinate and prevent duplication of genealogical efforts, and to undertake member research requests at a low cost. However, because of the growth of the Church and the rapid increase in genealogical activities over the next several decades, the board came to realize that the GSU research service could not continue to be provided for all members.[4]

By October 1961, the volume of requests had overwhelmed the research department, and costs were well beyond the payments being received. Department researchers were up to five years behind in completing requests. Board members proposed a number of solutions, including the suggestion "to establish a standard by which our library facilities could be used by other researchers,"[5] but attempts to resolve the problem first focused on internal solutions. Henry Christiansen suggested that the research department needed "50 to 60 new researchers and that it would be up to a hundred in the near future."[6] Two months later, the board voted to raise the charge for research to $2.50 an hour, effective January 1962.[7] By the next fall, GSU leaders were again discussing the overload of work in the research department,[8] and on 19 November 1962, the minutes state, "The research situation has not appreciably changed. We are unable to work out our backlog of research orders."[9]

The board then reoriented its focus from an internal solution of raising fees and adding employees to recommending professional researchers outside of the society to relieve the volume of requests. However, board members were concerned that GSU should only recommend qualified researchers. At the time, there was no way to know which genealogists had the necessary skills to produce quality work. In response, "Frank Smith and Henry Christiansen were appointed to meet and prepare suggested testing outlines in order to license researchers for com-

---

[2] Milton Rubincam, "The Status of Professional Genealogists," *The American Genealogist* 20 (July 1943): 2, 8.
[3] James B. Allen, Jessie L. Embry, and Kahlile B. Mehr, *Hearts Turned to the Fathers: A History of the Genealogical Society of Utah, 1894-1994* (Provo, Utah: BYU Studies, Brigham Young University, 1995), 11.
[4] Allen, Embry, and Mehr, *Hearts Turned to the Fathers*, 105-108, 185.
[5] Genealogical Society of Utah (Salt Lake City, Utah) "Board of Trustees Minutes, 1894-1975," vol. 7, 19 October 1961.
[6] GSU Minutes, 19 October 1961.
[7] GSU Minutes, 28 December 1961.
[8] GSU Minutes, 16 October 1962.
[9] GSU Minutes, 19 November 1962.

mercial research in [the GSU] library."[10] Almost a year later in April 1964, Eric B. Christensen passed the Danish exam and became the first Accredited Genealogist researcher.[11]

Professional genealogists responded positively to credentialing, and by the end of 1964, eighteen individuals held a total of twenty-four accreditations.[12] Two months later, Brigham Young University announced that all instructors of genealogical courses at the university were required to pass the GSU accreditation exam for their area of expertise.[13] Within a two-year period, the accreditation program quickly relieved the backlog of requests in the GSU research department, and on 13 April 1966, the board decided to discontinue patron research by the end of the calendar year.[14] As of 31 December 1966, eighty-eight professional genealogists held 110 accreditations in sixteen testing areas of the world.[15]

The Beginnings of Certification

While the Genealogical Society of Utah was developing the accreditation process between 1961 and 1964, the American Society of Genealogists was also responding to the need for lists of qualified genealogical researchers. At the society's 1961 annual meeting, Dr. Jean Stephenson proposed "that the Society consider the preparation of lists of persons apparently qualified to work in certain areas, such lists being compiled by means of a qualifying examination to be given, by mail, to applicants, and those who meet certain standards be recorded as having done so."[16] The following year, at the October 1962 ASG annual meeting held in New York City, "the Chairman [*sic*] of the Committee on Standards, Miss [Jean] Stephenson, reported that . . . the Library of Congress and The National Archives felt the American Society of Genealogists or the National Genealogical Society should furnish them with a list of competent genealogists and that with the increasing interest in genealogy some standards should be set up."[17] After considerable discussion, the society appointed a Committee to Investigate Certification of Professional Genealogists, chaired by Noel C. Stevenson, with Archibald F. Bennett and Dr. Jean Stephenson as committee members. The committee was to bring a concrete proposal to the next annual meeting.[18]

During the 1963 ASG annual meeting held in Boston, Noel Stevenson presented his committee's report,[19] and Walter Lee Sheppard Jr. was appointed as chair of the committee to carry out the recommendations.[20] As a result, the Board for Certification of Genealogists (BCG) was

---

[10] GSU Minutes, 8 May 1963.

[11] GSU Minutes, 5 May 1964

[12] 1964 annual list of Accredited Genealogist researchers created by the Genealogical Society of Utah and transferred to the International Commission for the Accreditation of Professional Genealogists on 31 August 2000.

[13] "Genealogy Teachers Get Exams," *Church News* (Salt Lake City, Utah), 6 February 1965, p. 6, col. 5, Web edition http://archive.deseretnews.com/historic.

[14] GSU Minutes, 13 April 1966.

[15] Annual lists of AG researchers created by the GSU, 1964-1966.

[16] John Frederick Dorman, Fredericksburg, Virgina, to Jill N. Crandell, letter, 18 July 2009, quoting ASG newsletters in his possession.

[17] Williams B. Saxbe Jr., American Society of Genealogists Secretary, Boston, Massachusetts, to Jill N. Crandell, e-mail, 15 July 2009, quoting ASG minutes.

[18] Saxbe to Crandell, e-mail, 15 July 2009.

[19] Henry B. Hoff and Malcolm H. Stern, "The American Society of Genealogists, The First Fifty Years: 1940-1990" (Philadelphia, 1990), 5.

[20] Saxbe to Crandell, e-mail, 15 July 2009, citing ASG newsletters.

incorporated in June 1964, and an additional credentialing program for professional genealogists had begun. The following year on 21 February 1965, Dr. Jean Stephenson became the first Certified Genealogist.[21]

Both the AG and CG credentials have been well-supported by the professional community since their inception. Advertisements in *The Genealogical Helper* included references to accreditation and certification as early as 1965,[22] and both credentials have been consistently displayed since that time.

Amazingly, there does not appear to have been any coordination or cooperation between GSU and ASG as both organizations simultaneously designed professional credentialing programs. GSU worked in Utah to resolve the issue of an overloaded research department, and ASG in Washington, D.C., responded to the request from the National Archives and the Library of Congress for lists of qualified researchers to distribute at their repositories. The solution to both issues involved establishing a method to evaluate the research skills of professional genealogists so that the sponsoring organization would have confidence in those individuals being recommended. In December 1964, Milton Rubincam included the following statement in his report to the ASG fellows:

> Although The American Society of Genealogists took the initiative in establishing the Board [for Certification of Genealogists], it worked closely in this connection with President Carleton E. Fisher of The National Genealogical Society, President Walter Muir Whitehall of The New England Historic Genealogical Society, and Past President Roy F. Nichols of The Genealogical Society of Pennsylvania. The Board for Certification of Genealogists . . . is an independent body and not connected with any other organization.[23]

It seems reasonable that if ASG had also coordinated with the Genealogical Society of Utah, then GSU would have been mentioned in this report. Neither the minutes of GSU nor the minutes of ASG make any mention of the other organization or indicate any knowledge of an effort beyond their own to create a genealogical credential.

In addition to the coincidental timing, Archibald F. Bennett could have been a coordinating link between the two programs. Mr. Bennett was an ASG fellow, and he was also a member of Noel Stevenson's committee that was appointed in 1962 to develop a proposal for a credentialing

[21] "BCG History," http://www.bcgcertification.org/aboutbcg/bcghistory.html, accessed 9 June 2009.
[22] *The Genealogical Helper* 19, (June 1965): 61 and (December 1965): 311.
[23] Milton Rubincam, Chairman of the Board of Trustees of the Board for Certification of Genealogists, Report to the Fellows of the American Society of Genealogists, 5 December 1964.

program. Mr. Bennett was from Utah, and he served as the secretary of the Genealogical Society of Utah from 1928 to the end of June 1961.[24] From that point forward, Archibald Bennett was in charge of the GSU genealogical library but no longer served on the GSU board, and he was not in attendance at meetings when the accreditation program was created. All assignments and reports to the board were handled by Frank Smith and Henry Christiansen.[25] Archibald F. Bennett died in 1965, and although many articles described his numerous genealogical accomplishments, none attributed any contribution to the accreditation or certification credentials.[26] On the surface, a link between the programs seems logical, yet the records of the time do not support that conclusion. It appears that a series of concurrent events came together in both the eastern and western United States, culminating in the creation of two unrelated professional credentials within the same few years.

The evaluation processes for accreditation and certification were unique from the beginning. The two sponsoring organizations approached their appraisal of researchers' abilities from different perspectives. Accreditation has always been based on expertise in a specific geographic locality, and applicants are required to submit a four-generation research project with its associated report. The application, once approved, is then followed by a

> ## The evaluation processes for accreditation and certification were unique from the beginning.

two-part written exam taken in person at an approved testing site, traditionally the Family History Library in Salt Lake City, Utah. The written exam is designed to evaluate researchers' knowledge, as well as their application of that knowledge in the analysis and evaluation of research problems. Upon successful completion of both parts of the written exam, an oral exam is conducted with several specialists in the applicant's area of accreditation. Because GSU has microfilmed records around the world and made them available for research in the Family History Library, accreditation has always been available for the United States and many foreign countries.

Certification is based on a portfolio submission from the applicant and does not require on-site testing. Researchers submit work samples, including a client research report, a case study, and a kinship determination project, as well as document analyses and research plans. The work samples are then evaluated by three to four judges who look for quality research, good judgment, accurate interpretations, adequate documentation, and an understandable report. Originally, the certification process focused on credentialing U.S. researchers, but BCG has since expanded certification to include special interests in foreign countries.[27] Although accreditation and cer-

---

[24] Allen, Embry, and Mehr, *Hearts Turned to the Fathers,* 95, 167-8.

[25] GSU Minutes, 1961-66.

[26] "A.F. Bennett, 69, Succumbs," *Deseret News* (Salt Lake City, Utah), 30 August 1965, A-10 and Arnold K. Garr, Donald Q. Cannon, and Richard O. Cowan, eds., *Encyclopedia of Latter-day Saint History* (Salt Lake City, Utah: Deseret Book Company, 2000), 87-8.

[27] Board for Certification of Genealogists Web site, http://www.bcgcertification.org.

tification employ different evaluation methods, both credentials seek to appraise the competency of genealogical researchers in skills essential to the professional. Both organizations require those who qualify to sign the organization's Code of Ethics.

Growth and Change in Accreditation

Accreditation exams were administered by GSU for thirty-five years, resulting in a steady increase in the number of genealogists holding the AG credential. However, at the end of 1999, GSU considered various options for ending its sponsorship of the accreditation program. The Utah Genealogical Association (UGA) was asked to submit a proposal for the creation of a non-profit organization to continue maintaining the credential independent of GSU, and on 25 February 2000, the UGA board created an Accreditation Committee. Jimmy B. Parker was appointed chairman, with Ray T. Clifford and Jill N. Crandell as committee members.[28] GSU also made arrangements with the Board for Certification of Genealogists to allow AG researchers the option to transfer an area of accreditation to certification with BCG.[29] The Genealogical Society of Utah officially transferred its sponsorship of accreditation to the International Commission for the Accreditation of Professional Genealogists (ICAPGen) on 31 August 2000.[30] At that time, letters were mailed to all current AG researchers to notify them of the change. During its sponsorship of the accreditation program, GSU granted a total of 546 accreditations to 477 genealogists.[31]

Jimmy B. Parker

During its first year of operation, the ICAPGen commission was chaired by Jimmy B. Parker, with Ray T. Clifford and Jill N. Crandell as commissioners. An advisory committee was also created, with Kory L. Meyerink, Louise LaCount, Karen A. Clifford, and George R. Ryskamp as members. Testing and renewals were suspended during the transfer of sponsorship. Testing began again on 15 October 2000, and five-year renewals for current AG researchers resumed 1 January 2001. Because the accreditation program was no longer supported financially by the Genealogical Society of Utah, it became necessary for ICAPGen to charge testing and annual fees. A year after the transfer of sponsorship, the bylaws for ICAPGen had been drafted and approved, and an election had been held, which resulted in the first full commission meeting on 1 December 2001 in Salt Lake City, Utah. At that time, Jimmy Parker resigned and Carolyn J. Nell was appointed commission chair. Additional executive committee members

---

[28] Utah Genealogical Association (Salt Lake City, Utah) Minutes, 25 February 2000.

[29] Thomas W. Jones, "BCG Invites AG Transfers!" *OnBoard: Newsletter of the Board for Certification of Genealogists* (September 2000): 17.

[30] Letter from Richard E. Turley Jr., Salt Lake City, Utah, to Jimmy B. Parker, 15 September 2000; held by ICAPGen, P.O. Box 4464, Salt Lake City, Utah 84110-4464.

[31] Annual lists of AG researchers created by the GSU, 1964-2000.

were Karen A. Clifford, first vice-chair; George R. Ryskamp, second vice-chair; and Jill N. Crandell, executive secretary; with commission members Ray Clifford, David Dilts, Ruth Maness, Kory Meyerink, Jimmy Parker, Larry Piatt, Paul Smart, and Marion Wolfert.[32]

Changes continued at a rapid pace. The Southern States accreditation region was divided into the Mid-South and Gulf-South regions, and emeritus status was approved for retiring Accredited Genealogist professionals in good standing. ICAPGen began the long process of registering the AG and Accredited Genealogist certification marks with the United States Patent and Trademark Office, completing the registrations on 9 December 2003 and 2 January 2007, respectively.[33] ICAPGen established a Web site, http://icapgen.org, and began sponsoring an annual conference for professionals. Classes at the conference include a track for individuals interested in becoming accredited in the future.

In recent years, the number of testing areas has continued to expand. Native American and African American testing have been added to the southern testing areas, and regional librarian accreditation is now available. In the western United States, testing areas have been added for the Great Plains, the Mountain West, and the Pacific States.[34] Historically, tests administered by the Genealogical Society of Utah were conducted exclusively at the Family History Library in Salt Lake City, Utah. For some, the travel expense prevented completion of their credentialing process. Recognizing this challenge, the ICAPGen commission approved the Genealogy Department of the Allen County Public Library in Fort Wayne, Indiana, and the DAR Library in Washington, D.C., as alternate testing sites, with plans to move to worldwide testing locations in the near future.

Over the years, the accreditation program has adapted to the progress of technology and its impact on today's research strategies. Techniques for locating and searching digitized sources could not have been imagined in the microfilm era of 1964. As the demand for professional genealogical research expands around the world, more areas of testing continue to be offered. Although there

> **ICAPGen is committed to maintaining the rigor of accreditation exams and the quality that the credential represents.**

have been changes in testing to stay current with the shifting needs of professional researchers, ICAPGen is committed to maintaining the rigor of accreditation exams and the quality that the credential represents.

---

[32] International Commission for the Accreditation of Professional Genealogists Minutes, 1 December 2001.
[33] United States Patent and Trademark Office, http://tess2.uspto.gov.
[34] "New Accreditation Regions, http://icapgen.org/Programs/new.htm, accessed September 2007.

24

When to Hire
a Professional

Tricia H. Petrey, AG

Your mother did it. Your grandmother did it. It's a pastime . . . a family project . . . a personal responsibility . . . and you're good at it! Why would you ever need to hire a professional? Genealogy is one of the most popular hobbies in the world, yet unlike most hobbies, all of the resources necessary for its pursuit are rarely at your fingertips. The truth is, there are few genealogists at any level who "do it all"; who have the time, resources, and ability to perform every aspect of research or family history they desire and still do it thoroughly and well.

It does not take long for the serious genealogist to realize that successful research and family history are most often a collaborative effort—and not just among fellow researchers and hobbyists. The most successful genealogists, and even research companies themselves, have learned the value of hiring other trained professionals in order to achieve their goals and simultaneously maintain a standard of excellence in their work. When lack of time, resources, or ability is the issue, hiring a trained professional brings the relief and satisfaction of knowing that your goals will be met in a timely and efficient manner with the standards you expect. In addition, exposure to professional methods and results can serve to advance your own skills as a genealogist.

Consider the following roles a professional may play in advancing your research goals and individual skills as a genealogist:

As a Partner

Professional researchers and research companies often market their services to beginners, or to those who would rather hire someone than do the work themselves. But what is not apparent is the number of advanced genealogists and family historians who regularly hire professionals for a variety of reasons, most often to access remote records or to conduct specialized research. When lack of time, resources, or skills is the issue, the professional acts as a "right arm" of sorts; he or she becomes a partner with the researcher in realizing goals that might not otherwise be accomplished.

A researcher living in New York City might hire a professional researcher in Salt Lake City to search through volumes of New York City vital records on microfilm. Not only is hiring the professional more cost effective and efficient than ordering the records onsite, but the researcher can be confident that the experienced professional understands the complicated indexes and records and will conduct the searches with an eye for the inconsistencies and variations inherent in New York City vital records. It is this trust that forms the basis for what becomes a partnership with the hired professional.

A seasoned family historian might be so busy gathering and compiling family records that she does not have the time to conduct the necessary painstaking research, or to prepare the detailed application required for membership in the Daughters of the American Revolution (DAR). By hiring a professional experienced in the preparation and research for such applications, she can focus her time elsewhere, confident that her application will be prepared with exactness and will meet all of the society's requirements. The professional she hires becomes a partner in the realization of her family's goals.

And then there's that Irish line, the Native American mystery, or that orphaned grandmother of your own. When you've taken the research as far as you can go and are experienced enough to know your limits, it's wise to call on a professional rather than spend countless hours spinning your wheels . . . or reinventing the genealogical wheel! If you wish to become skilled in that specialty area of research, a professional consultation could set you off on the right foot or spur you on when you've come to a standstill. There is wisdom in consulting an expert when you lack expertise.

From foreign language research and translation to the search for natural parents or living descendants, what one researcher does not have the time, resources, or skills for, an experienced career professional does. And in the end, that researcher is still able to maintain the high standards and quality of work he expects, as if he had been able to do the work himself. The professional is a trusted partner of the experienced researcher.

> # The professional is a trusted partner of the experienced researcher.

As a Technician

We've all seen the large glossy pedigree charts, beautifully published family histories, and expertly digitized photo albums that appear to go far beyond the capabilities of our own computer programs. Most of us have dedicated hundreds or even thousands of hours to family history research and would love the results of our research to be available to family, friends, and others around the world, if only we had the time to put it all together! Personal genealogy computer programs are continually evolving to provide you with a variety of options for publishing your family history. However, when it comes to producing high-quality, publishable material, most of us are limited by the type of equipment we own and the lack of technical skills required to produce the desired results. And ultimately the majority of us would rather be in the library than reading through detailed "how-to" manuals on graphic design, Web design, photo editing, and publishing.

There are professionals to help in every aspect of genealogy and family history, and the technical assistance available is not limited to computers. Experts might be hired for videography, oral interviewing, record preservation, and genealogy documentation. Most of these services are offered through larger professional research companies but can, of course, be found independently as well. From a small data-entry project to a full-scale, multi-volume family history incorporating all of these techniques, professionals are there to do what you do not have the time for, or the resources or inclination to take on. A professional can become the "technical arm" you need to share your family history with others.

> **There are professionals to help in every aspect of genealogy and family history, and the technical assistance available is not limited to computers.**

As a Mentor

There are obvious reasons to call upon a professional, but the less-obvious reasons may be some of the most valuable, particularly for the genealogist striving to advance his research skills. One of these reasons is to hire a professional genealogist for the sole purpose of being mentored.

Mentoring is a time-tested method for outstanding professional and leadership education. The word "mentor" immediately brings to mind any wise and trusted guide, such as a college professor or a counselor in a specific field of education. A mentor is often a master of a trade or a subject who inspires through wisdom, experience, and example. With regards to advanced genealogy, the adoption of a professional mentor could greatly enhance or direct your education and sharpen your skills as a researcher.

Most hobby genealogists, by nature, have a limited scope of research and experience, defined by their specific family lines or the projects required for course assignments to obtain a degree. Career genealogists, on the other hand, are repeatedly exposed to a variety of research problems and questions, which often require them to develop alternative research methods, or delve into lesser-known sources in order to find the answers. Over time, these experiences develop an expertise in the professional that is unmatched in the field. Repeated exposure to this kind of expertise in methodology, research, and analysis could prove very valuable on your path to achieving excellence as a genealogist.

The Personal Case Study

Consider selecting a difficult research problem, a "road block" of sorts, and then hiring one or more trusted and experienced career professionals who specialize in that area of research for a consultation or for a full research project. After providing details of what you may have already done in your own research on the problem, pay close attention to the educated strategies proposed in a consultation, or to the research sources, methods, and analysis used together in a full research project. This type of process will either help you to gain confidence in your own skills by confirming methodologies and sources you already suspected, or will expand your view of possible approaches to challenging research problems.

For example, in a Midwestern U.S. research project, a professional might introduce you to lesser-known religious groups in the area, or topographical features that could have affected the migration or settlement patterns of your family. The professional might do a combined study of local plat maps and tax records to prove relationships, or introduce you to valuable manuscripts or other collections that are key to research in that locality. Similarly, hiring a professional to tackle an early immigration problem might reveal lesser-known naturalization laws, unsuspected land records, and lateral research methods that shed light on your family's origins.

The professional research report you receive would not be unlike valuable case studies you've read or heard about in books, articles, and lectures. However, when the professional is hired by you, the insights gained are specific; they are tailored to your particular research problem. The detailed knowledge and use of local records might never be covered in a regional research article or lecture. Local research guides may list key sources particular to that area, but it is the professional researcher who reveals overlooked details of the records and sometimes unusual methods of using them together to solve a research problem. Because the project is personal and familiar, you are more likely to retain the details and methods the professional used and apply them to additional projects, enhancing your own research skills in the process.

> **It is the professional researcher who reveals overlooked details of the records and sometimes unusual methods of using them together to solve a research problem.**

The Written Report

Perhaps the most valuable aspect of hiring a professional genealogist as a mentor is the access to written reports for an in-depth research project. The level of education and experience of a professional genealogist is very often reflected in her ability to write a clear and thoughtful report, which outlines the research methodology and analyzes the results. Writing a report forces the researcher to stop and think. In fact, it is in the report-writing process, more than any other stage of genealogical research, that critical thinking and analytical skills truly come into play.

The whats, whys, and hows of each step taken in the research process require knowledge, not only of genealogy methods and sources, but of history, culture, law, environment, and even human behavior. The critical thinking comes in determining how these factors interplay and how they influence the choice of records searched. The analytical skills are required to determine the value of that interplay as evidence. Putting it all into words helps to ensure that the thinking is clear, the reasoning is sound, and the evidence is solid.

> The level of education and experience of a professional genealogist is very often reflected in his or her ability to write a clear and thoughtful report.

A professional research report differs from a published article or essay in that the research is usually still in process when the report is written. Therefore, the actual thought processes of the researcher can be more closely followed, broken down step by step. A well-written report is a glimpse into years of education and experience. It reflects the nitty-gritty of excellence—the skills that separate the good genealogists from the great genealogists. Reading the report with the intent to learn will reveal knowledge, thought patterns, and methodology, which you can use to enhance your own skills. The insights gained by hiring a professional as a mentor can be invaluable as a means of expanding your education. Repeat this process with a number of different related, or even unrelated, projects, and your insights will be multiplied.

Conclusion

Why in the world would you hire a professional? Why in the world would you not hire a professional, if your budget allows for it? The benefits of accessing the time, resources, and skills of qualified, experienced professionals only serve to lengthen your genealogical arm and expand your educational horizons, while maintaining the highest of standards. Whether genealogy is your lifetime hobby or your business pursuit, professionals fill a variety of roles on the path to achieving your goals.

For Further Study

Association of Professional Genealogists. "Hiring a Professional." http://www.apgen.org/
    articles/hire.html.

Cottrill, Natalie. "When, Why and How to Hire a Professional Genealogist." http://www.
    progenealogists.com/whentohire.htm.

Gormley, Myra Vanderpool. "When to Hire a Professional Genealogist." http://www.genealogy
    .com/20_myra.html.

25

ICAPGen Accreditation Process and Procedures

Carolyn J. Nell, AG, FUGA

Deciding to become an Accredited Genealogist[1] professional sets a researcher on a path headed for adventure. The journey is worthy of the reward: the prized AG credential.

Claiming the AG credential begins with competency testing, which applicants pursue on their own schedule. Hundreds of genealogists have taken the accreditation tests since 1964. By thoroughly adhering to the steps presented in this introduction, applicants will be prepared to successfully submit their application and proceed to the proctored tests and oral exam.

Prerequisites for Submission and Testing

Prior to beginning the accreditation process, applicants must meet two standards:

1. Select a geographical region in which to specialize. The geographical regions are listed online at ICAPGen Accreditation Regions, http://www.icapgen.org/icapgen/regions.

2. Complete a minimum of 1,000 preparation hours in research and education in the desired region of specialty. The forms for completing and recording these hours are online at ICAPGen Application Forms, http://www.icapgen.org/icapgen/applicationforms. Applicants with fewer than 1,000 hours of research experience and education in their selected geographic area generally do not pass the accreditation test. Most genealogists require even more than 1,000 preparation hours. Qualifying hours include those spent in researching record sources,

---

[1] Accredited Genealogist and AG are one credential represented by two registered marks with the United States Patent and Trademark Office (USPTO) in Washington, D.C.

reading methodologies, searching the Internet for records and contacts, visiting libraries, corresponding with clients or repositories, attending classes and conferences, and more.

The Testing Committee realizes some veteran researchers may have difficulty completing the Research Experience Table because the required information from previous years of research needs reconstructing. Under these circumstances, the applicants are to record the information to the best of their abilities. The oral reviewers may ask questions about the specific places and record types included on the Research Experience Tables.

Overview of the Testing Process

The ICAPGen accreditation testing process is divided into three distinct levels, which recognize the achievements of applicants at each level:

> The ICAPGen accreditation testing process is divided into three test levels, which recognize the achievements of applicants at each level.

- **Level 1:** a four-generation application project and accompanying application
- **Level 2:** a four-part written exam testing knowledge of record content and usage
- **Level 3:** a two-part written exam testing skill in data analysis, research planning, methodology, and report writing; and an oral exam

Level 1: Written Application

Level One includes the submission of the Accredited Genealogist application, which has three parts:

1. The Contact Information form[2] and accompanying fee
2. The Accreditation Application form[3]
3. The four-generation research project

To complete the four-generation research project, applicants find a family in their selected geographical region and trace its lineage for four generations. Since the purpose of the study is to demonstrate the applicant's research abilities, the families must have lived in the geographic area prior to 1900—for at least some portion of their lives. (For example, if the applicant selected the U.S. Mid-South geographical region, all four generations must have lived in one or more of the seven states in that region at some point.)

---

[2] The Contact Information form can be accessed at ICAPGen Application Forms, http://www.icapgen.org/icapgen/applicationforms.

[3] The Accreditation Application form can be accessed at ICAPGen Application Forms http://www.icapgen.org/icapgen/applicationforms.

The written report of this lineage study demonstrates the applicant's focus on accuracy, thoroughness, accountability, and professionalism. The report does not have to recite every step undertaken researching these families during the research process, but it should include all the important points drawn from the research. Especially important is the inclusion of evidence linking each generation to the next—this aspect of the report requires evidential proof to support conclusions presented: cite sources with standard footnotes and cross-reference sources on an accompanying research calendar.

A complete four-generation research report will include the following five elements:

1. A *pedigree chart* presenting a four-generation lineage prior to 1900 in the geographic area to be tested—the applicant must personally do the research.

2. A well-documented *family group record* for each of the four families presented on the pedigree chart and discussed in the written report.

3. A *research calendar* or log including all sources searched.

   The research calendar is a complete log of all research—both the positive and negative findings. To be of most benefit, researchers should enter each search *at the time of the research*. Procrastinating the entry of data can result in unrecorded sources and lost time in reconstructing the completed research.

   No set standard exists for the research calendar, but many computer templates are available online or at the Family History Library. Completed research calendar examples can be found at ICAPGen Work Samples, http://www.icapgen.org/icapgen/worksamples. Every research calendar should include fields for the following information:

   - Enter a *purpose* for each record accessed followed by the *results* of the research. A written record minimizes duplication.
   - Enter the date when researching a record.
   - Enter the names and locations of repositories.
   - Enter the source citation as if it was a footnote because by so doing, it can be copied and pasted where needed in the footnotes of the written report, or on the photocopied documents to show where they were identified. See Amy Harris's essay entitled, "Documentation and Source Citation" in this book for further information about formatting source citations correctly.

4. A well-written *report,* including the following sections (examples can be found at ICAPGen Work Samples, http://www.icapgen.org/icapgen/worksamples):

- *Research Objective:* Begin with a brief introduction stating the research objective and providing necessary background information on the ancestor.
- *The Report:* The body of the report explains the research and analytical processing by the genealogist for each of the four generations studied. Each step taken should relate to advancing the research objective. The report may incorporate subheadings to create divisions or transitions from one subject to another, which helps make the report easier to present and understand, and each subsection may appropriately contain brief summary sentences or paragraphs. Each genealogist will eventually adopt a reporting format to fit his professional style, but the recommendations presented by ICAPGen in the application for testing are fairly standard throughout the genealogy community.
- *Summary:* At the conclusion of the report, a summary section highlights the important research and restates conclusions in simple, concise statements.
- *Research Recommendations:* The report should also include recommendations for further research. These recommendations should be specific, including the type and location of any record considered for research—along with a stated purpose for that research.
- *Executive Summary Option:* Since the research report can become a lengthy document, applicants may choose to include an executive summary, a brief synopsis detailing important facts and main points of the research.

5. *Key documents supporting the research* must have reference numbers assigned to correspond with the research calendar and report footnotes. Key documents provide connections within a nuclear family, intergenerational connections, and extended family connections worthy of inclusion for the purpose of fulfilling the main goal(s) of the research.

The quality of the research report is as important as the quality of the research itself. Self-editing is a difficult but vital part of preparing a report for submission. Wise applicants will leave the report for a time before reviewing it to ensure it is of professional quality. Editing includes looking at the overall impression of the report (Does the content make sense? Are the explanations and analyses clear? Does the writing flow well? Is it easy to understand? Is the information easy to find?) and looking at the details (Do verbs and subjects agree? Are the verb tenses consistent? Is it written consistently in third-person voice? Are any words misspelled?).

Submitting the Accreditation Application Packet

Once the Contact Information form, the Accreditation Application form, and the four-generation research project are complete, the application packet is ready for submission. Applicants may access an online copy of the Application Checklist to ensure they have met all of ICAPGen's standards. The completed application can be submitted in two ways: (1) burning three CD copies of the complete application and its attachments and mailing them to ICAPGen or (2) uploading the application to the ICAPGen Web site. All supporting documents should be clearly identified and referenced within the report and on the CD. The application fee may be paid online via credit card, or a check may be mailed to ICAPGen at the address given on the application form and Web site.

Application Review Process

ICAPGen schedules application deadlines and test days several times each year. Please refer to ICAPGen.org for deadlines and test dates.

> ICAPGen schedules application deadlines and test days several times each year.

When ICAPGen receives a test application, reviewers confirm receipt of the application and issue an application number to the submitter. This application number is used in lieu of the applicant's name throughout the testing system to protect the identity of the applicant and preserve the integrity of the testing process.

The application packet is peer-rated by two independent AG professionals. This review process takes several weeks. For additional information on the rating criteria used, please see the current ICAPGen policies posted at ICAPGen.org. The raters review the submission from the perspective of clients and professional genealogists.

If the application passes review, the Testing Committee will notify the applicant and schedule a testing date for Level 2. If the application does not pass, the applicant will be encouraged to reapply at a later time and will receive suggestions for strengthening the future submission.

Level 2: Written Examination Part One

Testing for Level 2 includes a proctored four-part written examination. Exam sites are listed at ICAPGen.org. (Two additional written examination sections are tested in Level 3 to break up test time and enable applicants to concentrate on one set of genealogical skills at a time.) The Level 2 written examination sections test the applicant's knowledge of record content and usage. The four sections are as follows:

1. Document recognition
2. Handwriting (paleography)
3. Electronic databases
4. General questions and answers

Even though the written exam is open-book, there is little time for applicants to search for answers. Successful applicants know the subject matter and are able to quickly demonstrate the knowledge and skills they have already internalized. However, well-prepared applicants often create a binder containing summaries of key information and sample documents to bring with them on the day of the test.

All applicants are encouraged to visit the approved testing repository where they will be tested at least a day or two in advance to become acquainted with the holdings. Applicants benefit from knowing where books and films are located so they can access them quickly during the timed test. Most facilities have floor plan maps available to orient applicants to their holdings.

The first few sections of the exam are graded midpoint in the testing process. Only those applicants who score at least 80 percent on the early sections continue to the more difficult sections of the exam. In order to pass Level 2, applicants must have a cumulative score of 90 percent or higher on the entire proctored exam.

Applicants scoring a few points below the 90 percent may be given a special project designed to increase the applicant's knowledge or research skills in a specific area. If an applicant completes that project and resubmits before the next application deadline with a resulting 90 percent or better rating, the applicant passes Level 2.

Applicants failing the written exam receive suggestions regarding the areas in which they performed poorly; they may reapply to take the exam at a later testing date. Because the exam questions represent only a sample of the items researchers should know and be able to do, the subsequent exams will cover the same domains and tasks but will ask different questions.

Whether passing or failing the written exam, the applicants receive feedback on their performances with recommendations for improving—which includes areas of learning and skill development.

Level 3: Written Examination Part Two, and Oral Review

Level 3 includes the two remaining written exam sections and an oral review. The written exam tests the applicant's skills in data analysis, research planning, methodology, and report writing. The final sections of the written exam are as follows:

1. Brief pedigree evaluations
2. Research problem

After passing these sections of the exam with at least a cumulative 90 percent score, the applicant can schedule an oral review with a group of raters. The oral review panel consists of three or more members and usually includes one of the raters who originally reviewed the written application, a rater of the written exam, and another member of the Testing Committee.

These panel members strive to provide a consultative, positive learning experience where all of the participants—including the panel members—learn from each other. Items of discussion may include why the applicant chose a particular research strategy, as well as follow-up questions in specific areas identified as potential weaknesses on the written exam. The reviewers will likely address different aspects of the original application, the four-generation report, specific questions missed on the written exam, and/or concerns regarding any special assigned project (if one was assigned). They may also ask the applicant to provide more detail about the research experience included on the application forms.

The oral review lasts approximately three hours, allowing adequate time for extensive discussion. Applicants may request a short break during the oral review. During that break, the applicant rests while the reviewers compare their scores. At the conclusion of the oral review, the raters will confer and report the results to the applicant.

Earning the Accredited Genealogist Credential

After the application, written exams, and oral review are completed, applicants whose composite score is 90 percent or above earn the Accredited Genealogist credential.

> All who successfully complete the testing process become members of a special group of genealogy professionals and may proudly add the AG designation to their signature line.

All who successfully complete the testing process become members of a special group of genealogy professionals and may proudly add the AG designation to their signature line. They will also receive a wall certificate and pocket ID.

Ethics and the Accredited Genealogist Professional

The Accreditation Program is nearly fifty years old. During that time, much goodwill and trust has been built for those identified with the credential, and the good reputation of this credential must be guarded by all who are licensed to use it. Therefore, every AG professional is required to sign a professional code of ethics before he is awarded the actual credential.

> Every AG professional is required to sign a professional code of ethics before he is awarded the actual credential.

The ICAPGen code of ethics requires every Accredited Genealogist professional to maintain the professional standards of the organization. One AG professional's unprofessional or inappropriate actions can impact negatively on the entire body of Accredited Genealogist professionals. Those who violate the ICAPGen code of ethics become subject to the sanctions of the organization and may have their credential revoked. This code of ethics can be found at the ICAPGen Web site.

Summary

The process of becoming an AG professional is thorough but achievable—and once completed, the AG credential is rightfully a source of pride for all who have earned it.

The testing procedures described in this chapter provide an introduction to the process of accreditation and were accurate at the time of publication. To learn more, visit the ICAPGen

Web site, at http://www.icapgen.org, and attend the ICAPGen-sponsored mentoring workshops and the ICAPGen annual conference. For specific questions, contact ICAPGen by phone or e-mail.

www.ingramcontent.com/pod-product-compliance
Lightning Source LLC
Chambersburg PA
CBHW080328270326
41927CB00014B/3132

9 780971 670570